Ethnic and Intercommunity Conflict Series

General Editors: **Seamus Dunn**, Professor of Conflict Studies and Director, Centre for the Study of Conflict, and **Valerie Morgan**, Professor of History and Research Associate, Centre for the Study of Conflict, University of Ulster, Northern Ireland.

With the end of the Cold War, the hitherto concealed existence of a great many other conflicts, relatively small in scale, long-lived, ethnic in character and intra- rather than inter-state has been revealed. The dramatic changes in the distribution of world power, along with the removal of some previously resolute forms of centralised restraint, have resulted in the re-emergence of older, historical ethnic quarrels, many of which either became violent and warlike or teetered, and continue to teeter, on the brink of violence. For these reasons, ethnic conflicts and consequent violence are likely to have the greatest impact on world affairs during the next period of history.

This new series examines a range of issues related to ethnic and intercommunity conflict. Each book concentrates on a well-defined aspect of ethnic and inter-community conflict and approaches it from a comparative and international standpoint.

Rather than focus on the macrolevel, that is on the grand and substantive matters of states and empires, this series argues that the fundamental causes of ethnic conflict are often to be found in the hidden roots and tangled social infra-structures of the opposing separated groups. It is through the understanding of these foundations and the working out of their implications for policy and prac-tical activity that may lead to ameliorative processes and the construction of transforming social mechanisms and programmes calculated to produce longterm peace.

Titles include:

Stacey Burlet
CHALLENGING ETHNIC CONFLICT

Ed Cairns and Mícheál Roe (*editors*)
THE ROLE OF MEMORY IN ETHNIC CONFLICT

T.G. Fraser
THE IRISH PARADING TRADITION

Colin Knox
PEACE BUILDING IN NORTHERN IRELAND, ISRAEL AND SOUTH AFRICA

Colin Knox and Rachel Monaghan
INFORMAL JUSTICE IN DIVIDED SOCIETIES
Northern Ireland and South Africa

Brendan Murtagh
THE POLITICS OF TERRITORY

Marc H. Ross
THEORY AND PRACTICE IN ETHNIC CONFLICT MANAGEMENT

The Role of Memory in Ethnic Conflict

Edited by

Ed Cairns
University of Ulster

and

Mícheál D. Roe
Seattle Pacific University

First published 2003 by
PALGRAVE MACMILLAN
Houndmills, Basingstoke, Hampshire RG21 6XS and
175 Fifth Avenue, New York, N.Y. 10010
Companies and representatives throughout the world

PALGRAVE MACMILLAN is the global academic imprint of the Palgrave
Macmillan division of St. Martin's Press, LLC and of Palgrave Macmillan Ltd.
Macmillan® is a registered trademark in the United States, United Kingdom
and other countries. Palgrave is a registered trademark in the European
Union and other countries.

ISBN 0–333–75133–7 hardback

This book is printed on paper suitable for recycling and made from fully
managed and sustained forest sources.

A catalogue record for this book is available from the British Library.

Library of Congress Cataloging-in-Publication Data
The role of memory in ethnic conflict / edited by Ed Cairns & Mícheál D. Roe.
   p. cm.
  Includes bibliographical references and index.
  ISBN 0–333–75133–7
  1. Ethnic conflict. 2. Intergroup relations. 3. Memory—Sociological
aspects. 4. Time—Sociological aspects. I. Cairus, Ed., 1945– II. Roe,
Micheal D., 1951–

  HM1121.R65 2002
  303.48′2—dc21

2002029248

10 9 8 7 6 5 4 3 2 1
12 11 10 09 08 07 06 05 04 03

Printed and bound in Great Britain by
Antony Rowe Ltd, Chippenham and Eastbourne

Contents

Preface

The story behind this volume (as told in Chapter 10) goes back to at least 1995. However it could not have happened without the insights of several eminent colleagues and friends. Mike Wessells (from Randolph-Macon College) was one of the persons who suggested that research in this area would be fruitful and John Darby (then Director of INCORE at the University of Ulster) had the foresight to act on this suggestion and to help fund a small meeting on the topic the next year. In turn we were fortunate that Andy Dawes and Don Foster agreed to take time out from busy lives to facilitate the meeting, which was held at the Psychology Department, University of Cape Town.

Since then it has been a somewhat tortured path to the present volume. Along the way we have lost some of the original members of the group and gained some new contributors. We owe them all a debt of gratitude. On the production side we are especially grateful to Marian Cooper who acted as editorial assistant in the critical closing stages and to Betty Hemphill and Mary McLaughlin for their expert secretarial skills. Finally we are grateful to our publishers, Palgrave Macmillan for their patience.

Much has been written about the causes of intergroup conflict (usually referred to as 'ethnic' conflict). This book, while it is about memory and conflict is not trying to suggest that memory is a cause of conflict or indeed that conflict is a cause of memory. Instead in the following chapters we want to illustrate that there is a relationship, an important relationship, between memory and conflict. Each may be seen as one important 'cause' of the other. Drawing attention to this relationship we hope will increase interest in this area, especially on the part of psychologists, and will lead to further research, both academic and applied, which in turn bring us closer to understanding the dynamic of the many conflicts which make miserable the lives of so many people in the world today.

Notes on the Contributors

Daniel Bar-Tal is Professor of Social Psychology in the School of Education, University of Tel Aviv. He is a former President of the International Society of Political Psychology and recipient of the Otto Klineberg Intercultural and International Relations Prize of SPSSI. His latest book is *Shared beliefs in a society: Social psychological analysis* (2000).

Keith C. Barton is Associate Professor in the Division of Teacher Education at the University of Cincinnati and has served as a visiting academic with the UNESCO Programme in Education for Pluralism, Human Rights and Democracy at the University of Ulster, Coleraine. Barton's research has focused on history teaching and historical understanding among students in childhood and early adolescence. He has published articles on children's understanding of time, evidence, narrative and significance and he is the co-author, with Linda Levstik, of *Doing History: Investigating with Children in Elementary and Middle Schools* (2000).

Di Bretherton is Director of the International Conflict Resolution Centre at the University of Melbourne, Australia. Her main research activities have focused on conflict resolution and other interventions to prevent violence. Currently she is turning her attention more to the positive promotion of peace and reconciliation. She chairs the Committee for the Psychological Study of Peace of the International Union of Psychological Science, is President elect of the Division of Political Psychology of the International Association of Applied Psychology and is a member of the Foreign Affairs Council of Australia.

Ed Cairns is Professor of Psychology in the School of Psychology at the University of Ulster in Coleraine. He has been a visiting scholar at the Universities of Florida, Cape Town and Melbourne. He is a Fellow of the British Psychological Society and President of the Division of Peace Psychology of the American Psychological Association. He was editor (with Gary Ladd) of a special section in *Child Development* on 'Children: ethnic and Political Violence' and his last book, *Children and Political Violence* was published in 1996.

Patrick Devine-Wright studied psychology at Trinity College, Dublin before pursuing postgraduate studies in environmental and social psychology in the University of Surrey. His research interests emerged from an interest in the relation between the sense of place and identity in Ireland to an analysis of how processes of intergroup conflict in Northern Ireland shape popular understandings of history.

Brandon Hamber, a Clinical Psychologist, was co-ordinator of the Transition and Reconciliation Unit at the Centre for the Study of Violence and Reconciliation, Johannesburg, South Africa. A former visiting Tip O'Neill Fellow at the Initiative on Conflict Resolution and Ethnicity (INCORE) in Derry, Northern Ireland, he has written widely on the Truth and Reconciliation Commission and the psychological parameters thereof.

Ilse Hakvoort is a visiting researcher at the Department of Education at Göteborg University, Sweden, since November 1997. Her research interests focus on the development of children's conceptualisation of peace and war, learning and development in different socio-cultural contexts, storytelling, implementation of the convention on the rights of the child, conflict resolution and peace education.

Miles Hewstone is a Fellow of New College Oxford and University Lecturer in Social Psychology. He is a leading figure in European Social Psychology specialising in the field of intergroup relations. He is a former editor of the *British Journal of Social Psychology* and co-founding editor of the *European Review of Social Psychology*. He is a past recipient of the British Psychological Society's Spearman Medal, and has twice been a Fellow at the Centre for Advanced Study in the Behavioural Sciences, Stanford.

Christopher Alan Lewis is a Lecturer in Social Psychology, University of Ulster. He has a wide range of interests including the psychology of religion, the study of ethnic memories and conflict in Northern Ireland and the Czech Republic and issues related to Roma children in the Czech education system.

Alan McCully currently lectures in Education at the University of Ulster at Coleraine, where he contributes to pre-service teacher education and has responsibility for a Masters course in Education and Contemporary Society. Previously, he had twenty years experience teaching history and social studies in a Northern Ireland high school. His research interests and publications are around teaching controversial issues, education for citizenship and the relationship between history teaching and the formation of national identity.

Frances McLernon is a Lecturer in Social Psychology at the University of Ulster, Northern Ireland. Her doctoral research focused on Northern Irish children's attitudes to war and peace before and after the paramilitary ceasefires. Her work has involved a three-year research project investigating the role of intergroup contact in the processes of forgiveness and reconciliation in Northern Ireland, while her research interests include the development of social alienation among the Protestant/Loyalist community in Northern Ireland and an examination of the sociocultural experiences of men in Northern Irish society.

David Mellor is a Lecturer in Clinical Psychology at Deakin University, Melbourne, Australia. His main research activities are in the areas of racism and childhood mental health. He has published articles on ADHD, family therapy, group therapy for children, adolescent depression and risk taking, and perceptions of racism. He is an associate of the International Centre for Conflict Resolution at the University of Melbourne.

Louis Oppenheimer is Professor of Developmental Psychology at the Department of Psychology (University of Amsterdam). His research interests focus on social cognitive development and concern a wide range of topics. A major research theme deals with the development of the self-concept and self-system. A second research theme concerns peace research which has resulted in *How children understand war and peace*, (1999) edited in collaboration with Amiram Raviv and Dani Bar-Tal.

Mícheál D. Roe is Professor and Chair of Psychology at Seattle Pacific University, and for many years a research associate with the Centre for the Study of Conflict, University of Ulster. He works with Pacific Northwest Native Americans supporting their efforts for federal acknowledgement. He is active in APA's Society for the Study of Peace, Conflict, and Violence (Division 48).

Richard A. Wilson is Senior Lecturer in Social Anthropology at the University of Sussex. He has edited two collections on the anthropology of human rights, *Human Rights, Culture and Context* (1997) and *Culture and Rights* (2001). His present research is on the South African Truth and Reconciliation Commission, and his recent book is *The Politics of Truth and Reconciliation in South Africa* (2000). He is editor of the journal *Anthropological Theory*.

Part I
Introduction

1
Introduction: Why Memories in Conflict?

Ed Cairns and Mícheál D. Roe

> The importance of ethnic conflict, as a force shaping human affairs, as a phenomenon to be understood, as a threat to be controlled, can no longer be denied.
>
> Donald Horowitz (1985, p. xi)

Conflict between groups is a fact of life at the beginning of the new millennium. Of course it was not supposed to be this way. The ending of the Cold War was expected to herald a new world order. However, as Brown (1997) has pointed out, these 'great expectations have been dashed' (p. 80). This is because 'fierce new assertions of nationalism and sovereignty' have sprung up and the world is threatened by 'brutal ethnic, religious, social, cultural, or linguistic strife' (Boutros-Ghali, 1992, p. 6). Not all of these are strictly new conflicts. Some of them the media just did not bother about during the Cold War and so we in the Western world remained ignorant of their existence. So while the end of the Cold War led directly to the creation of many new conflicts, it also aggravated others that had lain dormant for decades or, exposed still older ones to the light of day.

Examples of current or recent intra-state wars include Bosnia, Ethiopia, Georgia (Abkhazia), Indonesia (East Timor), Lebanon, Russia (Chechnya), Rwanda and of course Northern Ireland. What has led to these conflicts grabbing the attention of the headline makers and television news editors is that these conflicts are essentially different from earlier wars. Today civilians, especially women and children, are increasingly in the front line. This is seen from the casualty statistics which reveal that while the First World War recorded 10 per cent civilian casualties; the Second World War some 50 per cent; in all subsequent wars around 80 per cent of casualties have been civilians. Or to put it another way – the ratio of soldiers to civilians killed in armed conflict has shifted from approximately 9:1 in the early decades of this century to 1:9 in recent conflicts such as Lebanon. What has grabbed the attention of the academic community about these conflicts on the other hand is the depth of feelings they appear to generate, their longevity and the challenge they present to those who would wish to explain this phenomenon plus the even greater challenge to those who would wish to control or end them.

In the series of essays we present here we wish to explore the relationship between memory and conflict. We do not, however, wish to give the impression that we think that memory is the only topic worthy of study in relation to conflict or indeed that it is the golden key to unlock our understanding of the causes of today's many intergroup conflicts. What we do believe is that memory is a topic which social scientists have tended to ignore in their attempts to understand 'ethnic' conflict. For example there is a temptation on the part of social psychologists to draw a simple analogy between methods used to reduce intergroup conflicts in the real world and those employed in the classical social psychology experiment by Sherif (1966) – but the boys in Sherif's study had no long-term history of animosity as do people in many of today's intergroup conflicts. Nor presumably did the feeling of dislike between the two groups of boys reach depths akin to those that led to genocide for example in Kosovo, or in Rwanda.

The role of memory in conflict has been ignored in spite of the fact that many writers have acknowledged that for people to be recognized as forming an 'ethnic community' they must (among other things) have shared memories (Smith, 1993). In other words there is a widespread recognition that ethnic identities are often historically constructed. And this construction Oberschall (2001, p. 130) notes can be an ongoing process, and a process that has become easier because of the proliferation of modern media, as for example in former Yugoslavia where 'nationalist claims played loose with historical truth and contemporary fact'.

While memory may play an important role in creating or recreating conflict, in reactivating it from the form in which it may have lain dormant, perhaps for several generations, this is not what we see as the most important role of memory in conflict. Instead, we believe that it is important to study the relationship between memories and conflict for their potential role in helping resolve conflicts. This is related to the fact that (Montville, 1993) such groups are often left with a sense of 'victimhood' that stems from unacknowledged and unreconciled historic losses. These in turn present a powerful barrier to traditional methods of peacemaking and diplomacy and create new senses of wrong and injustice thus creating the potential for future conflict.

The potential for future conflict is present because ethnic conflict often leads to violence that in turn invites collective revenge (Chirot, 2001). This revenge does not necessarily have to be based on some 'ancient' quarrel (although it may be); it can just as easily be based on a quarrel that is only one generation old. However long the time-scale, ethnic conflicts are always grounded in the past. The problem is that when one community takes revenge on another this in turn sows the seeds for continued violence. For these reasons, if ethnic conflict is to be brought under control, it is necessary to understand the role of the collective past in the collective present. This role is communicated via memories of the past, collective memories, which this volume will demonstrate play a major part in ethnic conflicts of many types and in many locations in today's world.

Because of the importance of the past, we hope that this volume will put the study of memories in conflict higher on the agenda for those who wish to search for ways of bringing about the long-term cessation of intergroup conflict. If this is to be done it will be necessary to come to terms in much more detail with phenomena social scientists have variously labelled *social memories*, *collective memories*, or *ethnic memories*. These are not new concepts but they are concepts that we would argue have been largely examined by mainstream social scientists. Further, while social scientific writings on social memory have been rich and diverse they are open to criticism, at times for their lack of theoretical grounding and at other times for their lack of empirical support.

The authors included in this volume represent attempts to address the roles of such memories, largely from an empirical perspective and in relation to conflicts from a variety of settings – South Africa, Western Europe, Australia, Northern Ireland, the United States and the Middle East. These are conflicts, which originate from a variety of past experiences, including dislocation and dispute over land, disenfranchisement of indigenous peoples, struggle for civil rights and world war but at the same time, share a common denominator in that all involve ethnic conflict at some level.

In Chapter 2, 'Theoretical Overview of Memory and Conflict', Patrick Devine-Wright provides an extensive review of relevant social science literature. He argues that examination 'of social aspects of remembering is not yet a coherent field of study in which research is integrated across disciplinary boundaries'; consequently, he structures his review according to the academic disciplines of sociology, social psychology, anthropology, history and political science. Juxtaposing concepts of collective memories, social memories and myths, Devine-Wright brings together a variety of methodologies, including the psychoanalytic, empirical quantitative, ethnographic and discursive. He closes his chapter by focusing the different disciplinary perspectives and methodologies specifically on remembering and forgetting in the context of ethnic conflict.

Part II contains chapters which provide applications of social memory seldom included in the literature on ethnic conflict; that is, the experience of indigenous peoples living as minority ethnic groups in the dominant cultures of their contemporary nation states. This failure to recognize the relevance of indigenous peoples' perspectives has been a significant oversight, for social memories and associated ethnic identities are central to the conflicts indigenous peoples experience today. In Chapter 3, 'Reconciliation between Black and White Australia: The Role of Social Memory', David Mellor and Di Bretherton address how the historical experiences of violence, dislocation and cultural denigration of Australian Aboriginal peoples are ever present in their social memories, and that these Aboriginal social memories are distinct from the knowledge of the past that dominant White Australia presents as *history*. The authors present this gap in perceptions of the past as a significant hindrance in achieving social justice and reconciliation within Australia.

In Chapter 4, 'Cowlitz Indian Ethnic Identity, Social Memories and 150 Years of Conflict with the United States Government', Mícheál D. Roe presents a paradoxical perspective on social memories in conflict settings. While focusing on groups' past experiences and distinctives may sustain and exacerbate conflict, it may also empower groups to maintain cohesiveness and continue to function until conflict resolution is achieved. Since early contact with 'White man' the Cowlitz Indian people of southwestern Washington state have experienced consequent and persistent conflict. The author argues that Cowlitz social memories and ethnic identity have empowered the tribe to face effectively a hostile White society and to resist a federal government intent on forcing its assimilation.

Part III includes two chapters which address the persistence of social memories and their impact on contemporary intergroup relationships; however, in the first, social memories are associated with ongoing ethnic conflict, while in the second, social memories are of a conflict long past. In Chapter 5, 'Collective Memory of Physical Violence: its' Contribution to the Culture of Violence', Daniel Bar-Tal's central thesis is that physical violence between ethnic groups which persists for a generation or longer changes the very nature of that intergroup conflict. Writing from the context of continuing Israeli/Palestinian violence, the author argues that selective social memories evolve from long-lived conflict, become institutionalized and transmitted across generations. These memories in turn contribute to conflict's intractability, resulting in a self-perpetuating negative cycle. Ultimately such social memories fill determinative roles in the formation of 'cultures of violence'. In Chapter 6, 'Will the Germans Ever Be Forgiven? Memories of the Second World War Four Generations Later', Louis Oppenheimer and Ilse Hakvoort examine the social memories of the Second World War, but among Dutch children and adolescents who live fifty years after the war's conclusion and who have no personal experience with ethnic or national conflicts. Addressing anti-German attitudes and feelings in these Dutch young people, the authors argue that social memories are not static and that each generation interprets such memories according to the prevailing 'zeitgeist', the nature of the content and personal experiences. Beyond specific memories, these authors argue that negative 'interpretative frameworks' also are cross-generationally transferred and that effective intervention into ethnic conflicts must break the cycle of such frameworks.

The fourth part of this book presents attempts at conflict resolution, not by putting the past behind, but by directly addressing social memories and their associated identities. In Chapter 7, 'History Teaching and the Perpetuation of Memories: the Northern Ireland Experience', Keith C. Barton and Alan McCully examine roles of formal education in perpetuating or ameliorating ethnic conflict. Specifically focused on the teaching of history to children and youth in Northern Ireland, the authors examine how such an academic discipline can assist young people's understanding of the roots of contemporary conflict, and whether or not the rationalistic inquiry-based methodology of history can be transferred to emotionally charged current situations. The authors close with a provocative proposal for how history education may contribute to decreasing ethnic tensions in Northern Ireland. That is, by history teachers intentionally addressing social memories and identity in their curricula with particular attention to elements of *shared identity*, and applying the strengths of a rational inquiry approach 'while grappling more directly with deeply felt personal and emotional aspects of history'.

In Chapter 8, 'Memories of Recent Conflict and Forgiveness in Northern Ireland', Frances McLernon, Ed Cairns, Christopher Lewis and Miles Hewstone present findings from an ongoing study of forgiveness in Northern Ireland's political violence. The authors extend beyond the role of forgiveness in reducing psychological distress of individuals in interpersonal conflict; they provide one of very few empirical examinations of forgiveness as intervention into intergroup conflict. Given that social memories of current and past violence are pervasive in nationalist and unionist communities in Northern Ireland, with both sides laying claim to victimhood, the authors propose intergroup forgiveness as a means of halting the historical cycle of revenge. They rather soberly conclude their chapter by noting that forgiveness of the other side has not yet achieved broad acceptance in the Northern Irish context.

In the final chapter of this section, 'Symbolic Closure through Memory, Reparation and Revenge in post-Colonial Societies', Brandon Hamber and Richard A. Wilson raise important questions about the adequacy of South Africa's internationally acclaimed Truth and Reconciliation Commission for traumatized individuals. In their analysis, the authors separate processes embodied in individual trauma work, national history-making and reparations offered by truth commissions, arguing that under some circumstances such processes may mutually reinforce each other, however, under other circumstances they can be disharmonious, incongruous, even counter productive. They present the value of truth commissions (at least for the psychological healing of persons) as limited and found primarily in creating a public space for the telling of subjective truths, and as such, providing for one form of closure.

In the closing chapter of this book, we review the variety of perspectives of our authors, extracting common themes and comparing and contrasting their less congruent conceptualisations. We also attempt to provide perspectives on future research and interventions in the hope that this volume will inspire other social scientists to take up the many challenges that our authors raise regarding the relationships between memory and ethnic conflict. Given that it is estimated that among the existing 185 sovereign states, few are ethnically homogeneous while around 40 per cent contain five or more ethnic groups, this is no small challenge.

2
A Theoretical Overview of Memory and Conflict

Patrick Devine-Wright

The past decade has seen a flowering of interest in the topics of memory and history both within academia and outside (Olick and Robbins, 1998). In parallel, there has been a heightened awareness of the link between processes of remembering and issues of ethnic conflict, reconciliation and conflict resolution, perhaps best exemplified by the actions of the Truth and Reconciliation Commission in South Africa (Asmal *et al.*, 1996). This chapter reviews recent scholarship on the subject of remembering and forgetting, emphasizing recent attempts to make the concept more social as well as the diverse ways in which researchers from different academic disciplines have approached the subject. I would argue that the study of social aspects of remembering is not yet a coherent field of study in which research is integrated across disciplinary boundaries. For this reason I have chosen to structure this review according to academic discipline, with a final summary of common themes that have relevance to issues of ethnic conflict.

Academic disciplines that research issues of remembering and forgetting include sociology, (social) psychology, anthropology, history and political science. In these disciplines, similar processes have different conceptual names, for example 'collective memories' in sociology, 'social memories' in social psychology and 'myths' in anthropology. A multiplicity of methodological perspectives is employed, including analytical, descriptive, empirical, ethnographical and discursive approaches. Probably the most important early figure in the literature is Maurice Halbwachs, a student of the sociologist Emil Durkheim, who published *Les Cadres Sociaux de la Mémoire* in Paris in 1925 (Halbwachs, 1925). It was the translation from French to English of Halbwachs' second book *'La mémoire collective'* (1980), which was originally published in 1950, that has contributed to the recent upsurge in research interest in this subject.

Before introducing each disciplinary area, some major themes that recur in the literature are briefly summarised. First, at a broad theoretical level, scholars have debated the relation between the present and the past (cf. Schwartz, 1991a; Shils, 1981), specifically whether the present is predominantly shaped by the past or vice-versa. Second, a distinction is made in the literature between active remembering (bodily action) and mental process (cognitive and emotional). Active remembering is embodied in the concepts of tradition and commemoration (for example, Hobsbawm and Ranger, 1983; Connerton, 1989; Devine-Wright and Lyons, 1997; Devine-Wright, 2001(a)). Mental approaches that look upon memory from a social perspective focus upon 'social memories' (for example, Lyons, 1996), 'collective memories' (for example, Halbwachs, 1950/1980) and 'myths' (for example, Malinowski, 1948; Smith, 1996).

Third, the role of emotions in remembering and forgetting is stressed by many scholars (for example, Mack, 1983; Irwin-Zarecka, 1994; Schudson, 1995; Frijda 1997; Devine-Wright, 1999). Fourth, sociological approaches have distinguished between the politics of public and private remembering (for example, Irwin-Zarecka, 1994), with explicit concern centred upon the contested and social nature of remembrance. Fifth, sociological approaches have focused upon the generational hypothesis, that is, the notion of a sensitive age-period in which people are more likely to remember experienced or learnt of events (Schumann and Scott, 1989; Pennebaker, 1992). Finally, researchers from several disciplines have elaborated the role of memory as a constituent of group and ethnic conflict and also an important aspect in the dynamics of reconciliation, forgiveness and conflict resolution (for example, Asmal *et al.*, 1996; Cairns *et al.*, 1998; Devine-Wright, in press (a)).

Processes of memory have traditionally been analysed by psychologists in a manner that exclusively focused upon the individual's mnemonic activities. Whether it was research informed by psychoanalytic or cognitive perspectives, remembering and forgetting was studied as an activity that individuals alone did (Middleton and Edwards, 1990). The amount of research carried out within these two research traditions is great. However, it has recently been challenged by writers who argue that memory must be analysed as a social process – that individuals do not inhabit isolated worlds but live socially, commemorate the past and actively make sense of the world through processes of social communication. The 'ancestors' of this alternative approach to memory were not psychologists but worked within the discipline of sociology.

Sociological perspective

Émil Durkheim (1912/1947) introduced the concept of 'collective representations' which referred to the set of beliefs and sentiments common to the average members of a single society which form a determinate system that has a life of its own. Maurice Halbwachs adapted this concept in his writings on the subject of social or collective memory (see for example, 1941; 1950/1980). Halbwachs believed that memories were both public and shareable, that remembering and forgetting were social processes and that there were as many collective memories in a society as there were social groups. This view fractures Durkheim's original position to embrace each and every different group that may exist in a society. He differentiated memory into two essential types: historical and autobiographical; the former referring to memory not learnt through direct experience but learnt through written records, artefacts, commemorations and so on, the latter to events personally experienced by individuals. He stressed how the environment groups dwell in is vital for communicating and symbolising memories from the past (1941); how social memories were important for maintaining the cohesion of the group and how a groups' memories will be determined by present contexts – that the beliefs, interests and aspirations of the present, which are held by groups, will shape the various views of the past as they are manifest in any historical epoch.

Collective Memory

Halbwachs argued for the fluidity of memory. Memory is socially constructed and reconstructed over time and is intimately related to people's sense of identity in the present context. This sense of identity was viewed as a product of social interaction as well as individual consciousness. Halbwachs stressed that he was not affirming the idea of a 'group mind', that while the collective memory endures and draws strength from its base in a coherent body of people, it is individuals as group members who remember (1950/1980). Thus, although remembering ultimately is a process carried out by individuals, it would be a mistake to overlook the shared and collective nature of remembering and forgetting, especially as they concern group members and experiences from the groups' history. Halbwachs' theoretical account of memory contrasts sharply with the orthodox psychological approach in shifting the unit of analysis away from individuals to one that embraces both individuals and social groups. This is the fundamental legacy of his work.

A review of subsequent research on the topic of collective memory indicates that Halbwachs' work was itself 'forgotten' by sociologists until the 1970s and 1980s (Coser, 1992). Subsequent writers have analysed the process of collective remembering at a number of different levels of inquiry, implicated by Halbwachs' theory – including families (Csikszent-mihalyi and Rochberg-Halton, 1981), institutions and organisations (Douglas, 1986), communities (Speller, 1992; Irwin-Zarecka, 1994), generations (Schumann and Scott, 1989) and national states (Schwartz, 1982; Smith, 1996). Furthermore, researchers have pursued Halbwachs' (1941) ideas that socially produced artefacts may be repositories of collective memories. Both Wegner (1987) and Schudson (1995) have pointed to dedicated memory forms, which are purposefully created (and destroyed) by social groups in order to socially influence the process of collective remembering and forgetting. The scope of these memory forms is wide (Schudson, 1995), embracing books, national and group holidays commemorating a particular event or historical figure (Zerubavel, 1991), monuments and statues (Lynch, 1972; Schwartz, 1982, 1991b; Nora, 1989; Johnston, 1994), souvenirs, place names, language, symbols and iconographic art, anthems, song and poetry (Schwartz, 1982), artefacts and museums (Uzzell and Stig-Sorenson, 1993).

Schwartz (e.g. 1982, 1986, 1991a, 1991b) followed Halbwachs' ideas with research focusing on an eclectic selection of mnemonic artefacts, including poetry (1986) and statues (1982, 1991b) and written texts (1991a). For Schwartz, the issue of past and present influence is of critical theoretical importance. His analysis is critical of Halbwachs' emphasis upon the determination of memory by present contexts. It is claimed that this depiction over-emphasises change, making the past seem more precarious than it actually was, in Schwartz's view. Schwartz countered with the view that memory can instead be analysed in terms of continuities in our perceptions of the past across time and to the way that these perceptions are maintained in the face of social change (also the view of Mead, 1938; Shils, 1981). Schwartz's analyses of the process of commemoration of historical figures in American national politics across time (for example, President Abraham Lincoln, Schwartz, 1991a; President George Washington, Schwartz, 1991b) posited the intermediary view that groups and societies are engaged in an ongoing dialectical relation between past and present – as aspects of collective memory.

Other American sociological researchers have pursued a more empirical approach in looking at collective memories at national level (for example, Frisch, 1989; Schumann and Scott, 1989). Building upon early theoretical work by Mannheim (1925/1952), Schumann and colleagues in a series of research studies (Schumann and Scott, 1989; Schumann and Rieger, 1992; Schumann *et al.*, 1997; Schumann *et al.*, 1998) have adopted an open-ended approach to investigate whether different generations of Americans and other nations possess different collective memories. Through empirical analysis, they concluded that there was persuasive evidence that distinct generations did possess unique collective memories, as manifest in different accounts of the significance of twentieth-century historical events. They argued that adolescence and early childhood constituted a critical period during which significant events can have a greater impact on historical knowledge than they do for people beyond this age period, although not all of the historical events investigated conformed to this pattern. Generational cohort differences were explained in terms of theories of adolescence (for example, Erikson, 1968), which assert the formative nature of such a life period. The impact of national media and autobiographical remembering was also acknowledged (Schumann *et al.*, 1998).

Frisch (1989) acknowledged that collective memory, as a process, involved societal and individual level processes that were interdependent in as yet imperfectly understood ways. His research is the result of a longitudinal analysis of American students' memories of figures from the American national past. At the time in the US, there was a perception that students' degree of knowledge of their own national history was inadequate. There were claims that the social cohesion of the nation would disintegrate (implying a direct link between history and identity) and the blame was usually placed upon the education system. The research indicated that beliefs about history were stable over the ten-year period of his research (1978–88) and were not directly due to people's formal education in the subject of history. Therefore, he concluded that 'collective cultural mechanisms' existed in parallel to the education system that informed people about their national history. Frisch interpreted these findings in terms of a system of civil religion, which he claimed the American national identity fulfilled for Americans.

There was remarkable continuity to Frisch's (1989) findings. His results indicated that George Washington and Betsy Ross (remembered as the creator of the national flag) were the most frequently remembered figures from history in every year of analysis. He claimed that these figures existed as ideals for Americans. Frisch's interpretation is largely influenced by anthropological theory. George Washington and Betsy Ross were figures of myth, which according to Frisch (1989), was 'the driving force behind history' (p. 1143). They constituted the 'mother' and 'father' of the nation, reflecting an ongoing American fixation with creation myths of national origin. The results suggest that other media outside of the education system are powerful in conveying ideas about the past. Frisch included images, including that of the national flag and Washington, which had been used by US advertising agencies to sell consumer products such as television sets. His results are a powerful testimony to the social nature of this form of remembering.

Commemorating the past

A further strand to the literature concerns the role of commemoration in remembering the past. It has been argued that commemorating the past is a behavioural process that defines the individual's location in the temporal continuity (Frijda, 1997). Commemorations are social occasions, in which group members gather together in order to focus upon past events, communicate a sense of common sense of social identification (Ignatieff, 1993) and legitimate social institutions and practices (Connerton, 1989). Through the commemoration, the individual participant is explicitly related to other group members who have existed in history. According to Schudson (1995), distantiation (the ebb of informational detail and loss of emotional intensity about the past which occurs in time) can be negated through commemoration. Bodily actions and performances such as marching and parading are an important characteristic of commemorations (Connerton, 1989). Connerton has claimed that these bodily movements constitute an important element of the process of collective remembering. The focus of the commemoration is often tragic; shared remembering of the dead of previous wars, for example, is said to be an important contributor to group cohesiveness and the individual's sense of belonging to the group (Jacobi and Stokols, 1983; Irwin-Zarecka, 1994).

Politics: remembering and forgetting

A persistent feature of more recent sociological accounts has been a stress upon the political aspects of social remembering and forgetting. These approaches directly relate the study of social memory with issues of political and ethnic conflict pointing to the manner in which social remembering selects and distorts the past in the service of present political interests (Gillis, 1994; Irwin-Zarecka, 1994; Schudson, 1995). Other writers have focused upon the manner in which the process of social remembering and forgetting is constrained by external social, political and ideological forces (for example, Butler, 1989; Ascherson, 1995;

Schudson, 1995). Individuals and groups in modern liberal societies are usually constrained in their ability to reconstruct the past in a manner that elites in more authoritarian societies are not (Butler, 1989; Ascherson, 1995). Constraints include the structure of the available pasts and the degree of conflict that exists about the past among a multitude of mutually aware individuals and groups; existing power relations between those relevant groups and finally, the integrity of journalists, historians and archaeologists, freedom of information and the existence of different groups free to make competing claims upon the past (Schudson, 1995).

Emphasis upon the dynamics of political functionality is relevant both to peaceful societies and contexts of ethnic, intergroup and international conflict. Writers have pointed to the manner in which social memory processes are shaped by the structure of societies and the relative status enjoyed by different social and ethnic groups. Schudson (1995) claimed that normal distantiation processes could be countered by present social grievances, citing the conflict in the former Yugoslavia. Irwin-Zarecka (1994) posited that, in effect, time collapses in a context in which historical moral accounts have not been settled. The passage of time in this case may actually serve to increase the emotional sense of grievance and the intensity of the collective memory for those concerned.

Victimisation

Mack (1983) and Irwin-Zarecka (1994) have written about the significance of processes of social remembering for subjugated and subordinate social groups. Their accounts have stressed the relation between social remembering and processes of emotion and social group identification. Social memories about the victimisation of the ingroup by members of the outgroup in history have been implicated in several social processes: the construction of rigid group boundaries between 'us' and 'them'; the process of engendering a sense of ingroup cohesion (Irwin-Zarecka, 1993, 1994); the process of outgroup derogation and dehumanisation (Mack, 1983); the process of ingroup idealisation and glorifying (Mack, 1983) and finally, a common ingroup sense of self (Mack, 1983). Socially shared emotional 'wounds' such as actual battlefield defeats were said to be particularly powerful in motivating the repair of national and collective pride through vengeful, violent military actions (Berlin, 1979). Mack's ideas (1983) suggest that the mobilisation of the past can play a powerful role in the context of intergroup and international conflicts because of the emotional and motivational force associated with collective memories and the possible relation between such emotions and collective actions. The relevance of such ideas for explaining forms of terrorism is explored further below.

A sense of collective victimisation might be situated in events that might have occurred generations before, as was the case with the social memory of Masada for Jews (Schwartz, 1982). Several factors were said to motivate a person who was a member of one group to take action against a member of an outgroup (Mack, 1983). These factors included the perceived social significance of the event; the individual's personal memories of their circumstances of learning about the event; their affective response and finally, their sense of belonging with the people who actually suffered. That group members socially construct an histor-ical event over time does not imply that the event never actually occurred, that it is completely 'mythical'. However, it does emphasise that interpretations of such occurrences and attributional judgements of blame and responsibility are open to social construction and are constructed and reconstructed over time, as present situations change.

Mack (1983) stressed the influential role of political leaders in such a process, claiming that group leaders often manipulate the sense of victimisation that is diffused within a group or nation in conducting wars against other groups or nation states. Aizpurua's (1992) description of Franco's victory parade in Madrid in 1939 might offer an example. Franco stands on a podium saluting the crowd below after the end of the Spanish Civil War. Aizpurua noted that he was surrounded by gen-erals but totally dwarfed by an immense mural of the ancient coat of arms of King Charles V and the heraldry of the royal houses of Aragon, Castile, Leon and Navarre. Other examples in the context of Northern Ireland were provided by Jackson (1992).

There is an explicit psychological element in Mack's analysis. Pro-cesses of idealisation and collective victimisation through the past were said to be social processes directly related to nationalism and people's personal sense of self. Idealisation of the actions of ingroup heroes and heroines was said to boost ingroup members' sense of self-esteem. The emotional 'wounds' experienced by other group members, with whom the individual possesses a sense of affiliation, was said to boost people's sense of collective belonging, thus resulting in increased cohesion of the group as a whole. Thus Mack's (1983) analysis was not solely confined either to the individual or to the societal/national level of analysis, but contained a sophisticated mixture of both. Self-esteem was argued to derive not only from personal life circumstances but also from the fate of one's group or nation state, thereby suggesting the significance of social aspects of the self-concept and social aspects of personal esteem. The 'wounds' of the past were conceptualised as attacks upon the esteem of national citizens. Group members who had experienced denials of self-worth both at personal and collective levels were claimed to be most likely to be motivated to engage in violent actions of revenge. The conjunction of personal and social circumstances provided by this analysis offers fruitful potential for further research.

The morality of remembering

Pointing out the instrumental and political functionality of the process of collective memory is also to elucidate a moral dimension, often implicated in processes of social forgetting (Irwin-Zarecka, 1994), for example, as has been studied in the context of German memory and history. In relation to German citizens' collective memory of the Holocaust, the passage of time has argued both in favour of and against a focus upon judgements of the morality of past actions (Schudson, 1995). The proximity of issues of identity, social justice, morality and political influence in relation to processes of social memory are manifest in recent attempts to deny the very fact that the Holocaust may have occurred (Lipstadt, 1993). There has been an ongoing debate in Germany about how a positive sense of national identity can be compatible with open acknowledgement by German society of their culpability in the phenomenon of Nazism (Maier, 1988). Manipulating memory in order to preserve a positive view of the self can involve transgressing ethical codes of conduct (Irwin-Zarecka, 1993, 1994), which might produce moral dilemmas for those engaged in selective remembering and forgetting. Moral aspects of processes of social remembering were said to be implicated in the dynamics of conflict resolution (Mack, 1983). Preoccupation with historical 'wounds' may act as a psychological barrier obstructing processes of conflict resolution. This might lead to reduced empathy for members of an outgroup; reluctance in admitting shared responsibility for past actions; refusal to recognize the legitimacy of the outgroup's perspective and opposition to the construction of a super-ordinate sense of common identification (Mack, 1983).

Other students of nationalism have focused upon issues of temporality and historicity in relation to the functioning of nation states and their citizens. It has been argued that a central characteristic of nationalism is the link between present and past. Anderson (1983), who defined the nation as an 'imagined community', stated that this psychological process of imagining served to maintain the cohesion of the nation state. He claimed that the imagined community of national citizens existed in relation to vertical and horizontal planes. The horizontal imagination linked the individual citizen with all those currently alive who were also members of the national group. Vertical imagining linked the citizen to all those members of the nation who had previously existed and future generations yet unborn. In sum these processes positioned the individual citizen in a linear temporal continuity from past to present and onwards into the future. In this sense, Anderson suggested that nationalism catered for a personal need for continuity over time and a sense of connectedness in the face of the inescapability of death. Citizens may be mortal, but the nation was perceived to be immortal, even though the constructed antiquity of modern nation states has been exposed by historians (for example, Hobsbawm and Ranger, 1983). Put this way, nationalism might be viewed as a form of civic religion, composed of a body of modern sacred mythology focused upon the institutions of state (Anderson, 1983).

In this vein, Smith (1984, 1996) has argued that ethnomyths, ethnic histories and territorial associations underlie the present global system of nation states. Smith defined the nation as a:

> named human population with shared myths and memories occupy-ing an historic territory or homeland, and possessing a common public culture, a single unified economy and common legal rights and duties (Smith, 1996, p. 561).

Smith uses the term ethnomyth in a similar manner to social or collective memories. His use of the term suggests a similarity between developed and less developed societies, with shared ethnomyths and memories serving as 'pre-modern cultural ties' (Smith, 1996) in modern nation states. It also reflects the manner in which Smith has borrowed theoretical concepts from anthropological scholarship of less developed societies and applied them to the study of nationalism in developed societies. Such myths can serve to maintain a distinctive identity for the group or nation as a whole, ensuring collective solidarity, the legitimacy of collective actions (Smith, 1984) and collective territorial attachments to ancestral homelands and sacred sites. In accounting for the upsurge in ethnic nationalism in the post-Cold War 1990s, Smith argued that shared myths and memories offer a firm explanatory basis for the power and variety of modern nationalism. Such ethnomyths were thought to complement existing sociological theories about the nationalism being derived from processes of industrialisation (Gellner, 1983), development of the mass media (Anderson, 1983), the interests of sub-elites (Giddens, 1985) and the ideology of modern democratic states (Hobsbawm, 1990). Smith contended that any understanding of modern nationalisms should look not only at the specific economic and political circumstances, but also the 'deep' ethno-symbolic resources which modern nationalisms command. An example cited by Smith is the nostalgic remembrance of a golden age (1984, 1996). The golden age refers to an era in which the group possessed glory, moral virtue and heroism. According to Smith, heroes and heroines provide models of virtuous conduct for present-day group members, their valorous deeds inspiring faith and courage in their oppressed or decadent descendants. Propagation of such myths by ethnic and national groups and their leaders was said to promote resurgence and renewal of national and ethnic identifications. This may be particularly likely in contexts of social change.

Anthropoligical perspective

Smith's use of the concept of myth (for example, 1996) is a reflection of the blurred boundaries between the disciplines of sociology and anthropology. This is particularly evident in relation to anthropological literature concerning the social functionality of myth. This literature is briefly referred to here. Anthropologists have typically theorised about myth from two bases: functional and structural (Overing, 1997). The functional approach stems from the writings of Durkheim, focusing upon the different functions of myths for groups and collectivities. Myths have been interpreted as social forms of explanation (for example, Frazer, 1918; Tylor, 1958), chiefly utilising the language of metaphor in personalising the forces of nature and in doing so, attempting to understand these forces and to create a shared sense of meaning. For example, Eliade (1963) detailed the ubiquity of origin myths, in which group member's constructed mythical fables and stories explaining the circumstances around the establishment of the group at the origins of time.

For Durkheim (1912/1947), myth was an element of the religious system, expressing in words what ritual expresses in actions; both have the social functions of maintaining and expressing group solidarity and cohesion. The content of the myth was important because it represented certain moral values embodied in social life that served as a guide to action; second, it reflected features of the social structure. Thus myths not only enable group cohesion but also define the group in a distinctive fashion, in the sense of possessing a unique myth that no other group possesses. The social sharing of sacred attachment binds the social group together and simultaneously differentiates it from other groups. Durkheim's ideas reflect the close relation of myth and ritual (similar to that pointed out between social memory and commemoration above), each considered different modes of communication about the same message, which are symbolic assertions, about the social structure of groups and societies (for example, Graves, 1955).

Charter myths

Of particular similarity to socio-political aspects of social memory processes is the scholarship of Malinowski (1948), who claimed that myths were used as a 'charter' which were beyond fact, reason, memory and ordinary time in order to legitimate and justify social institutions:

> ... myth, taken as a whole, cannot be sober, dispassionate history, since it is always made *ad hoc* to fulfill a certain sociological function, to glorify a certain group, or to justify an anomalous status.
>
> (Malinowski, 1948, p. 125)

More recent anthropological research has focused upon the role of charter myths in contexts of social change, for example among rural communities in Canada and Scotland (Cohen, 1975; 1985). Charter myths and traditional practices were said to increase in salience during the process of social change, in the transition of traditional cultures to modernity. Such myths were said to legitimise the continued power of certain leaders and to maintain the continuity of the community with the wider past and future, despite the imminent sense of social change (Cohen, 1975). Other forms of myth were said to reconcile inconsistencies, doubts and contestations in the everyday milieu, to idealise certain figures and to justify power relations among the group. In legitimating the right of a certain group to a particular territory, charter myths necessarily deny that same legitimacy to other competing myths devised by other competing groups.

Structural myths

The chief characteristic of Levi-Strauss' (1966) structural approach to myths has been the claim that myths function as a device that mediates and overcomes present contradictions or oppositions. The myths set up a set of irreconcilable contradictions in ideas and through their structural characteristics mediate them. As narratives, myths typically possess a beginning or moment of origin and a temporal diachronic sequence from the remote past in which later events are embedded and anchored to the immediate present context. The unfurling of events is often dramatic and imaginative, involving the establishment of oppositions and contradictions and their resolution. In referring to the past in order to legitimise the present, myths assume that the past has a force in the present and that the past is accorded a high status of its own. This was certainly the case in traditional societies, in which social status, claims to property and power and even the selection of marriage partners were structured by rules of descent. This is not to say that myths have no reference to the future, since myths of prophesy anchor the present in the future (Cohen, 1969).

It has been argued that processes of myth might also account for shared interpretations of the past in modern societies (for example, Barthes, 1957/1972). If this is the case, then the wider sense of the past that might be diffused within social groups in modern societies might bear similarity with processes of mythology as derived from the anthropological study of developing societies. This is Smith's (for example, 1996) assumption that was pointed out above. Levi-Strauss (1966) explicitly linked myths to what he termed pseudo-history, referring to ways in which representations of the French revolution served to overcome present contradictions in French society. Thus, myths are unlikely to be the sole property of traditional or 'primitive' social milieux. In the sense that myths relate the characteristics of the present to a series of significant past events and serve socio-political functions, for example, as charters for certain practices and institutions, then they bear clear similarity to processes of social remembering and forgetting.

Political science perspectives: memory and terrorism

Several political scientists that have studied the dynamics of terrorism have drawn attention to the role of memories in legitimating, motivating and idealising collective actions by the individual on behalf of the group (for example, Bowyer-Bell, 1978; Tölölyan, 1989). It has been argued that paramilitary groups in Northern Ireland and elsewhere have legitimised their actions through invoking a mythic past, replete with heroic martyrs (Bowyer-Bell, 1978; Tölölyan, 1989). Tölölyan (1989) was critical of accounts within political science that sought to explain terrorism through citing the personalities of the individuals involved. Instead, Tölölyan pointed to the role of beliefs about the past that are diffused within the cultures and belief systems of ethnic groups. Figures from the past such as these fulfil the function Graumann (1983) identified in representing ideal models that group members, particularly youths, may identify with. The status of historic figures as soldiers or freedom fighters idealise aggression and fighting, thus providing important legitimacy for those who are fighting in the present.

Scholars of terrorist publications and propaganda have provided further evidence. For example, materials published by Republicans in Northern Ireland, has indicated the important role of the past in provisional IRA propaganda (Tugwell, 1981). Similarly, Picard's (1991) content analysis of the *An Phoblacht* Republican newspaper over a period of twelve months revealed that the category 'commemorations, remembrances and obituaries' was the second most common category of content in the newspaper. Finally, Rolston's (1992, 1995) analysis of visual imagery in Republican and Loyalist wall murals in Northern Ireland suggested that the relation of current collective actions by paramilitary groups with past heroes is for purposes of legitimisation. Such research suggests that present day Republicans and Loyalists have used social memories associated with particular events and important figures from the past to legitimise terrorism in Northern Ireland.

Historical perspectives

Academic historians have recently begun to divert attention towards issues of memory (Thelen, 1989). These accounts have studied socio-political functions of history, including myths and traditions. For example, there is a clear degree of similarity between the sociological use of the term commemoration (as in Connerton, 1989), the anthropological use of the term 'ritual' (for example, Eliade, 1963) and historian's use of the term 'invented tradition' (Hobsbawm and Ranger, 1983). The concept of invented traditions have been defined as:

> a set of practices, normally governed by overtly or tacitly accepted rules and of a ritual or symbolic nature, which seek to inculcate certain values and norms of behaviour by repetition, which automatically implies continuity with a suitable historic past.
>
> (Hobsbawm, 1983, p. 1)

When traditions are said to have been invented, this continuity with a 'suitable historic past' is largely fictitious, reflecting historians' concern with issues of fact (Hobsbawm, 1983). In terms of political functionality, the invention of seemingly antiquated traditions was said to give the sanction of precedent either to a desired social change or the resistance of innovation (Hobsbawm, 1983). In such a process, social change is considered desirable or undesirable, according to the sanction of perpetuity. Historians (see Thelen, 1989) have claimed that the proclivity of such processes of invention, are most likely in social contexts of rapid transformation. This is similar to views made within anthropology (for example, Cohen, 1985) and social psychology (see Lyons, 1996). Probable or actual socio-political change can weaken social patterns for which 'old' traditions had been designed, producing new ones to which they are not applicable. Invented traditions, then, are most likely in situations of socio-structural change. Hobsbawm (1983) claimed that such 'traditions' chiefly have three functions: group cohesion, the legitimation of social institutions and practices and finally the diffusion of values, beliefs and norms.

Historians' interest in issues of remembering and forgetting exemplifies the degree to which issues of accuracy of memory are less of a focus in comparison to the socially constructed nature of memory. The postmodernist approach within cultural studies has emphasised the fractured nature of social life. Following on from this critical approach, the traditional study of history has been attacked as partisan, imprecise and ephemeral; as being a cultural artefact that is itself continually refashioned to accord with new needs. Objectivity and positivism in social scientific and historical research has been attacked by historians themselves (for example, Thompson, 1988). What has resulted is more of an emphasis upon memory and myth and the analysis of these phenomena tend to focus upon issues of hegemony and power in relation to the construction of histories, particularly national histories (see Alonso, 1988).

Social psychological perspectives

There is some similarity between the role of Maurice Halbwachs within the field of sociology and Frederick Bartlett within the field of psychology, in that both scholars were early pioneers of social aspects of remembering and forgetting in the first half of the twentieth century. Both also were 'forgotten' by the mainstream in their respective disciplines until relatively recently (Edwards and Middleton, 1987). Bartlett (1932/1995) stressed that the content and process of remembering was a social process. He noted how conversational and ritual behavioural processes were important aspects of remembering. Furthermore, he drew attention to the fact that membership of social or ethnic groups was important – that the act of remembrance did not occur in a vacuum, but was performed against a backdrop of social norms, institutions and networks of communication. Finally, he recognized the role of emotion in social remembering and forgetting.

Looking at more recent scholarship, it is apparent that empirical approaches to social memory are common, especially within social psychology. In terms of theoretical approach, the diversity that characterises social memory research across the social sciences is mirrored within psychology. A variety of perspectives may be identified, including social-cognition, autobiographical, identity, discursive, action theory and culture theory approaches. These differ in several aspects. First, there is diversity in the scope of 'social' aspects of remembering and forgetting. Second, the degree to which processes of identity are considered relevant to social remembering varies. Third, contrasting epistemological approaches are employed – discourse analysts, for example, advocate the study of language and conversational patterns, eschewing hypothesised mental or environmental structures. Finally, there is a clear divergence between direct or indirectly experienced events as the subject matter for social memory research. This divergence stems from orthodox psychological interpretations of memory applying empiricist epistemological assumptions, in which personally experienced events are counted as 'real'. Larsen (1988) citing Halbwachs (1950/1980) posited a more constructivist alternative based upon continental philosophy in contending that others can mediate an individual's knowledge, derived from a process of social construction. This latter approach opens up the possibility of more distant, non-experienced historical events as subject matter for social memory research.

Social-cognition

In terms of scale, the most microscopic focus belongs to that of the social-cognition perspective (see Clark *et al.*, 1990; Babey *et al.*, 1998). In this approach, researchers typically investigate whether the cognitive process of remembering is influenced by social factors. Questions addressed include how recall, as a process, differs between individuals, dyadic and four-person groups. The individual is the essential unit of analysis. This is also the case within the autobiographical memory perspective that has focused upon social aspects of personal remembering, particularly flashbulb memories (for example, Brown and Kulik, J. 1977; Finkenauer *et al.*, 1997). Flashbulb memories have been described as distinctly vivid, precise, concrete, long-lasting memories of the personal circumstances surrounding people's discovery of shocking events, such as assassinations of public figures.

(Finkenauer *et al.*, 1997, p. 191)

Such memories have been described as collectively shared across a group or society. Research has indicated an important emotional component to these memories, contributing to a sense of surprise and vividness (Finkenauer *et al.*, 1997).

Social identity theory

Group level empirical and theoretical approaches may be differentiated between those based upon theories of the self or identity and those that are not. Social identity theory (SIT, in Tajfel and Turner, 1986), which has been influential within the field of social psychology in the study of intergroup and ethnic conflict, has been applied in several empirical research studies concerning social memory research. Several of these studies have taken place in the context of Northern Ireland. These studies have produced divergent findings. McKeever *et al.* (1993) examined the memory of Northern Irish Catholics and Protestants for violent events that had occurred since 1980. They predicted that members of the two groups would remember this period differently, recalling different events and that divergent explanations for the 1981 hunger strikes would be given. In terms of methodology used, the authors combined open-ended and focused approaches. The results indicated that the Catholics were significantly more likely to remember Catholic deaths than the Protestants while both groups were equally likely to remember Protestant deaths. Second, for the prompted violent events, seven of whom involved Catholic deaths and seven involving Protestant deaths, the Catholics were more likely to remember the Catholic events while there was no significant difference in relation to the recall of the seven Protestant events. Finally, the attributions of responsibility for these events did markedly differ between the two groups. For example, in relation to the 1981 hunger strike, Catholics attributed blame to 'external factors', such as the 'government' while Protestants tended to attribute this event to 'internal factors' such as suicide. The authors suggested that group differences were produced by the increased salience of Catholic social identity resulting from minority group membership.

Cairns and colleagues (Cairns *et al.*, 1998; Cairns and Lewis, 1999) have also conducted empirical research in the Northern Irish context.

In the first study, university students in 1984 and 1995 were asked to date video clips of political events in Northern Ireland. Results contrast with those of McKeever *et al.* (1993) in that the events were similarly well remembered (dated) by both Catholics and Protestants. In the second study, group membership and a second factor – place of residence – shaped social remembering of a particular political event, yet it was Protestants who were more likely to remember this particular event. McKeever *et al.*'s (1993) assumption that group identity determines remembering is almost certainly an overstatement, as Cairns and Lewis (1999) point out, although all of the studies mentioned clearly suggest that social groups shape the construction of memories in contexts of conflict. It is likely that the status of the ingroup and the strength of ingroup identification both play a role in shaping social remembering and forgetting.

Further empirical studies of social memories that have been influenced by SIT (Tajfel and Turner, 1986) include a study of European's attitudes to political integration (Hilton *et al.*, 1996) and New Zealanders' attitudes to past and present political events (Liu *et al.*, 1999). Both of these studies are distinguished by the use of a social psychological theory of social knowledge – the theory of social representations (SRT in Moscovici, 1988). Both studies use ideas drawn from SRT to describe the dynamics of shared belief systems common to groups or societies – a likely characteristic of social memories. This research reveals the socio-historical context within which present-day intergroup relations are situated. Together they suggest that the application of social psychological theories to the study of social memories can produce beneficial insights and that future theoretical work is necessary to integrate theoretical tenets from diverse theories of identity, group conflict and social knowledge.

This was attempted by Devine-Wright (1999) who recognized the contested nature of claims for legitimacy in contexts of conflict. These claims relate not only to the shape of the existing social structure, often with an unequal distribution of power and resources across different social groups, but also to the strategies and methods employed by social group members to alter or preserve the socio-political *status quo*. It was argued that one strategy that might be employed by groups in contexts of conflict to bolster or undermine the legitimacy and stability of the *status quo* might be the propagation of social memories and active participation in commemorative rituals and traditions. The social construction of structural legitimacy is an overlooked research area within social psychology (Purkhardt, 1993), in which legitimacy is often assumed *a priori* and defined as temporally within artificial group studies in laboratory research contexts.

Devine-Wright (1999) argued that SIT (Tajfel and Turner, 1986) processes, including social creativity (in which members of social groups can redefine the dimensions of comparison between groups) and social competition (collective action to alter the social structure), might also involve social memory processes. For example, choosing to compare ingroup and outgroup in a past temporal period, rather than in the present context, may be a fruitful socially creative strategy to preserve a sense of positive ingroup distinctiveness and self-esteem for the individual group member. Second, social rituals such as commemorations may be fruitfully interpreted as forms of social competition, in that the enactment of 'traditions' may be an attempt by members of a high status group, for example, to preserve the socio-political *status quo*, prevent social change and maintain the status of the ingroup in society.

What is also suggested is that the use of commemoration as a collective strategy to influence the *status quo* can be a controversial action both at the intergroup level and at the intragroup level (Devine-Wright, 2001(a); Devine-Wright, 2001(b)). If some ingroup members perceive the commemoration to clash with important shared values and ideals, perhaps because of the manner in which it is conducted, then commemorating the past can reduce the cohesion of the group, alienating some group members from others. Empirical findings in the context of Northern Ireland supported this analysis (Devine-Wright, 2001(a)), suggesting that participation in historical commemorations was linked to willingness or refusal to accept social change.

Identity process theory

Lyons' (1993, 1996) approach to social memory is founded upon identity process theory (Breakwell, 1986). Breakwell theorised that identity was a process with biological, personal and social elements that develops in time, guided by four principles: continuity, distinctiveness, esteem and efficacy. Lyons focused upon the identities of groups rather than individuals, arguing that social remembering might be guided by the above principles serving to heighten the sense of continuity across time, distinctiveness, collective-esteem, collective-efficacy and cohesion of groups. Both Devine-Wright and Lyons (1997) and Roe (1998) have applied Breakwell's identity principles to processes of social remembering. Roe (1998) utilised them as a framework of analysis to interpret the social remembering of the Cowlitz Native Americans.

Devine-Wright and Lyons (1997) empirically investigated the symbolism associated with historical places in Ireland. It was hypothesised that such places were environmental referents for particular social memories related to national identities. The findings suggested that each of four places studied were related to the principles of esteem, efficacy, continuity and distinctiveness in the context of respondents' sense of being Irish. The places related to their sense of pride in being Irish (esteem), their feelings of continuity with Irish people from the past (continuity), their sense of uniqueness in comparison to other nationalities (distinctive) and finally to the practical achievements of previous generations (efficacy). The study corroborated Halbwach's assertion (1941) of the importance of the physical environment in relation to social memory processes. Irish people seemed to identify themselves with certain historical places because they symbolise the nation and what 'Irishness' is defined to represent. This is not to assert that all Irish people have similar beliefs about the places studied. Different interpretations of the places was interpreted as indicating that different versions of Irish history exist for different Irish people, depending upon their degree of active involvement in Irish traditional activities. The places were interwoven with, and emblematic of, different ways of remembering the Irish past.

Collective narrative

Pennebaker's (1992; Pennebaker and Banasik, 1997) empirical approach has defined collective memories as involving 'the ongoing talking and thinking about the event by the affected members of a society or culture'. Remembering is defined as a 'dynamic social and psychological process' (1992, p. 2). His empirical analysis focused upon memories of American public events like the Gulf war for American society. He concluded that collective memories were the result of an interactive process that took the form of a collective narrative, a consensual story about a particular event or person from the past. The emergence of a particular event in this narrative was said by Pennebaker to be shaped by the degree of long-term change caused by the event upon people's lives. Pennebaker also supported a generational interpretation of remembering (see Schumann and Scott, 1989, above), claiming that major national events will affect people of different ages in different ways. Those between the ages of 12 and 25 will be most affected. As a result, people tend to look back and commemorate the past in cyclic patterns occurring every 20–30 years.

Pennebaker's societal level focus and empirical results offer many fruitful hypotheses for further research. Cross-cultural research can verify whether these findings can be demonstrated outside of the cultural context of the United States. His emphasis upon emotional events and the way in which people collectively make sense of them through inter-personal conversation is a useful contribution to the literature. His focus is specific in that it is upon very recent events and the way in which people collectively cope with them and understand them within short periods of their occurrence. Whether memories that refer to events that occurred beyond people's lifetimes and personal experience relate to similar social processes deserves further empirical research. Furthermore, describing the collective memory as a collective narrative perhaps places an emphasis upon the consensuality of memory that might be problematic when analysed empirically.

Discourse analytic approaches

In contrast to the approaches mentioned above is the discourse analytic perspective (for example, Edwards and Middleton, 1987; Middleton and Edwards, 1990). This perspective adopts a strongly constructivist perspective focusing upon conversational discourse as the sole process of remembering and forgetting. Referring to Bartlett (1932/1995), discourse analysts have taken the position that the accuracy of recall is unimportant. More significance is attributed to how versions of events are constructed in conversation, how they are shaped and fitted to the particular context and what the participants in the interaction accom-plish – such as to establish identity, claim membership of a group, to blame, to justify and so on. (Middleton and Edwards, 1990). Researchers focus upon conversation in order to elucidate how cognitive processes are represented in language rather than how conversation is represented cognitively. Specification of putative universal mental models of memory is considered unimportant (Middleton and Edwards, 1990). The impli-cations of such an approach is a welcome emphasis upon social, ecological, pragmatic and rhetorical functions of remembering and forgetting. It is a reminder that traditional sociological and psychological approaches to memory are normative in emphasis. It is often assumed that group members share social memories in a fairly homogenous manner. Discourse analysts might argue that multiple interpretations may be the norm rather than the exception and that this must be taken into account in any social-psychological accounts of the phenomenon.

A focus upon interpersonal interactions as a unit of analysis in memory research is a feature of the model of transactive memory developed by

Wegner (1987). Wegner (1987) was critical of psychologists for an over-emphasis upon cognitive processes of memory, consistently ignoring 'external memory', that is the manner in which human beings utilise objects/individuals as external storage media for information. Wegner (1987) focused upon how the interdependence between people in a group forms a transactive memory system encompassing the memory systems of individuals and the processes of interpersonal communication between them. Certain people within social groups can become specialised experts, functioning as memory stores and used as a memory resource by other members of the group. Such a transactive system was viewed as a group information-processing system. This analysis is useful in broadening the focus of memory beyond a purely individualistic focus to that of small groups. However, it is not clear to what extent his theory could apply to larger scale groups or categories in which interpersonal communication between all of the members is unlikely, if not impossible. Theorising about social remembering in such collectivities requires going beyond the interpersonal level of analysis.

The final social psychological perspectives to be mentioned are those of action theory and culture theory (for example, Scribner and Beach, 1993; Straub, 1993). Both approaches are firmly based within the tradition of psychological memory research. They reflect attempts to overcome dualistic problems: whether memory be conceptualised as 'structures' that occur within the confines of the head (for example, Anderson and Schooler, 1991) or as 'structures' that are distributed across the social and physical environment beyond the individual (see Stokols and Jacobi, 1984). Action theorists adopt an intermediary position that is an attempt to reach beyond this self-other/inside–outside dichotomy, emphasizing an interactionist position that encompasses environmental influences upon memory and vice-versa in a mutually influencing dialectical system. According to the authors, it is neither possible nor advisable to separate social and cognitive processes. This approach is an echo of Bartlett's research on remembering and forgetting (1932/1995) in its emphasis upon a holistic account of human mentality, encompassing emotional processes. It also echoes Breakwell (1994) and Doise's (1986) ideas about the study of social psychology that have recommended analysis at different levels.

The culture theory approach to social memory (for example, Straub, 1993) is similar to the above in that 'action' is seen to be simultaneously the result of the intentional mental reflections of an individual and a flexible, functional and symbolic constituent of the 'cultural action field' which is open to multiple meanings, options and valences.

This approach is similar to the discourse approach in that memory is seen as a linguistic, symbolic construct. It is an important constituent of culture, articulated in and created through the 'narration of stories'. Recognition and acceptance of the past is part of a process of generating the surrounding world and the individual's identity in that world. Straub (1993) claimed that remembering is a structured, dynamic and constructive process. Texts, documents and symbolic objectivations are not storage facilities for the past. They do not carry meaning passively; rather they are the impulse 'for subjective semantic operations, for reflection and recollection'. With this in mind, collective memory is conceptualised as a framework and structural basis for the creative and communication-based production of collective experiences. Social recollections are conceptualised as 'actions' of groups that are only to the extent memory-related actions to which the collective memory provides social and cultural traditions in the form of materialised or institutional starting points for the co-construction of mutual pasts. Collective memory then becomes a changeable repertoire of both action-structuring and action-determining possibilities.

Relating memory and conflict: a summary

Several disciplinary perspectives have linked processes of remembering and forgetting with issues of ethnic conflict. Scholars have noted how memories can be used to legitimise or delegitimise social institutions and collective actions. Anthropologists noted the 'charter' function of myths in relation to social change – either justifying change or attempting to obstruct it (for example, Malinowski, 1948; Cohen, 1985). Historians have described how traditions come to be 'invented' in order to legitimise socio-political claims (see Hobsbawm, 1983). From both disciplines, a picture emerges of how beliefs about the past can be constructed and mobilised to serve socio-political purposes. This is significant for contexts of ethnic conflict, in which social change is usually desired by one of the conflict parties. It also explains why memories can be the subject of controversy in contexts of conflict. There is a behavioural dimension to this issue also. Devine-Wright (2001(a)) noted the potential role of historical commemoration, using the Orange parades in Northern Ireland as an example, in legitimising or delegitimising the social structure, representing a form of collective action that actively attempts to influence the socio-political *status quo*. In this vein, scholars have noted how terrorists seek to legitimise violent actions by referring to the past (Bowyer-Bell, 1978; Tololyan, 1989). The link between legitimacy and memory reflects the temporal nature of ethnic conflict and the manner in which group leaders can seek to manipulate and distort memories for group purposes (for example, Mack, 1983; Schudson, 1995).

An important issue that relates to the legitimising role of memories noted above concerns the issue of identity. Many scholars have noted the link between memories and identity (for example, Mack, 1983; Gillis; 1994; Devine-Wright and Lyons, 1997; Cairns and Lewis, 1999; Liu *et al.*, 1999). It has been asserted that social identifications shape the nature of people's beliefs about the past. Members of ethnic groups in contexts of conflict are likely to share accepted ways of seeing history. Members of different groups are likely to have significantly different beliefs about the past. At the individual level of analysis, remembering and forgetting have been linked to processes of self-esteem (Mack, 1983). The threat to self-esteem posed by memories of past conflict defeats have been claimed to be used to mobilise and motivate present day group members to engage in collective acts of vengeance on behalf of the group (Mack, 1983).

Reconciliation between ethnic groups and the role of memory in this process has received increased attention (for example, Falconer, 1988; Fennell, 1993; Asmal *et al.*, 1996). Scholars have debated whether remembering the past serves to help reconciliation between conflicting groups. Two views emerge. First, Devine-Wright (1999) suggested that certain constructions of history, used to legitimise actions in a context of conflict, were unhelpful in a climate of emerging peace and reconciliation, serving only to entrench divisions between groups and preclude the possibility of forgiveness. In this context, it may be necessary for common ways of remembering the past to be 'forgotten' and new constructions to emerge that are more in tune with changing societal contexts. Second, a powerful argument has been made about the need to prevent forgetting, for example by the Truth and Reconciliation Commission in South Africa and scholars of German history and the holocaust. This argument reflects the moral and political nature of processes of remembering and forgetting. In South Africa, moving from a social climate of apartheid and conflict to one of peace requires that those who have been prevented from remembering must be allowed to do so for moral reasons (Asmal *et al.*, 1996). Only when these acts of remembrance have occurred can reconciliation and forgiveness take place.

The contrasting nature of these arguments for forgetting and for remembering the past illustrates the complexity of links between memory and ethnic conflict that operate at multiple levels of analysis, from personal to collective. This review has evidenced the rich diversity across the social sciences, particularly within social psychology and sociology, into topics concerning memory, history and ethnic conflict. Existing research suggests that the study of such processes can play an important role in explicating both the dynamics of ethnic conflict and conflict resolution. What is necessary is a consolidation of the diverse approaches into a more coherent body of literature and further empirical research focusing upon issues of forgiveness and reconciliation. As is clear from contributions to this volume and other writings that focus upon memories and reconciliation in diverse geographical and social contexts (for example, Falconer, 1988; Fennell, 1993; Asmal *et al.*, 1996), there is much scope for future theoretical and empirical scholarship. Such development contributed by social scientists can make a positive contribution to practical attempts to resolve ethnic and intergroup conflict.

Part II
Memories of Aboriginal Pasts and Current Conflicts

3
Reconciliation between Black and White Australia: the Role of Social Memory

David Mellor and Di Bretherton

This chapter presents the premise that within the Australian nation are divergent social memories, and that these memories relate to different senses of self, group identity and needs of the present. It is argued that such constructs are important considerations in the process of reconciliation between black and white Australia. After providing a brief historical/ political background to the current conflict between black and white Australia, we briefly discuss the role of social and cultural factors in shaping the way in which people interpret, remember and recall events. Finally, we present and discuss the findings from two recent studies that suggest the manner in which memories of historical events are culturally encapsulated may impede the understanding and resolution of social conflicts.

The meaning of reconciliation in Australia

History tells us that Australia was 'discovered' by Captain Cook, who claimed it for England in 1770. Despite the fact that at the time there were approximately 750,000 Aboriginal people living on the continent (White and Mulvaney, 1987), the land was considered by the English to be *terra nullius* – that is to say, empty. Eight years later, the first fleet arrived, bringing with it a few hundred convicts who had been shipped out, because of a shortage of prison space in England. From the white Australian perspective, the subsequent colonisation is represented as a process of taming a new and inhospitable land, bringing agriculture, technological development and culture. From the Aboriginal perspective, colonisation began a process of dispossession, attempted genocide and a cultural genocide that continued up to and throughout the twentieth century.

The white settlement of Australia can be conceptualised as military 'conquest'. In such a conquest, suggests Ho (1985), the indigenous population is confronted with two choices: unconditional surrender or extermination. Among members of both the indigenous population and the colonisers, myths or prejudices about members of the other group appear spontaneously, and function to emphasize the belief that there are indeed major differences between the groups. Social identity theory is useful to explain this phenomenon. Simply put, the conquerors see the 'good' (including culture) belonging to themselves and the 'bad' belonging to the conquered. Ho argues that in order to survive the conquered must accept this interpretation. A higher level of congruence between the two groups in their views about themselves and each other helps to stabilise the relationship between them, and reduces the possibility of overt conflict between them. However, it may also lead to decimation of the well-being and culture of the conquered. In Australia for example, new diseases such as smallpox, syphilis and measles, against which the indigenous population had no immunity, were introduced with white settlement. After 150 years of white occupation, the indigenous population had fallen from approximately 750,000 to only 60,000. Of the original 200–250 distinct languages that were spoken, at least 50 are now lost. Another 100 or so are spoken only by a small number of elderly people, and as few as 30 languages are used in everyday life and passed on to the current child generation.

Stability, based on dispossession, cultural oppression and domination, characterised the relationship between white and black Australia up until 1967. At that time, a referendum among white Australians decided that recognition should be given to Aborigines as citizens. Since then there has been considerable discussion about the relationship between black and white Australia. In 1979, the National Aboriginal Commission, a government advisory committee, suggested that a treaty between Aboriginal and non-Aboriginal Australians be drawn up. However, the idea lapsed until the 1988 bicentennial celebration of the discovery and settlement (or dispossession) of Australia neared. At this time, the Prime Minister, Bob Hawke, put forward the idea of a 'compact' as a possible goodwill gesture to Aboriginal people. Subsequently, he promised a treaty between Aboriginal and white Australia, suggesting the centenary of Federation in 2001 as the likely date for such a treaty.

The issue of a treaty, however, remains unresolved due to a lack of consensus and commitment. Opposition has come from many quarters. Some believe a treaty would unite the Australian population, others that it would divide. Unresolved questions include: what form should a treaty take? Which voice or voices should represent the diversity of Aboriginal groups in Australia to negotiate and sign a treaty? How should the interests of those opposed to a treaty be addressed? How should a treaty be implemented in a federal system where states have explicit rights? Finally, what would ultimately be achieved by a treaty more than 200 years after occupation/dispossession? Current Prime Minister John Howard has argued that the idea of a treaty is absurd, because a nation cannot make a treaty with itself.

Today, the concept of a treaty has been put to one side and the process currently advocated is reconciliation. The Black American writer hooks (1993), who discusses racism, sexism and healing in her critiques of hierarchical social relationships, describes reconciliation as relating to our capacity to restore harmony to that which has been broken, severed and disrupted, implying not only that there is damage to be repaired, but also that there was at some previous stage an harmonious relationship. However, the relationship between black and white Australia has never been harmonious, so the idea of restoring the relationship to harmony is misleading, and the term 'reconciliation' seems to be something of a misnomer in the Australian context. Despite this, it has now been cemented into common discourse through media and political references and has taken on the broader meaning implied by hooks.

The reconciliation process aims to improve relations between white and black Australians at the community level through increasing understanding of indigenous history and culture, from the time of white settlement to the present. The objective is to foster an ongoing national commitment from the mainstream community to co-operate with Aboriginal people and to address Aboriginal disadvantage before the centenary of Australia's federation, in 2001. Sadly, this target is nowhere near being met.

Our analysis of the reconciliation process presents it as having three stages: (1) coming to terms with the past; (2) taking responsibility in the present; and then (3) working together to make a better future. It is clear that memory plays an important role in coming to terms with the past, and that if there is a lack of agreement about the past; it is difficult to move forward towards reconciliation. An examination of the literature on memory suggests that a chronological account, where past memories generate present stances is too simplistic to be a useful basis for understanding reconciliation processes. In reality, present stances influence what is remembered and what is forgotten in both individuals and groups. Therefore, an alternative analysis of memory is required.

Memory

Since the first psychological studies of memory were conducted, psychologists have viewed memory as an active process of representation (see Devine-Wright, this volume). Rather than an objective recording device, which can be rewound and replayed like videotape, it is has been shown to be influenced by subjective elements. Information that is already within the memory system, and the way in which individuals perceive and interpret new information shape what becomes encoded, stored and retrieved. That is to say, individuals construct their own memories. As described by Bruner (1994), 'Self is a perpetually rewritten story. What we remember from the past is what is necessary to keep that story satisfactorily well formed' (p. 53). Contemporary evidence that not only the events of the past, but also the circumstances of the present, influence the process of recollection has been highlighted by recent debates about the 'false memory syndrome', where therapists are thought to have implanted memories of childhood abuse in client's minds (Pope, 1996).

Memory differs from documented history in that it is more subjective, fluid and mobile. As a rule the content of everyday memories is not systematically recorded, nor are the sources of recollections documented. Memory then does not passively receive and store perfect perceptual representations but rather actively constructs representations of varying correspondence with external events and continues to work on these constructions. Rather than 're-collecting' stored data, the mind 're-creates' the past from a bank of images, which are themselves in motion.

Devine-Wright (this volume) notes that historically psychologists have analysed memory in a manner that exclusively focused on individuals. However, if individuals inhabit a social world, commemorate the past together and make sense of their lives through social communication, then the cultural and social aspects of memory also need to be considered. Bartlett (1932/1995) characterised the precise role of the relationship between social factors and memory as follows:

> Every social group is organized and held together by some specific psychological tendency, which gives the group a bias in dealing with external circumstances. The bias constructs the special persistent features of the group culture and this immediately settles what the individual will observe in his environment. It does this markedly in two ways. First by providing that setting of interest, excitement, and emotion which favours the development of specific images, and

secondly, by providing a persistent framework of institutions and customs which act as a schematic basis for constructive memory. (p. 255)

The sociologist, Durkheim (1912/1947), referred to the shared beliefs and feelings of a society as 'collective representations'. These collective representations do not form a reified fixed entity, like Jung's (1969) collective unconscious, but rather are observable interactions and products such as stories, commemorations and discourses. Halbwachs (1992) suggested that such *social memories* are important for maintaining group cohesion: 'A group's memories will be determined by present contexts – the beliefs, interests and aspirations of the present which are held by groups, will shape the various views of the past as they are manifested in any historical epoch'. (p. 2)

In situations of conflict the emotional function of the social past is heightened. Mack (1983) analyses memory in contexts of conflict from a psychodynamic perspective of psychohistory. His proposition, that social memory serves the needs of group cohesion and identity, provides a point of convergence with the work of social psychologists such as Tajfel (1982). National myths and versions of the past serve, Mack says, to maintain national continuity and cohesion and to strengthen attachment to the land (and hence claims to territory). He suggests that intergenerational transmission of historical triumphs and grievances may be carried out by parents, the education system, the media and literature. Similarly, Feagin and Sikes (1994) also note the importance of history but suggest that as well as being stored in individual memories and family stories, experiences of oppressed people are also stored in group recollections.

We will use the term *social memory* to describe the accounts of the past, which are shared by a group. As demonstrated in Devine-Wright's (this volume) analysis of the research on memory, the content of social memory is not objectively accurate recollections of the past. Not only is social memory biased by group processes, it is also vulnerable to the idiosyncratic tendencies of individual memory. Social actors are human beings and are fallible in their initial understanding and representation of events. Social actors refine stories in the re-telling. Pieces of content can become dissociated from their sources. Emotions shape recollection and representation. A strong sense of conviction is not a reliable guide to the objective truth of the account.

Memories and reconciliation: empirical studies

In our work on reconciliation in Australia, we have been interested in the role of social memory and other cognitive functions. In particular, we have been interested in the kinds of memories that characterise the two reconciling groups: white Australians and Aborigines. We have conducted two studies that provide insight, one with Aborigines and one with white students.

Aboriginal perspectives

Respondents to our study (Mellor, 1998; Mellor *et al.*, 2000) of what Essed (1990, 1991) termed *everyday racism* made it clear that for Aborigines, current experience cannot be divorced from historical context and that social memories are vital. As expressed by one respondent,

> All me ancestors y'know an' that. My father and his father, his grandfather pass stories on y'know and runs in that family, old stories like that. Oh, it just hurts. Even when you just read about, it y'even got tears an' everythin'. You're just readin' about it, and thinking about it. It still hurts mate, y'know? You can never take away the pain, no matter how long. Give us land, get our land back, whatever, still won't take away the pain. The oldies still feeling it today mate. They, they've been there and done that, an' trapped an' seen all the other people die. Their stories are, they tell 'em on down to the young people, y'know like today. See with my kids, I'll tell 'em too. Y'know? Still keeps goin'.

In this study, 32 indigenous Australians aged between 20 and 54 years participated in in-depth interviews about their experiences. Recognizing that Aboriginal people are a small and much-studied minority that is wary of being exploited by researchers, we employed a qualitative method that focused on listening to their concerns. Following Finch's (1993) suggestions on how to avoid relative power relationships influencing such interviews, the formal structure of the interviews was limited to open-ended questions and the interviews were conducted on the participants' own 'territory' (that is, at community centres and meeting places, or in their homes). Interviews were audio taped so respondents could talk informally in a relaxed atmosphere.

The method of allowing respondents to talk freely about their experience, and letting research categories emerge from the data, was a rich way of approaching the subject. Interestingly, we asked respondents about their personal experiences of racism, but they consistently reframed the question and began talking about past injustices that applied collectively to their people. Three core aspects of the past emerged as being particularly central. These were the dispossession of

Aboriginal people, subsequent treatment of Aboriginal people and the (now-ceased) practice of removing Aboriginal children from their families. Each of these is presented and discussed briefly below.

Dispossession. Two recent High Court cases have sharpened the national focus on dispossession. These are known as the 'Mabo' and 'Wik' decisions. The 1992 Mabo decision rejected the notion that Australia was *terra nullius* at the time of white settlement. However, despite moving the issue forward for Aboriginal people, the decision was limited because it stated that native title could only be recognized if Aboriginal groups can demonstrate an unbroken connection with the land. This condition is impossible to meet for those groups who have been removed from their traditional lands and prevented from returning to it. However, as Galarrwuy Yunupingu, chairman of the Northern Land Council has argued,

> Native title is not a piece of paper or words in a book. It is our living Aboriginal culture. It is our songs and our dances, painted on our bodies and written in the sand. It is our law, which has been unchanged for thousands of years. If it is taken away, then we have lost everything. (1997, p. 15)

While it was the hope of many that the Mabo decision would offer some potential for reconciliation between white and black Australia, theories of symbolic racism would predict the opposite. According to McConahay and Hough (1976) symbolic racism in the US is a reaction to policies and actions that represent the gains or demands made by Blacks, and are elicited by issues such as affirmative action, black candidates for public office, and public welfare. Opposition to such issues is justified in terms of 'traditional' values such as equality, fairness, individualism and self-reliance. In Australia, the return of land to indigenous Australians had the potential to be seen in a similar way. That is, giving something to people who are not trying to help themselves, not making a genuine effort on their own and therefore not deserving of the land, because their use of the land violates traditional European values about the way land should be used. Indeed, rather than creating 'a nation at peace with its soul', the Mabo decision did seem to unleash such racist sentiment, with various members of the white community arguing that the dispossession of Aborigines had been inevitable, that the nation was at risk of reverting to a 'stone age culture of 200,000 people living on witchetty grubs' (see, *The Melbourne Age*, 19 June

1993), and that Aborigines should trade back the blankets and trinkets given to them at the time of European settlement in exchange for their land.

The Wik decision, handed down in December 1996 followed a claim by the Wik people from the Cape York Peninsula for native title to Crown lands leased to pastoralists. Four of the High Court's seven judges found that native title and pastoral leases could coexist. However, they added that where there might be a conflict between the two interests, the pastoral lease would prevail. Various lobby groups, including State governments, pastoralists and mining companies applied pressure for legislation to extinguish native title rights as the only way of clarifying the question of certainty of title. This triggered a new round of bitter debate as the national government procrastinated over the issue, and various High Court challenges to the legislative outcome, whatever it might be, have been flagged.

Such opposition to Aboriginal land claims does not give recognition to the connection between the past and the present. Current social arrangements, which privilege some and not others, were based on and are still influenced by, the doctrine of *terra nullius*, the denial not only of Aboriginal rights but the Aboriginal peoples' very existence. That the indigenous respondents in our study see white people as denying the connection between the past and present is demonstrated by the following extracts from the interviews with two of our participants.

> I mean, you know, they invaded Australia when we were there. I reckon they should be waking up to themselves and start realizing that they wasn't the first people in Australia. You know they claimed this, and by the queen, and by the court judge, or whatever they were supposed to be doing.

> You know, that in European consciousness they didn't even acknowledge what had happened.... A lot of white people go about their business and they don't even realize that they are standing on people's freedom, that they are hurting people.

Further, the respondents see echoes of the doctrine of *terra nullius* in both government policy and current attitudes:

> I mean the government today, they just don't understand that we, as indigenous people, really, all we want is to be recognized that we are true Australians! They should give us, you know, that dignity that we

are the true, well they say, the true dinky-die Aussies. You know it's good to say that you are Australian, which we are proud to say. Well if you're bothered to say you are Australian, be proud of it, be proud of us, we were the people that were here first.

Treatment of Aboriginal people since colonization.   The treatment of aboriginal people since colonization is also highly salient in the memory of the contemporary indigenous population. For example, one participant in our study argued that white people do not know the whole story of colonisation:

> More often than not, they don't know the whole story. They only know the part of the story that they want. You know? You know what I mean?

Another participant was more forthright about what the white people do not know, and how the impact of the past lingers on indigenous people:

> And um, yeah, it's just that a lot of people don't realize that, you know, 200 years ago people were slaughtered. I mean they were shot and just left where they are. You know, and they say we got it easy, you know? I mean you know we hurt too.

A third participant recounted other means by which such genocide was carried out:

> Years ago, the white fella used to give you flour and damper for free labour and they used to get sick of you, and they used to put acid in the flour. Yes, they used to put acid in the flour, and watch their stomach explode. And they'd laugh about it! Nobody knows about that today. It's easy for them to sit there and laugh and say 'they got shot, they're dead', the ancestors, when we know it's gone on and on.

In fact, some feel the continuity of these atrocities:

> It's been happenin' two hundred years. Australia's the youngest country in the world, mate. Y'know? Two hundred years!... Oh, so many (massacres) in just one area, in Gippsland, everywhere, all around Australia mate. Still feels like that today, y'know. White Australia has a black history.

Further, others marvel at the ease with which these atrocities were neglected by current society in the face of the slaying of 35 people at the Port Arthur outdoor museum, Tasmania in 1996.

> They [the media] make reference to the fact it is the greatest massacre in the world, but they don't count the Aboriginal massacre. They just look at themselves. I don't want to take anything from them, from the tragedy that happened, but I just think now that if people looked at the white people, what do you think happened to the black people when their people were massacred?... They hardly even acknowledge that our people were massacred, like in Tasmania. It just gives you a bit of an insight into our tragedy. Of what has happened to the blackfellas.

The removal of children.   According to the Human Rights and Equal Opportunity Commission's (HREOC, 1997a) report of the National Inquiry into the Separation of Aboriginal and Torres Strait Islander Children from their Families, indigenous children have been forcibly removed from their families and communities since the very first days of the European occupation of Australia. Most present-day Aboriginal families have been affected in one or more generations by the removal of children. Depending on which state authority oversaw the removals, between one in three and one in ten indigenous children were forcibly removed from families and communities across Australia between 1910 and 1970. The report concluded that indigenous families and communities have endured 'gross violations of their human rights, and that these violations continue to affect indigenous people's daily lives' (Human Rights and Equal Opportunity Commission, 1997b, p. 33). These violations were seen by the Inquiry as an act of genocide, aimed at wiping out indigenous families, communities and cultures.

Haebich (2000) reports on the ease with which Aboriginal children could be taken away from their families. In Western Australia, police could enter communities at will and take children, filing reports to the child welfare authorities later. In Queensland, only a ministerial warrant was needed. In some states under child welfare laws the burden of proof that the child was neglected was low. Haebich argues that the recency of these policies is demonstrated by the fact that the 1950s and 1960s were a time when adopting a black child was not unusual, and at one point having a black baby in the house was the 'in' thing. She states that at this time the faces of cuddly black babies and Aboriginal children sent to the city for holidays beamed from the pages of papers, particularly in Victoria.

The *Stolen Generation* Inquiry saw itself as of fundamental importance in validating the stories of generations of indigenous people who until now 'have carried the burden of one of Australia's greatest tragedies' (Human Rights and Equal Opportunity Commission, 1997b, p. 33). In effect, it allowed the social memories that provide the framework for the indigenous standpoint in the reconciliation process to be explained. It also allowed white Australians, perhaps for the first time, to see the sense of loss and grief experienced in an ongoing manner by generations of Aborigines when their children were forcibly removed from their families. Because the majority of white groups do not experience this everyday social reality of Aborigines, the white viewpoint is one of detachment. In contrast, the Aboriginal view is derived from the shared experiences of their community because there is hardly an Aboriginal family that was not affected by child stealing. One of our Aboriginal respondents reported as follows:

> I used to have a fear of white people, because we had white people chasing us to put us away. So we had fear. When we were sleeping on river banks, my mother would put a camp where, a long way from the road, you know, in a clear way, so she could see a car coming. You could have a back door. You know? A little hut with a back door, and then just run out the back on the river, or swim the river, if the police came down. It was always a fear. A life of fear.

Another respondent reports the trivialisation of the issue by whites:

> You only have to read through the papers. I have read through there, and anything about Land Rights...you know, 'they shouldn't get that'. The children have been taken away – 'they shouldn't worry about that'. But they don't go back and know the effects of what happened.

In the manner described by Ho (1985), we white Australians want to see ourselves as good and remember our white ancestors as good. As one Aboriginal interviewee told us:

> They're still in Australia today, y'know, keepin' it dark, not sayin' much about their history, are they? That's why you don't get many white Australians today gettin' up and talking about their past 'What

about my ancestors?' an' all that, 'cos they know what they done. That's why they won't get up an' say anything.

In summary, the record of the past for indigenous people is better seen as social memory, rather than history. Stories of the experiences of dispossession, attempted genocide, removal of children and social dis-location are told and passed on, rather than systematically documented. While they are not part of the millennia-old oral traditions like the stories of the dreamtime handed down from mother to daughter, father to son, in an unchanging traditional setting, these social memories are made up of more recent stories of uprootedness, persecution and social rupture that are shared within the broader kinship system. The social significance of these memories is in the sharing. For the indigenous community, social memories constitute 'our' story, and in the current social context, social identity is built around them.

These Aboriginal social memories contrast with the accepted Austra-lian history. Such history is recorded in official texts or other tangible media, and observations and ceremonies of remembrance tend to enshrine and reinforce it. In the main, what is recorded and celebrated is the story of white settlement, privilege and triumphs. Even when oral historians attempt to put stories together to find out what 'really happened' their emergent findings are authenticated against existing records to establish 'the truth'. When existing records are biased or incomplete, 'the truth' is only relative.

The White perspective

Our study of racism pointed to the need to understand the past as well as the present. Initially we, like our indigenous respondents, considered the contrast to Aboriginal social memory to be white history, the official story of white settlement. As we became more sensitive to the complex relationship between individual and social memory we began to wonder what in fact diverse groups of white Australians remember about the past, and we decided to collect some empirical data.

It was neither culturally appropriate nor cost effective to use the qualitative narrative approach we adapted to meet Aboriginal needs. Rather, following the methodology of Cairns and Lewis (1999) who used an open-ended approach to investigate the social memories of subjects in Northern Ireland, we asked a convenience sample of 40 first-year psychology students to describe the three most significant events in Australia's history. The students volunteered to participate in the study as it offered them an opportunity to fulfil the research participation requirements of their year. As they were attending one of the more prestigious universities in Australia, they were drawn from the upper end of the achievement spectrum for young Australians. It would be expected then that they are knowledgeable about current affairs, and somewhat progressive when compared to the general population. Twenty-four of the students reported that both of their parents were born in Australia, nine students had one of their parents born in Australian, three students were Australian-born to parents who were born elsewhere in the world, and the remaining four students and their parents were born in different countries overseas. There were no Aborigines in the student sample.

As they identified their three most significant events in Australia's history, the participants were asked to state why each event is significant, the source of the information, and where and how they learned about these events. Rather than following Cairns and Lewis (1999) and searching for memories of a particular event, we evolved content categories from the data. The first category was defined by economic and political events. It contained 42 responses, of which events related to the Federation of Australia in 1901 were the most frequently cited. However, the National Council for the Centenary of Federation would be most disappointed to learn that there were only nine, of a possible 120 mentions of the Federation, suggesting that it is not very salient. A variety of other economic and political events made up the remaining 33 responses. These varied from the gold rush of the 1850s to the abolition of capital punishment. The reasons given for choosing economic/political issues were the establishment of independence, humanitarian concerns and the building of the 'national character'. It is noteworthy that Aboriginal issues rated poorly in this list. The 1967 referendum, which gave Aborigines the right to vote, was mentioned only twice, as were the stolen generation and the High Court Mabo decision. The reasons given as to why these were important were that they recognized prior mistakes by white settlers.

The second category related to the (European) discovery, settlement and colonisation of the country. While a few respondents thought the initial discovery was a most significant event, the majority of responses focused on issues of colonisation. The significance of colonisation was seen to be the establishment of the socio-political and cultural basis of the nation (for example, English roots rather than another European nation, the lack of a class structure and the genesis of the Australian character). However, less than 25 per cent of the 34 responses recognized that the settlement by Europeans signified the dispossession of

Aborigines. Some referred to the changes that settlement began, others saw the duality of the process and a small number noted the dispossession.

The third category of significant events and issues was defined by wars – perhaps reflecting acceptance of the military nature of the colonisation and Australia's recent history. Seventeen responses were in this category. While the two world wars were seen to be significant because of the large losses of life, they were also considered to be important in, again, defining the national character. Associated social change, particularly in the role of women was also seen to be significant. Notably, the frontier wars that followed European settlement described by Yarwood and Knowling (1982) were not recognized in the responses of the participants.

The fourth category related to the bicentennial celebrations in 1988. One reason for the prominence of this category may be that it occurred when many of the participants were in primary school, and a considerable part of the curriculum was devoted to it. And as reflected by the data, the bicentennial year celebrated the non-indigenous history, with only two participants referring to the dual aspects of the events of settlement. The final rather mixed category included natural disasters such as Cyclone Tracey, which destroyed Darwin in 1972, sporting achievements such as the 1983 Americas Cup victory, and the 1996 Port Arthur massacre in which 35 people were killed.

These data indicate that despite the Prime Minister's fear that activists and sections of the media are promoting 'black arm band' history, the university students in this study had a Eurocentric understanding of Australian history and failed to note the double-edged nature of historical events. While the students themselves were from diverse non-indigenous backgrounds, their view of history was 'white', with the core concerns of Aboriginal people being rarely mentioned. Given that this sample was made up of academically advantaged young people, the implications are rather stark. Our data were collected through an open-ended, qualitative approach, which allowed for issues salient to the participants' memory to be accessed. No doubt had they been asked direct questions about the stolen generation, for example, they would have been able to discuss some of the issues involved. However, the fact that such issues did not arise spontaneously suggests that they are not the most salient aspects of history stored within the memory of these participants.

Implications for reconciliation

Current formal processes in post-apartheid South Africa are posited on the view that public acknowledgement of the truth is key to the whole

process of reconciliation. However, if truth is seen as somewhat subjective then the problem of whose or which truth remains. The black
majority in South Africa can put weight behind its stories, and reveal an
underside to recent history, which challenges the official story of the
past. As our data have shown, in Australia the Aboriginal *minority* can
all too easily be forgotten. For example, when the *Stolen Generation*
report was released to the public, many Australians claimed that they
knew nothing of the practice of removing children from their families
with the explicit purpose of reducing the Aboriginal population.
Haebich (2000) recently demonstrated that this lack of awareness was
not, or should not have been, the case because there is a long history of
public debate about these policies. Haebich's research reveals 70 years
of opposition to the removal of Aboriginal children expressed through
editorials, columnists, letters to the editors and stories running on the
front pages of newspapers. Haebich suggests that in the early part of the
century the opposition was not continuous but came in bursts of
concern. However, by the 1950s and 1960s it was extensive. The many
voices of opposition and protest in the newspapers indicate a level of
public awareness and concern that has not been acknowledged in
contemporary debate. Haebich's claim is consistent with our own data.
Despite copious publicity given to the release of the *Stolen Generation*
report less than one year before our study was conducted and the centrality
of the issue to Aboriginal people, it received only two mentions from
the non-indigenous student group.

The Reconciliation Convention in Melbourne in 1997 gave Australians a chance to reflect on the history of our nation; a history, which
our Prime Minister, John Howard, tells Australians to be proud of. He
has no time for 'black arm band history' – a sentiment echoed by
former state premier Rob Borbidge, who recently proclaimed 'The
whole sorry industry has gotten a bit out of hand. If some people spend
their lives moping around about what happened in the past, that's their
business' (*The Melbourne Age*, 27 May 1998, p. 1). Indeed the government
has implemented an advertising campaign that aims to make people
proud of their (white) heritage.

Our studies suggested that the indigenous and non-indigenous social
memories are not the same. Their views of history are influenced by the
standpoints determined by unequal power, and the subsequent oppression of one group by the other. The relative freedom experienced by
generations of white people allows for a series of social memories of
particular events that are related to national character. These commemorate and reinforce the history of white settlement and colonisation.

While such memories are comfortable to the majority population, they are in marked contrast to the unmet need of the minority. In the Aboriginal community bitter memories of loss and dispossession, passed down through generations, mark the continuity of cultural oppression. Frustration with the lack of acknowledgement of these memories was expressed by many of our indigenous participants. For example

> The schools aren't . . . teaching children about the true history and just, you know, our worth as a people. It's not there in the history books. I mean the curriculum doesn't say that this is part of your learning or part of the teaching. They're electives. They can elect to know about us if they feel inclined.

While it seems clear that the parties to reconciliation in Australia have different social memories of the Australian past, this difference relates not only to the content of memories but also to the processes involved. The dominant white narrative is enshrined as history through schooling and other socialisation processes that are periodically reinforced by the media and annual ceremonies such as the celebrations associated with Australia day and with ANZAC day when Australia's fallen soldiers are remembered. This history is the accepted story and is corroborated by evidence uncovered by historians. In contrast the Aboriginal perspective is better described as a shared network of narratives of personal experiences of the community that date back at least to the advent of white settlement. This 200 year old history is experienced *as if* autobiographically. Abuse of community members in the past as well as the present is recounted as abuse of oneself. For example,

> And I'm very angry, and frustrated that I'll never get rid of it. It'll die with me, because I won't be able to. I've still got all this anger because it is still in my eyes what happened to my family, and others in my family, not just my mother.

By contrast, the dominant white group, with its greater individualism, does not feel this personal connection with the collective past. What happened to other people in the past is experienced as not belonging to the self, not 'my' responsibility, and hence no apology is needed. The white past is thus distal, and remote, and easily selectively forgotten, whereas the black past is proximal, keenly felt and constantly remembered. This is a history that we in the mainstream do not routinely read about or acknowledge. To become aware of this history, we need to hear the narrative of indigenous people, and try to understand what the events recalled mean for the lives of the individuals affected by it. But to challenge the white version of history, we need evidence that may not be recorded in the manner familiar to historians.

In contending that there are diverse social memories between the parties to the reconciliation process, we recognize that there is also diversity within these groups. This is of particular note within white Australia. 'White' is an adequate descriptor of the official historical narrative, but non-Aboriginal Australia is made up of many more groups than the descendants of the original British settlers. It seems that in-coming migrants from diverse cultural backgrounds tend to accept the official history and for the purpose of reconciliation are conceived of as white. If this supposition were true then it would help explain why Aboriginal people experience more racism than immigrants do (Mellor, 1998). It could be that Aboriginal people are perceived as more threatening to white identity because they challenge its historical justification.

Lack of knowledge of and agreement about the past is an obstacle to reconciliation. However, provision of information about the past will not necessarily lead to accord between conflicting parties. Rather, the past can be seen as another arena for contestation, for the past is recalled in the present, and in the present what is remembered and what is forgotten is shaped by social and cultural forces (Bartlett, 1932).

Conclusion

In discussing social memories of the two parties to reconciliation in Australia, we have pointed to asymmetries in the content and type of memory, which relate to the difference in power between black and white. One of the misleading features of the process of reconciliation is that it does imply two parties who are equally responsible for the past and can be called upon to forgive and forget. In the Australian context, framing the conflict in this way is not helpful. To achieve harmony it will be necessary to begin reframing the issues in a way that gives more power to Aboriginal people, as well as promoting the study of Aboriginal issues as a key element of reconciliation. Further, there is a need to develop reflective understanding of the roots of white identity. Helms (1990, 1995) provides a framework for this. Finally, there is a need to give more place to the Australians who are neither indigenous nor the descendants of early British settlers. Instead of automatically co-opting them into the 'white' side, they need to be disaggregated from it. Rather than encouraging the Australian public to forgive and forget, we should perhaps be encouraging a process by which the different views of history can be brought to compliment each other. Such a process may result in all members of society having the opportunity to understand how the past both shapes and is shaped by our diverse identities.

4
Cowlitz Indian Ethnic Identity, Social Memories and 150 Years of Conflict with the United States Government

Mícheál D. Roe

Introduction

In a comparative study of Pacific Northwest Native Americans (or American Indians) attempting to regain some semblance of their former lands and resources, anthropologist Kenneth Tollefson argued that:

> land, or some other form of a tangible estate which includes water, property, and other natural resources, is indispensable to the economic and social well-being of tribal people.... Dislocated tribal people generally seek some tangible estate in order to maintain their common fund and their system of values (Tollefson *et al.*, 1996, p. 321)

In this analysis, Tollefson introduced three types of contemporary Native American – estate relationships: (1) tribes which signed treaties and now live on resultant reservations; (2) tribes which did not sign treaties, but gained access to reservation lands; and (3) tribes which signed treaties, but never received tribal reservations or allotments *as tribes* on other reservations.[1] This third type of tribe has yet to achieve any tangible estate. The Cowlitz Indians of southwestern Washington state represent a fourth type of Native American experience. The Cowlitz composes a *non-treaty* tribe, which never received a tribal reservation and has yet to achieve a tangible estate. In spite of 150 years of conflict with the United States government, during which time they were forced from their land, pressured to assimilate and even today remain in uncertainty regarding their federal recognition as a tribe, the Cowlitz have maintained individual ethnic identity, tribal identity, and tribal authority.

Ethnic identity and ethnic or social memories may appear paradoxical in settings of political conflict. Working through similar psychosocial mechanisms, they may hinder or facilitate peacemaking processes, or both. That is, while focusing on group distinctives may sustain and exacerbate conflict, it may also empower groups to maintain cohesiveness and to continue to function until conflict resolution is achieved. One of the challenges in working for resolution of ethnic conflicts is to diminish the negative effects of ethnic identities and social memories, without eliminating their positive contributions. In reality, such objectives can make peace processes more attractive to the principals, since ethnic groups in conflict rarely are interested in giving up their cultural identities and histories. Ethnic identity and social memories have provided for both personal and community stability and empowerment for the Cowlitz Indians described in this chapter, and it has been precisely that continuity in their identity and memories which has perpetuated conflict with the United States government – a government that had intended that the Cowlitz simply assimilate into mainstream American society and no longer raise challenges to it.

In contrast, since the day in 1855 when the Cowlitz refused to sign a treaty with the US government, they have vigorously confronted federal, state and local governments, even inviting arrest as they exercised rights denied to them. Persistent conflict has been the Cowlitz reality. For example at the federal level, in the early 1900s Cowlitz pursued a number of land claims with an unresponsive US government. They obtained the introduction of twelve separate bills in US Congress, only to have their one success vetoed by President Coolidge in 1928. With the Indian Claims Commission established in 1946, the Cowlitz formally submitted a petition in 1951. In 1969, a compromise decision was reached, however, due to disagreement in how the judgment fuds were to be disbursed, those funds have yet to be released.

The Cowlitz Tribe was designated for termination in 1953, however, the termination bill failed to pass Congress. At this point the Bureau of Indian Affairs (BIA) of the United States Department of Interior, without statutory authority, began treating the Cowlitz tribe as if it had been terminated. With the federal acknowledgement process established in 1978, the Cowlitz formally submitted a petition in 1982 and a revised petition in 1987. At the present time, their federal recognition is being challenged in a board of appeals. As a consequence of their unrecognized status, in the 1920s the state of Washington began to enforce off-reservation fishing and hunting regulations against the Cowlitz. The tribe successfully forced the state to issue necessary Indian identification cards to tribal members. When the state dropped the Cowlitz from the card programme in 1976, they filed suit against the state and won back their rights through a United States Court of Appeals decision in 1981. At the local level, in 1957 the Cowlitz entered suit against the city of Tacoma over proposed construction of hydroelectric dams on the Cowlitz River. They lost the suit and as a result fish runs were destroyed and archaeological sites inundated. In 1978, the Cowlitz again confronted local authorities to protect archaeological sites from the construction of a new hydroelectric dam on another stretch of the river. In contrast to the earlier conflict, the local public utilities district worked with the Cowlitz throughout the 1980s to protect the tribe's interests. However, conflict has reemerged. As recently as the June 2001 Cowlitz tribal meeting, the general membership supported a proposal to bring suit against the local city power company to open up the Cowlitz River for fish passage (that is via fish ladders at the hydroelectric dams).

In this chapter, the foundation for such persistent conflict will be examined by exploring Cowlitz ethnic identity and social memories. Two approaches will be utilised. The first will provide an historical and modern community analysis of the Cowlitz experience of acculturation, applying the comprehensive model of John Berry at Queens University, Ontario (see Berry, 1980, 1997). The second will be an analysis of Cowlitz social memory, based on the social psychological model of Evanthia Lyons at the University of Surrey (Lyons, 1996; Devine-Wright, this volume).

Acculturation

The history of Native Americans is replete with ethnic conflicts occurring both before and following Euroamerican contact, and certainly conflict well describes the relationship between Native Americans and the United States government throughout its relatively short existence. As with all aboriginal peoples during times of peace or conflict, the Native American experience has been one of acculturation. Acculturation refers to the process of culture change, which results from direct and continuous contact between two or more cultural groups (Redfield *et al.*, 1936). Although acculturation influences are mutual, it is well recognized that most changes occur in the less dominant of the group.

Models of acculturation

Early models conceptualised acculturation as a simple linear process, which ultimately ended in a rather diffuse category of *modernity*. This type of model presented the interval between traditional culture and modernity as a continuum on which a cultural group was located. In the case of native peoples, the basic assumption was that contact over time with the encroaching dominant culture would result in the native group moving along the continuum until it passed a point where it became more modern than traditional; that is, it became more like the dominant culture than its aboriginal past. Once beyond this point the members of the native group were considered assimilated and no longer representative of their original culture. Unfortunately the application of this model is all too common today with proponents 'treating acculturation exclusively as assimilation' (Berry, 1980, p. 9). They attempt to evaluate native peoples by observing how much of their aboriginal culture is evident, translating that evidence into a location on the continuum, and then analysing the location's relationship to that 'point of no return'.

Research from the past 30 years has demonstrated the inadequacy of the linear model, and consequently the inadequacy of a process, which attempts to locate a cultural group on that linear continuum. Models today recognize that acculturation is multidimensional, multivariate, and multiple endpoint in nature (for example, Weinreich, 1988; Trimble, 1989; Ward and Rana-Deuba, 1999; Berry, 1997).

The complex nature of acculturation is well represented in Berry's model (see Berry, 1997). This conceptualisation delineates a variety of categories of variables: (1) phases of acculturation; (2) types of acculturating groups; (3) nature of larger society; (4) modes of acculturation; (5) endpoints or goals of change; (6) sociocultural characteristics of acculturating group; and (7) psychological characteristics of acculturating individuals. Modes of acculturation and endpoints or goals of change are particularly relevant to this analysis of the Cowlitz, so they will be described in greater detail.

Modes of acculturation

Arguing that acculturation is not synonymous with assimilation, Berry presents acculturation as an adaptation process designed to decrease conflict between cultural groups. He argues that four modes of acculturation exist and that they are defined according to two dimensions. The first dimension relates to ethnic distinctiveness, and the second to inter-ethnic contact. The valuing of both a distinct ethnic identity and inter-group contact defines the *integration* mode of acculturation. Not valuing a distinct ethnic identity while valuing inter-group contact defines the *assimilation* mode of acculturation.

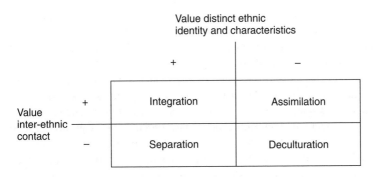

Figure 4.1 Modes of acculturation

Source: J.W. Berry (1997) 'Immigration, Acculturation, and Adaptation', *Applied Psychology: An International Review*, 46, 5–68.

Valuing a distinct ethnic identity and not entering into inter-group interaction defines the *separation* mode of acculturation. Finally, the loss of ethnic identity coupled with alienation from larger society defines the *deculturation* mode of acculturation. These are diagrammed in Figure 4.1.

Endpoints or goals of change

Three alternative goals of change are particularly relevant to native peoples. Berry and his colleagues in their research among the James Bay Cree Indians of Canada isolated these; they include the goals of *continuity*, *change*, and *synthesis* (Berry, 1984). *Continuity* is evident in the persistence of traditional ways (that is, ways prior to Euroamerican contact), and it is also evident in a cultural group which is no longer traditional but whose goals emphasize a 'more characteristic' ethnic way of living. *Change* represents attempts to become more like the dominant culture, while *synthesis* is an attempt to select the best of both worlds.[2]

Native Americans and acculturation

At the time that Columbus landed on the shores of North America, it is estimated that there were between two and ten million indigenous people, living in over 300 distinct cultures and speaking over 200 languages. The cultures were various and well adapted to the different environments of the forests in the east, mountains and deserts of the southwest, rainforests and salt water of the Pacific northwest, and so on. The preceding centuries saw the rise and disappearance of many cultures, and the rise and social transformation of many others (Fowler, 1972; Nabokov, 1991). That is, acculturation had been occurring long before the first contact with 'white man'. In the Pacific northwest, for example, regular inter-tribal contact was occurring along the Columbia River near the present day town of The Dalles in Oregon state. Here substantial trade was occurring between Indian peoples of the northwest, plains, and sometimes from as far east as the Great Lakes (Nabokov, 1991). To facilitate communication among such a diverse group of Indians, a 'universal' trade language developed, the Chinook jargon, elements of which are still in use in the region. Today about two million Native Americans, Eskimos and Aleuts live in the US on over 175 reservations and about 200 Alaskan villages.

Also today exist between 150 and 175 unrecognised Native American tribes in the United States.[3] Their members are ineligible for most Indian services and programmes, and as groups they experience none of the prerogatives of sovereignty available to recognized tribes. Some of these unrecognised tribes never signed treaties with the US government. With others, the US government simply abrogated the treaty agreements. In most cases, the government does not consider present day members of these tribes to be Indians, but assimilated descendants of Indians. In western Washington State alone, there were seven such tribes as recently as April 1996: the Snohomish, Snoqualmie,[4] Samish,[5] Chinook, Steilacoom, Duwamish and Cowlitz. In fact, their names are a part of the local geography; for example, the Cowlitz River, Snohomish County, Snoqualmie Valley, the town of Steilacoom and so on.

In order to change its status, an unrecognised or unacknowledged tribe must receive a positive determination from the Branch of Acknowledgement and Research (BAR) of the BIA. The federal acknowledgement process requires that the petitioning tribe meet seven criteria (25 Code of Federal Regulations, 1978): (1) documentation continuously identifying the tribe from historical times to the present as 'Native American'; (2) evidence that the tribe constitutes a *modern community* of Native Americans; (3) evidence that the tribe has maintained continuous political authority over its members; (4) submission of the tribe's governing document or documents; (5) submission of a membership list with evidence for each member of her or his descendancy from the aboriginal tribe; (6) evidence that members are not also members of another Native American tribe; (7) evidence that the tribe was not the subject of congressional legislation which, expressly terminated its relationship with the federal government.[6]

Experience of the Cowlitz Indian Tribe

History

The aboriginal Cowlitz Indians were an interior tribe of what is now southwestern Washington State. To date, evidence has been uncovered indicating continuous human habitation in the Cowlitz region for some 7000 years. At the time of first Euroamerican contact, Cowlitz villages extended along the Cowlitz River from near Mount Rainier to the Columbia River. Others also lived in the Lewis River area between Mount St Helens (the volcano that erupted in 1980) and Mount Adams. In general the Cascade Mountain range provided the eastern boundary to Cowlitz lands. Those Cowlitz inhabiting villages along the lower Cowlitz River spoke Salish as did most of the western Washington tribes; those Cowlitz inhabiting the upper Cowlitz and Lewis River areas either spoke Sahaptian, characteristic of native peoples east of the Cascade Mountains, or were bilingual (Irwin, 1979; Ray, 1966).

Based on extensive field work among the Cowlitz Indians which commenced in the late 1920s, Ray (1966, 1982) argued that the Cowlitz were unique among tribes of western Washington and Oregon. The Cowlitz had no access to salt water, visiting the coast very rarely, and the Columbia River held relatively little economic relevance to them. Salmon were important to the Cowlitz, but this food source occupied a relatively smaller place in their economy than with other tribes in the region. Their lands contained great geographic contrasts, from prairies to river valleys to the forests and slopes of the Cascade Mountains. In the midst of these contrasts, the Cowlitz economy was particularly dependent on the small, widely scattered, but numerous open prairies. Of all western Washington tribes, the Cowlitz was the most accomplished hunters, had the greatest dependence on roots as diet supplement and utilised horses the most. Finally, the Cowlitz was the most cohesively organised of western Washington tribes.

The yearly cycle of the Cowlitz people began in the spring when they left their cedar longhouses along the streams and rivers and travelled by canoe and horse to the prairies to dig camas bulbs and gather the roots, bark and grasses from which they would make baskets, mats and fishing nets. With the arrival of summer they moved into higher country for berry picking. The autumn salmon run brought the Cowlitz back to the rivers. Hunting and some fishing were practiced all year round (Irwin, 1979).

Records of early contact between Euroamerican explorers and Cowlitz Indians began with the 1805–06 Lewis and Clark expedition. Trappers and traders followed and a Hudson Bay station was established on Cowlitz Prairie. Around 1830 an epidemic of 'intermittent fever' decimated Indian populations along the lower Columbia and lower Cowlitz Rivers. Cowlitz Indians were among the victims with whole villages wiped out. Their numbers never recovered. The 1840s saw major encroachment by white settlers into Indian lands throughout the region, and increasing Indian discontent (Ruby and Brown, 1981). Cowlitz Indians experienced confrontations with settlers, dislocation from villages, trespass and even the plundering of their graves. In spite of these violations, the Cowlitz did not enter the 'Indian Wars' of the 1850s. The result of those wars was a plethora of treaties and the displacement of many Pacific northwest tribes to reservation areas. The 1855 Chehalis River Treaty offered to the Cowlitz required that they leave the Cowlitz Prairie and River, and that they resettle in the alien ecology of dense rainforests on the salt-water coast among a traditional enemy, the Quinault Tribe (Proceedings, 1855). The Cowlitz refused to sign any treaty, which required that they leave their aboriginal lands, consequently, they resolutely declined to enter a treaty relationship with the US.

At the turn of the twentieth century Special Indian Agent Charles E. Roblin evaluated the Cowlitz of the past as follows.

> The Cowlitz tribe was a powerful tribe, and in the early days constituted the 'blue blood' of western Washington. They were independent, fearless and aggressive; and they refused to subordinate themselves to the white man by entering into a treaty with him. Their descendants have the same qualities, which placed their ancestors in the position of leaders. (Roblin, 1919)

Tollefson (1992) suggested three alternatives for Indian survival during this period. They could either: move to inadequate reservations, form new Indian communities in less accessible areas, or move out of the area entirely. The Cowlitz followed a variation of the second alternative. With no treaty and no land base the Cowlitz were unable to maintain their aboriginal economy, and were forced to enter into the mainstream economy of the dominant culture to survive. In the early years of the twentieth century Cowlitz cultural distinctiveness was not only discouraged, it was literally outlawed. In the mid twentieth century an unsuccessful attempt was made to terminate the Cowlitz Tribe through legislation. In spite of this failure, the BIA administratively terminated the tribe on grounds that it no longer existed as a culturally distinct group (Beckham, 1987). The BIA claimed that the Cowlitz had assimilated; in contrast, the Cowlitz never relinquished their tribal identity or authority. That is, their acculturation was via the integration mode, and this form of adaptation continues today (see Beckham, 1997).

Modern community

The Cowlitz modern community was explored in a series of three studies associated with the federal acknowledgement process. These are described in depth in Roe (1991, 1992). The first study consisted of 1989 oral histories from key elders and a subset of Tribal Council members. Judith Irwin collected these data through semi-structured, face-to-face interviews.[7]

Based on a content analysis of these oral data and other documents, a second study was designed to assess six domains indepth: (1) participation in tribal meetings; (2) tribal efforts to protect its members' interests; (3) social interaction of tribal families; (4) tribal leadership; (5) ethnic identity; and (6) involvements as a tribal member but beyond tribal boundaries. A subset of then current and past Tribal Council members participated, producing in most cases quite extensive written protocols. These protocols were content analysed according to the six domains delineated above. The domains of Social Interaction and Ethnic Identity were found to be particularly relevant to the Cowlitz modern community study, and so they were the primary areas analysed and interpreted. The Social Interaction domain provided content related to tribal gatherings, tribal communication, leadership and decisionmaking, and social networks. In this latter category, sociometric techniques provided information regarding interpersonal preference and behaviour. The Ethnic Identity domain provided content related to self-identity, cultural knowledge and practices, and relationship to aboriginal lands and river.

The final study was focused on the general membership of the Cowlitz Tribe. Based on the results of the second study, a short, structured survey was designed and administration procedures standardised. The items examined four domains: (1) Tribal meetings; (2) Informal Social Interaction; (3) Tribal Authority; and (4) Ethnic Identity. The survey was designed to be administered by phone or face-to-face interviews. The interviewers were Tribal Council members who received an introduction to the instrument and the data collection process during a brief training session following a tribal meeting. The choice of using Tribal Council members as data collectors reflected the importance of decreasing participant–interviewer distance in cross-cultural research (for example, Pareek and Rao, 1980; Munroe and Munroe, 1986) and the importance of participant–researcher links in increasing response rate (Warwick and Lininger, 1975). In addition, an attempt was made to assign to Council members those participants who were family or friends. Data were collected on 90 enrolled members of the tribe, 18 years of age or older. These participants represented a 57 per cent response rate of the original sample selected.

Only a subset of the results is presented in the tables following. These results are particularly relevant to Cowlitz tribal authority, ethnic identity and social memory. Given the non-parametric nature of the data, a series of Chi Squares were performed, corrected by the Bonferroni inequality to protect against type 1 errors. (For a complete examination of the results, see Roe, 1992.)

Data in Table 4.1 demonstrate the high importance placed on the tribal leadership, not only to administer formal and informal tribal business, but also to maintain cultural traditions and tribal identity. Data in Table 4.2 demonstrate the high importance placed on variables of personal ethnic identity and collective 'memories' of historical and cultural experiences and practices. Taken together these data are consonant with the *integration* mode of acculturation.[8] These data, in conjunction with oral data to be presented shortly, also support *synthesis* and *continuity* in Cowlitz goals of change. That is, in their acculturation process they have retained important elements of Cowlitz culture while

Table 4.1 Level of importance: roles of Cowlitz Tribal and Council Chairs

Role	Level of importance					
	% No	% Some	% Average	% Above average	% High	*n*
Administering tribal business	1.2	2.3	5.8	15.1	75.6*	86
Maintaining tribal harmony	0.0	1.2	7.0	18.6	73.3*	86
Representing tribe to community	1.2	1.2	4.7	18.6	74.4*	86
Continuing Cowlitz cultural traditions	2.3	0.0	10.5	15.1	72.1*	86
Strengthening Cowlitz tribal identity	0.0	0.0	4.7	10.5	84.9*	86

Bonferroni inequality: $\alpha_0 = \alpha_T/Q$. Given $\alpha_0 = .05$ and $Q = 5$; $\alpha_0 = .01$
* Statistically significant comparison, Chi Square $p < .001$.

Table 4.2 Level of importance: Cowlitz Ethnic Identity

Element of Identity	Level of importance					
	% No	% Some	% Average	% Above average	% High	*n*
Identifying self as Cowlitz to others	1.1	2.3	14.9	16.1	65.5*	87
Knowing Cowlitz history and culture	1.1	2.3	8.0	18.4	70.1*	87
Passing on Cowlitz culture to next generation	2.4	1.2	11.9	8.3	76.2*	84
Practicing traditional Native American cultural ways	13.9	8.9	35.4	10.1	31.6*	79
Honouring spirits of Cowlitz ancestors	5.9	5.9	17.6	14.1	56.5*	85
Honouring and communing with all creatures	3.5	7.0	17.4	15.1	57.0*	86
Being on or near the Cowlitz Prairie	9.3	8.1	26.7	14.0	41.9*	86
Being on or near the Cowlitz River	7.0	5.8	23.3	15.1	48.8*	86

Bonferroni inequality: $\alpha_0 = \alpha_T/Q$. Given $\alpha_0 = .05$ and $Q = 8$; $\alpha_0 = .006$
* Statistically significant comparison, Chi Square $p < .001$.

accepting elements from the dominant culture, and they have empha-sized a 'more characteristic' Cowlitz way of living. *Continuity* is evident in members' 'characteristic Cowlitz' attitudes and behaviour toward the Cowlitz River and Prairie. They communicate a sense of relationship and place with their aboriginal land. *Synthesis* is evident in their main-taining Christian beliefs side-by-side with elements of Native American spirituality (see Lame *et al.*, 1972; Capps, 1976; Weaver, 1998). In particu-lar, these elements relate to the Cowlitz relationship with the spirits of their ancestors, their respect for and relationship with the Cowlitz River and Cowlitz Prairie, and for some, the practice of traditional ceremonies (for example, longhouse ceremonies, sweat lodge, drumming, cleansing with smoke and eagle feathers).[9]

The Cowlitz succeeded in their battle for recognition by the US government, Formally signed by a representative of the BIA on 14 Feb-ruary 2000. The following statement was published in the United States

Federal Register on 18 February 2000 along with substantial supporting documentation.

> Pursuant to 25 CFR 83.10 (m), notice is hereby given that the Assistant Secretary [of Indian Affairs] acknowledges that the Cowlitz Indian Tribe...exists as an Indian tribe within the meaning of Federal law. This notice is based on a determination that the tribe satisfies all seven criteria for acknowledgment...(Gover, 2000).

This is a positive final ruling. However, currently the Cowlitz Indian Tribe is in the midst of a challenge by the Quinault Indian Nation, which is contesting the finding before the Indian Board of Indian Appeals. The Quinault Indian Nation is the present day equivalent of the Quinault Tribe among whom the Cowlitz would have been required to live according to the 1855 Treaty described earlier.

Social memory

Members of groups share ethnic or social memories, and they become context and content for what will be jointly recalled and commemorated in the future (Middleton and Edwards, 1990), with social forgetting just as socially constructed as social remembering (Irwin-Zarecka, 1994). Sociological and psychological writings on social memory have been numerous and variable (see Devine-Wright, this volume). Emerging from this literature is a new social psychological model of social memory, which applies Breakwell's Identity Process Theory to group identity (Lyons, 1996). Identity Process Theory is framed around content and value dimensions, assimilation-accommodation and evaluation processes, and identity principles of distinctiveness, continuity, social value and autonomy (Breakwell, 1986, 1996b).

Lyons' (1996) model proposes that groups are likely to construct, sustain and reconstruct memories in such a way as to show their *continuity, collective self-esteem, distinctiveness, efficacy* and *cohesion*. This model provides a framework to explore the ethnic identity and social memories of the Cowlitz Indians and their relationship with the US government. (Throughout this section, direct quotes from Cowlitz people will be used to illustrate the principles under discussion.) Lyon's notion of *continuity* is demonstrated when members explain their group's present identity with consistent constructions of the past; for example, the Cowlitz people consistently assert their 'Indianness' and their relationship to their aboriginal ancestors.

My spirit is Indian and I do what is expected. I pray, I try to honor the spirits of the animals and vegetables the Creator provides.

[Being near the Cowlitz Praire and River] we always felt a sense of belonging, because we always knew we were Cowlitz.

[Being near the Cowlitz Praire and River] I always know I'm walking where my ancestors lived and my ancestors are very much a part of me.

Enhancing *collective self-esteem* is demonstrated, for example, in claiming famous persons, as members of ones own ethnic group. For the Cowlitz, recognition of their past 'blue blood' status among western Washington tribes and the frequent claim of descent from early Cowlitz chiefs fulfil this purpose. The most common claim is descent from Chief Scenewa, who was a Cowlitz leader in the early 1800s, although tribal members also name Chiefs How-How and Kish-Kok.

Distinctiveness guides the process of remembering the uniqueness of ones people in rituals. The Cowlitz fulfils this criterion through the practice of traditional ceremonies and the telling of traditional folklore and myths. For example, the Cowlitz begin every tribal meeting with the spiritual leader, often holding a 'talking stick',[10] telling a Cowlitz legend; and recently the tribe published a book of Cowlitz legends to ensure their preservation. *Group sense of efficacy* is enhanced by memories of victories, while defeats are forgotten or at least not a central focus. The Cowlitz perceive themselves as collectively efficacious (see Bandura, 1982), and their collective efforts over the decades have resulted in important accomplishments for the tribe. The implications of these accomplishments are revisited regularly at tribal meetings in the course of conducting tribal business. Recent examples include a very large monetary award as a result of a land claim suit, ongoing work on aboriginal sites with state archaeologists, and active consultation with Washington State in developing the Mount St Helens interpretive center (see Roe, 1994).

Finally, *group cohesion* is served when groups construct their past in ways that emphasise unity rather than division. Even in the midst of internal conflicts, the Cowlitz accomplish cohesion in part through their persistent focus on family continuity over generations and family ties between current tribal members. The Cowlitz Indian modern community consists substantially of family networks; most Cowlitz learned of their heritage and culture through family members. Most knew their family lineage, attended tribal meetings with family members, considered renewing family ties to be a primary purpose of the tribal meetings, formally and informally gathered with Cowlitz family members outside of tribal meetings and considered Cowlitz family members to be among their closest friends. In addition, most considered it important to continue to honour the spirits of deceased Cowlitz family members. This salience of family connections confirms Fitzpatrick's (1986) observations of the Cowlitz Indians, and is in line with her argument that interaction through kin networks is 'typical for Salish [Indian] people whether they live on reservations or not' (p. 213).

An additional process occurs between the Cowlitz, which facilitates cohesion, but is somewhat at odds with Lyons' argument for a group sense of efficacy described earlier. That is, sharing memories of past events in which one's ancestors were victimised. It is not uncommon at tribal meetings for a tribal member to stand up and address all present, angrily describing a past disenfranchisement of a family member at the hands of the US government – the same government, which for a century and a half refused to acknowledge the Cowlitz. Most have similar family memories and share the expressed anger in solidarity, perceiving the government at least in part as an external common enemy (see Rubin *et al.*, 1994). Related to corporate anger, is corporate grief shared at each tribal meeting, when the Cowlitz stand in silence with heads bowed in deference to the memory of Cowlitz elders deceased since the previous meeting. As one tribal member sighed, 'another elder passed on without seeing his tribe recognized'. It is not uncommon for the corporate grief to rekindle the corporate anger with the realization that again an elder died who never had access to the resources available to Indians in recognized tribes. (For additional discussion of this sense of collective victimization, see Mack 1983.)

Two hypotheses emerge from Lyons' (1996) social application of Identity Process Theory, which are particularly relevant to Cowlitz – United States government relations. First, 'when a group's identity is threatened by challenges to its values and what it stands for, then the continuity and cohesiveness principles will dominate' (Lyons, 1996, 26). A focus on continuity and cohesiveness leads both to an emphasis on the past and to entrenchment of identities. Among the Cowlitz this is evidenced in the persistent practice and/or sanctioning of traditional spirituality in terms of personal relationship to land (that is, prairie and river), and the honouring of spirits of ancestors. This is evidenced also in the maintaining or reviving of traditional practices. Particularly clear examples are found in the attitudes of many Cowlitz people toward desanctification ceremonies. That is, the ceremonial removal of a sacred valence surrounding aboriginal sites, particularly graves, before the contents are disturbed.

> The desanctification ceremonies are meaningful to me as a way to apologize to our ancestors for disturbing their area and to enlist their help as we try to uncover information about the past. These rites help me to be aware of my link with them and my responsibility in the present to help keep the Cowlitz people alive.

> I feel the spirit of our people, living and dead, remains with the land that has been given to us by the Creator and lovingly cared for century after century . . . [desanctification] is a proper way to pay honor to the spirit of our ancestors and to respect the ground that has been home to our people for thousands of years. It is a way for the tribe to pay respect to the ancestoral spirits; honor the site where our people have been known to occupy, and a means of gaining and granting permission for the ground to be open.

The second hypothesis emerging from this model states that 'where the group's identity is threatened in terms of recognition of its existence by others, then the distinctiveness principle will dominate because what makes a group distinct is likely to provide the rule of inclusion and exclusion for the group' (Lyons, 1994, 36). Given the long history of governmental refusal to recognize the Cowlitz as an Indian tribe, this hypothesis has particular poignancy. Evidence for this hypothesis is found in the Cowlitz blood quantum requirement for tribal enrolment, in their knowledge of their personal lineages and in their unyielding claims of being Indian people. This was rather dramatically demonstrated in responses to a set of questions, which addressed Cowlitz ethnic identity and the possibility of the BIA ultimately refusing to acknowledge the Cowlitz tribe.

> We will stand together and go on being the Cowlitz Indian Tribe the way we always have. We are Cowlitz Indians no one can take that away.

> My identity as a Cowlitz Indian will not be affected by whether or not the government comes to officially acknowledge the tribe. I know in my heart that the tribe exists, regardless of what the government paper work says. I will continue to be a proud member of my tribe for the rest of my life.

We have learned patience through willpower and know that one day we will persevere and take our rightful place in the 'Circle of All Native Americans'.

In a more defiant tone reflective of the historical relationship between the Cowlitz and the US government, one tribal member stated that such a decision by the federal government would 'make [him] even prouder'.

Recently Lyon's theory was considered in conjunction with the experience of Australian aboriginal peoples. Bretherton and Mellor (Bretherton and Mellor, 1998; see also Mellor and Bretherton, this volume) questioned the applicability of Lyon's model to a people not limited to a linear perspective of time, and for whom personal and ethnic identities are inseparably linked with *place*. The Cowlitz relationship with their aboriginal lands is a good example of Bretherton and Mellor's observation. Cowlitz intimacy with the land can be interpreted as a construction of their past which does emphasize unity, so conceivably this fits within Lyon's *group cohesion* criterion; however, it is also a very real experience in their present. Within Berry's model this relationship can be described as an example of both *continuity* (that is, a characteristically Cowlitz way of relating to the land) and *synthesis*.

Being at [settings important in Cowlitz history] brings to me feelings of warmth and compassion for times past in history. They all give me a spiritual link to the Big Picture and I sometimes see it in visions that come when I close my eyes.... Our Grandfathers walked there and still do in spirit. White society can only glimpse this through the eyes of an intruder.

To me it is wonderful to walk among the spirits in the land of my ancestors.

Such themes emerged in Fitzpatrick's interview data of the Cowlitz as well. She described the relationship as 'loyalty to the aboriginal land area' (1986, p. 256; see also pp. 260–7); however, 'loyalty' did not appear to be a sufficient term for the images, which arose from responses in the Roe (1991, 1992) studies. Participants in these studies communicated a personal, metaphysical interconnectedness with the land, river and ancestors. They communicated an intimate sense of place, which transcended geography.

The river is all I know. I was reared on it, fished it, swam in it, bathed in it, hunted it, know it for it's treachery, and therefore respect it, and am very familiar with the power of it's spirit. The river talks to me and I am able to talk to it.

The Cowlitz River is the catalyst to my heritage. I sometimes fish there–not for the fish but for the closeness to centuries of history. I sometimes see that old Cowlitz fisherman, spear in hand, waiting for that salmon to swim by.

The river is a linkage with the former history of the Cowlitz people and is a recognition that their spirit lives on in the lives of the present day Cowlitz. The river, for me, is alive with a spirit that inspires and speaks of the Creator's work. I feel close to my people, to the creation and to the One who made all things. There is a spiritual bonding that takes place when near the river.

The Cowlitz Prairie to me is my motherland. . . . Visiting my motherland is like being home.

[The Cowlitz Prairie] represents a continuity of tribal involvement. It represents a special relationship with Earth Mother. I have a sense of being part of a community, past and present that has special meaning for me.

Additional insights into ethnic identity, social memories and the roles of place and non-linear time can be gleaned from the tribe's responses to the acquisition of acreage on the Cowlitz River. Following monetary compensation for destruction of a portion of its aboriginal lands, in 1989 the Cowlitz tribe purchased 17 acres on the Cowlitz River. This decision raised conflicts among tribal members for a number of reasons. It violated the traditional value that one cannot buy back that which no person can own, that is, the land. Others expressed frustrations about the great discrepancy between the few acres purchased and the vastness of their aboriginal lands; the injustice of being forced to pay for a piece of the very land from which the Cowlitz were violently forced; and that the transaction was the result of a settlement with a private utility company, and not with the US government. On the other hand, for the first time in 150 years the Cowlitz had a land base, albeit a miniscule one. The Tribal Council chair at the time described the meaning of the property as 'permitting the people to feel the presence of their ancestors in the soil.' He saw this as a marker event, the consequences of which have lead to greater commitment by tribal members to Cowlitz traditional practices. Others express similar perspectives.

[The acreage] has special significance to me for it places a link to the past that was always missing. . . . I have deep feelings when I walk that land. The past comes forward when I watch members of the Cowlitz silently touch this area. A thousand words cannot adequately describe those looks, steps, and gestures that are individually portrayed.

[The acreage] makes me feel a greater connection to the land along the Cowlitz River, having now a place to focus on, to travel to and stand on, to experience the nature and peace that my tribal ancestors felt inhabiting that area.

This role of place and non-linear time in ethnic identity and social memories demonstrates the importance of the land to native peoples. Undoubtedly, the Cowlitz continuous access to their prairie and river since the onset of 'white man' encroachment has supported the continuance of such identity and memory. Returning to Tollefson's concept of tribal estate, although the Cowlitz have yet to achieve a significant *land-based* tribal estate, their *social and psychological* tribal estate (including their ethnic identity and social memories) has been perpetuated in their cultural values, social interactions of their extended families and access to aboriginal areas (see hypothesis three in Tollefson *et al.*, 1996, p. 336).

Conclusion

There is irony in that Cowlitz ethnic identity and social memories have maintained a sense of community and empowerment, and as a consequence, have maintained 150 years of conflict with the government. The persistence of those same ethnic identity and social memories have supported the maintenance of a modern community of Native Americans, and as a consequence, have fulfilled the US government's own criteria for acknowledgement, in spite of its past attempts to deny the Cowlitz such a status.

Many Cowlitz possess feelings of justifiable anger with the US government; some harbour deep bitterness. Assuming the Cowlitz prevail in the Quinault challenge at the Board of Appeals, they will be acknowledged by the US government as a sovereign nation. This acknowledgement will carry significant symbolic meaning in that it can be interpreted as a public avowal by the US government that it was wrong in its past dealings with the Cowlitz people, and it will be a confirmation of both corporate tribal identity and personal ethnic identity. This acknowledgement will also carry significant pragmatic meaning, as the Cowlitz will gain access to land, a substantial land-claim judgement award, and entitlements and grants reserved for Native Americans. It will be interesting to see how such a public acknowledgement and access to resources (perhaps filling a function similar to reparations) will affect reconciliation and 'healing of memories' for Cowlitz individuals (see Montville, 1993; Hamber and Wilson, this volume).

The Cowlitz are a twenty-first century Native American people steeped in the everyday world of the 'white man'. They live and work in towns and cities, their leaders regularly travel to Washington DC to lobby, give testimony in Congressional hearings, or to argue their case in federal courts. Many of these self-same Cowlitz continue to perceive as permeable the barriers between the past and present and between the material and the ethereal. This is captured well in the Cowlitz annual 'river float', which includes paddling canoes down the Cowlitz River, visiting sacred sites, sleeping on 'Grandmother Earth', prayer and traditional ceremonies. A Cowlitz leader describes the river float as a spiritual journey and how, not too long ago, each morning before they set off from the shore a large osprey glided out from the forest, circled the participants and then flew downstream as their *tomanawas* or spirit guide.

Notes

1. That is, as in contrast to allotments distributed to individual Indians.
2. Although Berry's acculturation model has been very influential over the past 25 years, it has its critics. For example, Ward and Rana-Deuba (1999) argue that psychological acculturation and sociocultural adjustment are at least as important as Berry's four modes of acculturation in predicting adaptation outcomes.
3. As of 13 February 1997, the Branch of Acknowledgment and Research of the Bureau of Indian Affairs had received a total of 185 petitions for federal recognition (Branch of Acknowledgment and Research, 1997).
4. In August 1997, the Snoqualmie received a positive determination by the Branch of Acknowledgment and Research of the Bureau of Indian Affairs. Their case was unsuccessfully challenged by the Tulalip Federated Tribes in the Department of the Interior's Indian Board of Indian Appeals, and in 2001 the Snoqualmie became a federally recognized sovereign nation of Native Americans.
5. The Samish were originally denied acknowledgement in 1987. The tribe appealed the decision in federal court and won their case. They were finally, officially recognized in April 1996.
6. Unfortunately, this petitioning process has possessed inherent cross-cultural and sociological weaknesses. These include (a) requiring continuous 'paper

trail' records from oral-tradition peoples; (b) assuming a political organisation of unified tribes under the authority of chiefs, when this organisational model often was forced on Indian participants by the US representative during treaty negotiations; (c) assuming that a 'modern community' of Indians requires residences in close geographical proximity, which not only is an outdated conception of community, it has also been difficult for unrecognized tribes to fulfil, since they were forced from their land and into the dominant white economy; and (d) assuming that acculturation is synonymous with assimilation.

In addition, the Federal Acknowledgment Process has not been administered so as to meet its mandate (Slagle, 1989). The BAR was organised in 1978 to work on tribal petitions as a part of the BIA. By the beginning of 1997, 185 petitions for acknowledgement had been received by the BIA. At that time the BAR had acknowledged only 12 tribes and had denied acknowledgement to 13 others. That is, the BAR had reviewed on average only slightly more than one petition a year, and tribes eligible for acknowledgement had apparently been denied 'without recourse to any other process and sometimes without justification' (Inouye, 1989). In response to such criticisms, in February of 1994 the BAR published new regulations regarding the federal acknowledgement process, which it argued would help applicant tribes (Procedures, 1994). In contrast, critics replied that the new rules were likely published simply to stall BAR reform legislation at the Congressional level, and that the newly published criteria and their operations were quite similar to the past inadequate standards.

7. Interestingly, Irwin recently was honoured by being adopted into a Cowlitz family and by receiving honorary membership in the Cowlitz Tribe – both through traditional ceremonies.

8. Within a multicultural society such as the present United States, the integration mode not only is adaptive (see Berry, 1984), in comparison to the other modes of acculturation it is associated with the most positive indices of mental health (Berry, 1994).

9. *Cowlitz* means 'seeker of the medicine spirit' and originates in the traditional practice of vision quests to seek out a spirit helper known as a *tomanawas*. Some Cowlitz today still seek *tomanawas* guidance.

10. A carved staff affording authority to the speaker with the expectation that all present are to attend respectfully.

Part III
Conflicting Memories and Time

5
Collective Memory of Physical Violence: its Contribution to the Culture of Violence

Daniel Bar-Tal

Many social scientists suggest that intergroup conflicts are an inevitable part of human social life (for example, Coser, 1956; Levi-Strauss, 1958; Burton, 1969; Galtung, 1969; Mitchell, 1981). Indeed, the history of civilisation is filled with continuous and numerous intergroup conflicts,* and the twentieth century has witnessed some of the most vicious and atrocious inter-ethnic and international conflicts in history (see, for example, the list of conflicts published by Richardson, 1960; Beer, 1981).

Intergroup conflicts are not of a unitary type; one way to evaluate them is to categorise them according to their intensity and severity. In this vein, Kriesberg (1993, 1998) suggested the classification of conflicts on an intractable–tractable dimension. At the intractable pole of the dimension are conflicts in which engaged parties resist a peaceful resolution and perpetuate vicious cycles of violence. At the tractable pole of the dimension are conflicts in which the parties involved use institutionalised and acceptable avenues of confrontation, routine negotiations to resolve disputes and avoid violence. Intractable conflicts are characterised by seven features: (1) they persist for a long time – at least a generation; (2) they are violent, involving killings of military personnel and civilians; (3) the parties involved perceive their conflict as irreconcilable; (4) various sectors of participating parties have vested economic, military and ideological interests in the continuation of the conflict; (5) the conflicts are perceived as zero sum in nature; (6) the issues in the conflicts concern basic needs which are perceived as essential for the parties' survival; and (7) the conflicts occupy a central place on the agenda of the parties involved (Kriesberg, 1993, 1998; Bar-Tal, 1998).

Those features should be seen rather as continuous variables, whereas any one case of conflict can be described and evaluated along each

77

dimension. The total value of the seven features may indicate that a conflict is extremely intractable, but the weight of the features may vary among themselves and even change from conflict to conflict. Nevertheless, it is the basic premise of the present chapter that the longevity of the conflict together with its violent nature are two interwoven, salient characteristics which underlie the conflict's viciousness and intractability (see Brecher, 1984; Gochman and Maoz, 1984; Goertz and Diehl, 1992). The present chapter will elaborate on the societal–psychological implications of these two characteristics. In general, it is proposed that when in prolonged conflicts people are killed or wounded, then these experiences frequently and dramatically change the nature of the conflict and constitute weighty obstacles to its peaceful resolution. The conflict between Protestants and Catholics in Northern Ireland, and Israeli–Arab conflict can serve as two examples of the detrimental effects of the longevity and violence on their resolution. These two characteristics will now be discussed.

Longevity

The length of the intractable conflict is of special importance. There is a major difference between conflicts which last a short time and conflicts that persist for at least a generation, sometimes decades and even centuries. The long duration of the conflicts implies that attempts to resolve them have failed and they often are perceived as irreconcilable. In addition, over the years, the parties involved have accumulated increasing amounts of prejudice, mistrust, hatred and animosity. However, the important implication of the longevity relates to the evolvement of collective memory. Over the years, groups involved in conflict selectively form collective memories about the conflict. On the one hand, they focus mainly on the other side's responsibility for the outbreak and continuation of the conflict and its misdeeds, violence and atrocities; on the other hand, they concentrate on the self-justification, self-righteousness, glorification and victimisation. This collective memory is institutionalised and maintained by the groups in prolonged conflict, who transmit it through the political, social, and cultural channels and institutions. This memory is also imparted to the new generations through the educational systems and is incorporated in the societal ethos, thus contributing to the group's social identity (Bar-Tal, 2000). An example of a long intractable conflict is the Israeli–Arab conflict, or more specifically, the Israeli–Palestinian conflict, which has lasted about a century. The long duration of this conflict has had a determinative effect on the emerging cultures of both societies, which are greatly imprinted by the ongoing hostility.

Physical violence

The other important characteristic of intractable conflict is physical violence. Physical violence includes the killing and wounding of human beings as a result of the hostile activities carried out by the parties involved. While the killed and wounded are almost always members of the military forces, physical violence is often inflicted on civilians who do not directly participate in combat. Also, particularly important in the context of inter-ethnic or international conflict is the fact that although individuals perform violent acts, the violence is initiated and carried out within a social system. That is, the social system provides the rationales and the justifications for the violence, system's organisations train the individuals to carry out violent acts, and social mechanisms and institutions glorify the violent confrontations. In the case of the Israeli–Palestinian conflict, the violence has claimed many lives. For example since 1948 approximately 20,000 Israeli Jews have been killed and many more have been wounded. The number of killed Arabs, including Palestinians, is probably considerably multiplied.

In sum, the combination of longevity and violence is a well-established prescription for the intractability of the conflict. The human losses and the evolvement of collective memory, a process that incorporates the memory of those who fell in the conflict, underlie the development of the culture of violence that characterises protracted and violent conflicts. Before continuing, however, it is necessary to elaborate why physical violence has such profound effects on the nature of intergroup conflict.

The meaning of physical violence

The meaning of physical violence is related to the sanctity of life, the emotional meaning of the loss of life, the irreversibility of those losses, the desire for vengeance and the need to rationalise violence. Each of these points will be discussed separately.

Sanctity of life
The maintenance of life is perhaps one of the most sacred and universal values in human culture. Alternatively, killing, or severely physically hurting another human being is considered with some exceptions the

most serious violation of the moral code (Donagan, 1979; Kleinig, 1991). The commandment 'Thou shall not kill' is a widely accepted precept and is probably one of the most important for most, if not all, societies (Feldman, 1992). Societies tend to adhere to this commandment devoutly, creating norms and enacting laws, to preserve it. In modern times, the right to life has become a basic principle; under most circumstances, no person is allowed to take the life of another person. Taking a human life, especially of the innocent, is an unforgiven sin, in almost all situations. Those who violate the moral and legal codes regarding the sanctity of life are severely punished. Some societies even take the life of the killers, which is viewed to be the most severe punishment that can be meted out to the transgressor.

As long as the conflict is limited to verbal statements and even hostile acts are without human loss, the conflict remains on a lower level of confrontation. However, once one party in the conflict kills and/or wounds a member of the other group, or both sides suffer losses, the conflict moves to another phase. In this context of taking the life of soldiers, despite them being trained to kill and preparing to be killed, is perceived as a violation of a moral code (Osgood and Tucker, 1967). Thus, the killing or wounding of military personnel leads to the escalation of a conflict. In this vein, of special importance is the harming of innocent civilians, which is viewed by the parties as particularly painful because it is considered to be a severe violation of the moral code. These cases fuel even further the conflict, forcing the parties to take special action to prevent further violence to them and to punish the perpetrators. The described dynamics are well reflected in the Israeli–Palestinian conflict. Both sides – the Israelis and the Palestinians – are very sensitive to human losses inflicted by the other side and at the same time, mutually delegitimise each other, by claiming that the other side does not respect the sanctity of life.

Emotional involvement

Violence increases the emotional involvement of the parties engaged in intergroup conflict. Group members are deeply and emotionally touched when compatriots are killed and wounded, especially when the loss is sudden, untimely and intentionally inflicted by other persons. In principle, the closer the relationship to the injured or deceased, the more intense is the emotional reaction. But, in the case of violent, intergroup conflict, even when those killed are not personally known, the personal relevance of the human losses is intensified. The killed and/or wounded are perceived as compatriots, kin, as group members, who have been harmed. That is, in these cases, the physical violence is perceived as a group matter and group members view the losses as group losses, with the victims acquiring a social identity within the group's perception of the events.

In modern societies, this perception and emotional involvement is a consequence of socialisation processes in modern societies, which extend the concepts of kinship (that is, patriotism, nationalism) towards personally unknown society members (for example, Fox, 1994; Billig, 1995; Johnson, 1997). More specifically, societies make special efforts to inculcate patriotic and nationalistic feelings through methods that include the use of fictive kin terms such as 'sons', 'brothers and sisters', 'brotherhood', 'motherland', or 'fatherland' in reference to members of the society and the land (see for example, Halliday, 1915; Johnson, Ratwik and Sawyer, 1987). Through this method, members of a society are encouraged to form a sense of belonging, feelings of closeness and a sense of mutual responsibility and solidarity. It is, therefore, not surprising that individuals are personally touched when members of their society fall as a consequence of violence in the context of intergroup conflict.

In most cases, the whole society mourns those killed in intergroup conflict. They are considered as society's martyrs, because they fell as a result of societal cause. Their death, thus, is viewed as the group's loss and, therefore, group members feel emotional involvement. It should be noted here that the loss of compatriots frequently turns the conflict into relevant experience for many society members. It is so, because many issues of disagreement between the parties in conflict are difficult to understand and are irrelevant to the lives of society members, but death of compatriots is an experience that concerns every society member and turns the conflict into concrete reality. The conflict then becomes a relevant part of society members' lives and absorbs a new personal meaning.

The above description is well founded in the case of the Israeli–Palestinian conflict. Almost every group member, killed by the other side, causes the Israeli Jews and the Palestinians to be greatly emotionally involved. The death touches every group member, and those killed in the conflict are considered to have made a sacrifice for the benefit of the entire group.

Irreversibility of the situation

Loss of life has particular importance in the conflict process because of its irreversibility. That is, while suitable compensations and compromised solutions can be found for various disagreements, nothing can compensate for death. Therefore, the conflict escalates in tandem with the human costs incurred. The parties involved in the conflict find it difficult to justify compromises in view of the human losses. Although comprises were possible prior to the deaths, the parties now find it difficult to justify such an option. Their positions become fixated, a situation that perpetrates the conflict.

The desire for vengeance

Killings within the context of intergroup conflict serve as a basis for vengeful acts. 'An eye for an eye' is a basic norm in many societies, and may even be considered a moral requirement. That is, the society's members feel an obligation to harm physically members of the group in conflict, in retribution for the inflicted violence. Thus, once group members are killed, it is difficult to settle the conflict peacefully, before avenging those killed. Turney-High (1949), when analysing the causes of primitive warfare, pointed out that:

> Revenge is so consistently reported as one of the principal causes of war that it requires detailed analysis. Why should the human personality yearn to compensate for its humiliation in the blood of enemies? The tension-release motive plays a part here: Revenge loosens the taut feeling caused by the slaying or despoiling of one's self, clan, tribe, nation. Even the hope for revenge helps the humiliated human to bear up, enables him to continue to function in a socially unfavorable environment.... Revenge, or the hope of revenge, restores the deflated ego, and is a conflict motive with which mankind must reckon with universally. (pp. 149–50)

As Turney-High implies, the call for vengeance is not unique to primitive societies. It is a universal phenomenon. Members of a society demand vengeance when society suffers human loss as a result of intergroup conflict. For example, Rutkoff (1981) quotes French poems written during the Franco-Prussian War of 1870–71, that call for revenge. One of them reads:

> Revenge will come, perhaps slowly
> Perhaps with fragility, yet a strength that is sure
> For bitterness is already born and force will flow
> And cowards only the battle will ignore. (Cited p. 161)

In the case of the Israeli–Palestinian conflict, the human losses usually stiffen the opinions of both sides, causing demands to punish the other side. The losses in intergroup conflict are almost always perceived as unjustified; moreover, there is an identified, concrete and specific perpetrator (the other party in conflict) who has to be punished for his act. That is, vengeance is perceived as a matter of national or ethnic obligation, an expression of responsibility to those that were killed. It is, therefore, seen even as a matter of national honour to punish the opponent, so as to 'prevent' future losses by showing the perpetrator that violence against the group will not be tolerated. In fact, Scheff (1994) suggested that vengeance is one of the most important psychological bases for international conflict. In his view, vengeance is a result of the denial of emotions such as shame, guilt or alienation. These emotions are especially aroused in situations when parties in conflict incur human loss. According to Scheff (1994), in most cases the parties deny these emotions and raise their voices for vengeance.

Need for rationalisation and delegitimisation

Physical violence against human beings requires an explanation for those who carry it out as well as for its victims (for example, Grundy and Weinstein, 1974). It stems from the basic need to live in a meaningful and predictable world, as well as in a just world (Katz, 1960; Lerner, 1980; Reykowski, 1982). In view of the ascribed sanctity to life and its violation, which takes place in physical violence, the participants need to justify these. The performers require reasons to carry out the violent acts and the victims need reasons why they must incur losses. As 'the victims' retaliate and become perpetrators of physical violence against their adversary, a cycle of victimisation and rationalisation of that state begins to evolve.

McFarlane (1986), for example, provided an anthropological analysis of the explanations used by people in rural areas of Northern Ireland for the violence of the Catholic–Protestant conflict. To explain the abnormal acts of violence such as murders, bombings, and so forth; the villagers insisted that these violent acts were aberrations performed by outsiders. The relevance of his findings is of importance for the present analysis as those justifications, explanations and rationales are based on the contents that delegitimise the opponent (Eldridge, 1979; Mitchell, 1981; Bar-Tal, 1990a; Worchel, 1999). Delegitimisation is defined as a categorisation of social groups into extreme negative categories that essentially deny their humanity (Bar-Tal, 1989). Such a classification suggests that the adversary is evil, malevolent, immoral and inhuman. This is the most economic and comprehensive way to explain why human lives are taken and why they should continue to be taken. Bar-Tal (1998) provided an illustrative analysis of mutual delegitimisation between the Israeli Jews and Palestinians. Both nations have resorted to a list of different delegitimising labels and have used different social institutions to propagate this delegitimisation.

Summary

The above analysis suggests why violence constitutes a significant element in intergroup conflict: violence changes the nature of the conflict because the loss of human life and the performance of violent acts have special meaning for society's members. Violence often escalates the level of intergroup conflicts; when it continues for many years, violence has a crucial effect on the society as the accumulation and sedimentation of such experiences in collective memory penetrates every thread of the societal fabric. The collective memory of physical violence serves as a foundation for the development of a culture of violence. In turn, the culture of violence preserves the collective memory of the human losses, as well as the perceived cruelty, mistrust, inhumanity and evilness, of the enemy. By doing so, it rationalises the continuation of the conflict and makes an imprint on the reality perceived by society members. The relationship between collective memory and the culture of violence is discussed in the next section of the chapter.

Collective memory and culture of violence

As indicated, a culture of violence develops in response to the experiences of physical violence accumulated during intergroup conflicts, and is based on the subsequent evolved collective memory that preserves those experiences and their meanings. This development is almost inevitable in view of the human losses that the society incurs through decades of conflict and the participation of its members in the violent acts. These powerful experiences touch society members emotionally, involve them, and permeate societal products, institutions and channels of communication, which then serve to maintain them as collective memory. With time, a cultural pattern evolves that has at least three identifiable facets: (a) the formation of societal beliefs that concern intergroup violence; (b) the appearance of rituals and ceremonies that commemorate the slain compatriots; and (c) the erection of monuments to honour the victims.

Societal beliefs

Societal beliefs, defined as cognitions shared by a society's members on subjects and issues that are of special concern to the particular society and that contribute to the sense of uniqueness and social identity, are developed and disseminated in light of the significant experiences of society members (Bar-Tal, 2000). The contents of societal beliefs may concern societal goals, collective memories, self-images, aspirations, images of out-groups, and so forth. They are organised into thematic clusters, with each theme consisting of a number of beliefs. They often feature on the public agenda, serve as a salient referent for decisions made by the leadership and influence courses of action.

When physical violence continues for a long time, it contributes significantly to the formation, dissemination and maintenance of four themes of societal beliefs, that are part of the society's ethos of conflict (Bar-Tal, 2000): beliefs about the conflict; beliefs about the delegitimacy of the opponent; beliefs about the victimisation of the own group; and beliefs about patriotism. Other societal beliefs might issue in the process of an intractable conflict, as Bar-Tal (2000) suggested in his analysis of the ethos of conflict, but these four beliefs are apparently formed in direct response to the human losses resulting from physical violence. Each of the societal beliefs will be discussed in turn.

Societal beliefs about the conflict

These beliefs contain, in the main, the collective memories that evolved from the experiences related to conflict. They include the causes for its outbreak, the reasons for its lack of resolution, the major events that shaped the conflict, particularly malevolent acts perpetrated by the adversary and the sacrifices that the ingroup incurred during the conflict, including its heroes' sacrifices. These beliefs are one-sided and selective (see for example, the analysis of the Israeli and the Palestinian beliefs in Bar-Tal, 1990b). They serve the needs of the society's members to view themselves as just, righteous, humane and moral, and provide explanations of the present situation. Connerton (1989) pointed out 'our experience of the present very largely depends upon our knowledge of the past. We experience our present world in the context which is causally connected with the past event and objects.' (p. 2) In short, the beliefs encased in collective memory help to make sense of the present reality. But, in order to fulfil this function, the past is reconstructed and re-appropriated to serve the current needs and attitudes of society's members (Kammen, 1991; Halbwachs, 1992).

Societal beliefs about delegitimising the opponent

Human losses through intergroup conflict, especially losses of innocent civilians, and the necessity to inflict harm on the opponent, facilitate the formation of societal beliefs about delegitimisation (Bar-Tal, 1989, 1990a). Delegitimising societal beliefs fulfil several important epistemic functions. First of all, the related beliefs explain to society why it has incurred such human loses, especially among civilians. Epithets such as 'murderers' or 'vandals' point to the reasons why the adversary can perform such inhuman, immoral and atrocious acts against the 'human beings' belonging to the ingroup. At the same time, these beliefs also justify the ingroup's acts of violence, its revenge! Because of their inhuman qualities, the opponents should be punished for their violent acts and/or they should be physically prevented from performing future acts of violence. Both arguments rationalise violence against the opposing group, including its civilian population.

For example, as noted in the context of the violent Israeli–Palestinian conflict, both parties extensively participated in labelling. Israeli Jews labelled the Palestinians as terrorists, murderers, Nazis, anti-Semites, or blood thirsty, while the Palestinians used such labels as sadists, Nazis, imperialists, colonialists, terrorists, or aggressors to delegitimise Israeli Jews (see Bar-Tal, 1988). The Vietnamese supporters of the Viet Cong and Americans carried out similar delegitimisation during the Vietnam war, which claimed many thousands of human lives (White, 1970).

Societal beliefs about the group's own victimisation

As the number of human losses grows, societies develop beliefs about being victimised by the opponent. These beliefs focus on the losses, deaths, the harm, the evil and atrocities committed by the adversary while they delegate the responsibility for the violence solely to the 'other'. This self-perception focuses on the sad and wretched fate of the group and frames its victims as martyrs. The dead and wounded become the salient, concrete evidence of the group's status as a victim.

For example, in the context of the violent Northern Ireland conflict, both the Catholics and Protestants perceive themselves as victims of the other party. The two groups focus on the terrorism of the other side, selectively, while collectively remembering the violent acts, and blaming the opponent (Hunter, Stringer and Watson, 1991; Wichert, 1994). The same focus can be found in the case of the Israeli Jews and Palestinians. Both groups perceive themselves as victims in the conflict. This self-assigned status is not necessarily indicating weakness. On the contrary, it provides strength *vis-à-vis* the international community, which usually tends to support the victimised side in the conflict, and it often energises society members to avenge and punish the opponent.

Societal beliefs of patriotism

Human loss instigates the intensification of societal beliefs of patriotism, which in turn emphasizes commitment, pride and loyalty towards the ingroup and the country (Bar-Tal, 1993). In response to the scope of the losses, these beliefs call for mobilisation and sacrifice. They may even demand the willingness to die for one's country, a necessity when societies are involved in a violent conflict. Without the willing participation of individuals, violent conflicts cannot continue. Societies thus make special efforts to impart patriotic beliefs to its members, beliefs which inspire the readiness to make their ultimate sacrifices for their homeland. As a tribute to these sacrifices, the killed and wounded are revered and memorialised in patriotic myths and rites. Some are portrayed as heroes, as models. New generations are then socialised in their light. In this respect, patriotic beliefs explain and justify the sacrifices the society members are called upon to suffer.

An example of the attempt to impart patriotic societal beliefs during violent conflict can be found in Israeli society. In view of the continuous violence, living in Israeli society requires much devotion, commitment and sacrifice (Galnoor, 1982). Different channels, methods and institutions have been used to develop commitment and loyalty to the state and the Jewish people (Eisenstadt, 1973). They nourished a heritage of wars and battles and glorified heroism (for example, Sivan, 1991). Military heroes received a special place in the social Parthenon and the society commemorated those fallen in military service in public ceremonies. This approach was extended to the treatment of Jewish history. Historical fighter-heroes and their patriotic acts were presented as models for identification and admiration (for example, Liebman and Don-Yehiya, 1983).

The evolution of these four themes of societal beliefs about conflict delegitimisation of the opponent, self-victimisation and patriotism is, then, directly related to the intensity and length of the violence endured. As the violent conflict becomes protracted, these beliefs become embedded in the societal repertoire and enter the collective memory. They are frequently presented through societal channels of communication. Thus, as for the public agenda, they are disseminated through cultural, educational and societal institutions. That is, these described societal beliefs become 'enduring products' which appear as recurrent themes in literature, textbooks, films, theatrical plays, paintings and other cultural products (Bar-Tal, 2000; Winter, 1995). In consequence, they become more and more central to the personal repertoire of the society's members. These beliefs, therefore, represent the epistemological pillars of the culture of violence, as they are widely disseminated, maintained through time and imparted to the new generation.

Memorial to the conflict

Human losses from violent conflict generate the appearance of monuments and cemeteries, specialised, permanent sites dedicated to preserving collective memories (see Ignatieff, 1984; Winter, 1995). These sites combine three important characteristics: they are located in a particular defined place, their construction consists of durable structures providing symbols for the society's members and they materialise the collective memory. As such, they become an inseparable part of the culture of violence. As Mosse (1990) pointed out:

> War monuments commemorating the fallen, symbolised the strength and manliness of the nation's youth and provided an example for other generations to follow. (p. 35)

Indeed, memorials fulfil important functions to perpetuate the memory of the fallen and inspire the remaining society members with the will to continue the conflict and fight the enemy. In a specific case, Levinger (1993) pointed out that 900 of the war monuments in Israel were constructed to immortalise fallen soldiers. These monuments, in her opinion, have an ideological function, including justification of the war, heroism and martyrdom. Similarly, Almog (1992) pointed out that Israeli war memorials serve as didactic tools to convey messages of commitment to the heritage by those who fell, namely, commitment of the people to continue to protect the nation and to hold on to the land for which the fallen have sacrificed their lives (p. 63). In essence, this message supports continuation of the conflict. In a brochure edited by Shamir (1976), and published by the Israeli Ministry of Defence, the contributors discuss various aspects of this practice. The major points presented in this brochure touch upon the societal obligation to immortalise the fallen soldiers, the ways of doing so, the special power entitled to the bereaved families and the will expressed by the fallen soldiers to continue in their footsteps to secure the existence of the Israeli state (see also Witztum and Malkinson, 1993).

The monuments and cemeteries, then, are constant and enduring reminders about the losses suffered in conflict, the sacrifices made by patriots and heroes and the malevolence of the opponent. In one sense and during certain periods they represent concrete investments in the continuation of the conflict.

Rituals and ceremonies related to conflict

Rituals and ceremonies related to the violent conflict, which commemorate particular battles, wars and especially fallen members of the society, are another expression of culture of violence. Rituals and ceremonies consist of speeches, acts (such as parades, guards exchanges), music, decorations and displays presented at a particular time and place for the purpose of communicating the meanings attached to the conflict. They symbolically express beliefs, values and attitudes towards the violent conflict. They glorify battles and wars, the heroism of those who participated in the events, the martyrdom of those who fell, the malevolence of the enemy and the necessity to continue the struggle in fulfilment of the patriotic 'will' of the fallen.

Thus, in times of conflict, and especially intractable conflict, rituals and ceremonies contribute to the continuation of the conflict. Their contents fuel public animosity towards the enemy while urging the society's members to fulfil their patriotic duties in the conflict. As such, they serve as an important socialisation and cultural factor, ideologising the conflict. Although ostensibly, meant to perpetuate and invigorate the collective memory, rituals and ceremonies, together with the monuments and cemeteries come to eternalise the collective memory of the society in effect shed light on the present. Monuments and cemeteries acquire with meanings through the rituals and ceremonies performed in their space. For example, Ben-Amos (1993) in analysing the place in French collective memory of four national monuments in Paris, pointed out that their importance lies in the meaning ascribed by the ceremonies conducted at the sites. In other words, the encounter between the monument and the ceremony (depending on the particular generation), significantly contributes to the construction and maintenance of the collective memory for the specific period in which it transpires.

In this vein, Handelman (1990) provided a detailed analysis of the official state ceremony performed in Israel on Memorial Day. This day is dedicated to those who 'sacrificed their lives for the existence of the State', both soldiers and civilians. The ceremony constructs a sense of belonging to one large family whose sons were lost in conflict. It reminds individuals of their duty not to forget the fallen and their acts. Recently, in an extensive piece of work, about the commemoration of the fallen in Israel during 1948–56, Azaryahu (1995) pointed out the linkage between the ceremonies and the sites (that is, military cemeteries and war memorials) and the evolving nature of the official state rituals. He emphasised that during the years investigated, which were at the peak of the Israel and Arab conflict, the rituals had special importance to impart patriotic commitment to the Israelis. They came to transmit the legacy of heroes' sacrifice, needed in view of the continuation of the violent conflict.

Conclusions and implications

This chapter suggests that violence and longevity contribute to the intractability of conflicts. The fact that a society incurs human losses, especially those losses that occur over a long period of time, is a powerful experience in itself and attains a special meaning for society's members. As a result, with time, a culture of violence evolves which makes the conflict more resistant to peaceful resolution. Cultural products evolve especially in response to physical violence, which claims human loss of compatriots and motivates the society's members to carry out acts of physical retribution. Specifically expressions of a culture of violence, which consists of societal beliefs about delegitimation of the opponent, societal beliefs about the conflict, the group's victimisation and about patriotism, as well as the sites of memorials and the practice of rituals and ceremonies dedicated to the conflict fuel the continuation of the conflict.

Cultural products (memorials and rituals and ceremonies) are necessary outcomes of violent conflict. In contrast, societal beliefs concerning conflict, delegitimisation and victimisation may be formed under circumstances other than violent conflict, and patriotic beliefs develop under all conditions due to society's need to survive. However, in the context of protracted violent conflict, all four societal beliefs flourish intensively and extensively. That is, these beliefs preoccupy a central place in the societal repertoire, are incorporated within the collective memory and are disseminated as the violence continues over an increasing number of years. Within a culture of violence, memorial sites, rituals, and ceremonies support the four societal beliefs, making them more accessible, relevant and concrete. On the other hand, the societal beliefs provide the conceptual framing for the creation of memorial sites, rituals and ceremonies. That is, the beliefs provide the contents elaborated in the rituals and the ceremonies, which serve as a prism through which society members attach meaning to the acts and the artefacts.

The culture of violence has a number of implications, which have a direct influence on the course of the intergroup conflict. First, the culture of violence fixates collective beliefs on the four societal beliefs we have discussed. The experience of loss from the conflict become engraved in the memory of a society member, while the beliefs provide the lenses through which the society explains that loss as it justifies its violence. In prolonged conflict, when the losses are heavy, the probability that one member will be personally acquainted with at least one fallen person grows; such experience ties them to the conflict. That is, the conflict becomes concrete and relevant to them.

But, society's members not only remember the fallen, they also remember why they fell and their unfinished mission of the fallen. With time, these memories are institutionalised in rituals and ceremonies, and thus is maintained and reinforced (Connerton, 1989; Halbwachs, 1992). In addition, as the conflict is protracted, more of the society's members personally participate in the violence. Participation strengthens the power of the experience and reinforces the centrality of the societal beliefs. It is thus not surprising that as the conflict continues, the experiences related to the violence enter the collective memory. In essence, the collective memory focuses on those experiences, which support the culture of violence. Society members, therefore, remember especially the violence of the opponent, how it was initiated, the atrocities, and, of course, their losses. In contrast, they tend to forget their own acts of violence.

Second, the human losses and the resulting culture of violence are in certain respects, investments in the continuation of the conflict. Because it is impossible to compensate individuals for loss of life, the society feels an obligation to adhere to its original goals, otherwise the sacrifices made will be viewed as being in vein. This logic applies especially to those who lose someone close to them. The survivors often resist compromise, which they perceive as a betrayal of the fallen. They often assume that early compromises could have saved lives, but since the society has decided to adhere to its original goals, sacrificing compatriots in the conflict, there should be continuation of this adherence.

From another perspective, societal beliefs serve as the cognitive and effective foundations of the conflict by providing explanations and justifications for its continuation. In essence, these beliefs represent the ideological bases for the conflict. Society members who hold these beliefs are compelled to continue the violence once they have accepted its rationale. Furthermore, once these beliefs become embedded in the societal repertoire, it is difficult to change them. These beliefs of conflict, delegitimisation, own victimisation and patriotism arouse emotions (fear, hatred and anger towards the opponent, feelings of self-pride, esteem and pity) but also evoke behaviour geared to persevering it's own goals, avenging loses, hurting the opponent and sacrificing one's own life for the group.

Finally, and most patently, the evolution of a culture of violence instigates vicious cycles of violence. Violence leads to increasing violence, as the survivors are feeling a growing obligation to avenge the fallen. Clutondem, an ideology, which rationalises the continuation of the conflict gains in complexity and strength. During these cycles, it is often difficult to differentiate between the trigger and the reaction, as each act is eventually interpreted as either. Nevertheless, the parties in conflict always view their behaviour as acts of defence and reaction. Poole (1995), when analysing the distribution of violence in Northern Ireland, concluded that the vicious circle is a continuous process, having no end. Lulls may occur, but they come to an end:

> – when the killing recommenced, it was concentrated in exactly the same places as before. The local social reproduction of a culture of political violence can apparently lie dormant for many years, even well into the next generations. However, it merely disappears from immediate view – and only until the next time. (p. 43)

This analysis is not meant to suggest that violent conflicts cannot be resolved peacefully. Many such conflicts were resolved after prolonged violence. Under unique conditions, which require further discussion, violence may sometimes facilitate conflict resolution in light of the human costs involved in the continuation of the conflict. The basic thesis of this chapter suggests, however, that when violence continues throughout the decades it constitutes a determinative factor *per se* in intergroup conflict. It changes the nature of the conflict. Therefore, it is of special importance to understand not only the specific acts of violence, but also the psychological and cultural bases which underlie them. These bases play a crucial role in violent conflicts because human beings, as thinking creatures, need to rationalise their acts. The present chapter is an attempt to contribute to the elucidation of these bases by focusing on the evolvement of the collective memory of physical violence, which has a determinative role in the formation of culture of violence.

Note

* Throughout the chapter the term intergroup conflict will be used, but it refers mostly to inter-ethnic and international conflicts.

6

Will the Germans Ever Be Forgiven? Memories of the Second World War Four Generations Later

Louis Oppenheimer and Ilse Hakvoort

> Historical phenomena are like stones, which, when thrown in the pond of memory, create increasingly wider circles in proportion to their weight (von der Dunk, 1990, p. 7).

In general, memory is perceived as the mental faculty that permits individuals to acquire, retain and retrieve knowledge related to their own personal experiences and forms an important part of individuals' identities. The concept of collective memory involves the assumption that both groups and societies have memories (Halbwachs, 1950/1968) and subsequently, that the collective memory of a society (for example, represented by museums and memorials) forms an important part of a society's culture. A relation is assumed between collective and individual or personal memory by which individuals' memories of events may conflict with the larger society's representations of the same events, and by which different subgroups within a diverse society may represent or remember common experiences differently. The purpose of the present study is to discuss the relationship between collective and personal memory and attitudes towards others on the basis of studies conducted with Dutch children and adolescents.

Collective memory versus personal or autobiographical memory

As was noted previously, collective memory is not necessarily identical to personal or personalised memory. In a study of the collective memories of Germans and Japanese about the past half-century, Schuman, *et al.* (1998) noted that none of the central events of the Second World

War (for example, the annihilation of the Jews and the atomic bombing of Hiroshima) were often mentioned as parts of the collective memory of the older age cohorts (that is, people who experienced the war). Instead, personal suffering as a result of the war's impact on their personal lives figured predominantly in the memories of these individuals. According to Schuman *et al.* (1998), similar findings from other studies suggest that 'ordinary individuals ("the general public") are usually much more concerned with the impact of events on their own personal lives than they are with the events and symbols that occupy much of the attention of intellectuals, political leaders, and academic investigators' (p. 451).

Hence, collective memory may not correspond with personal or autobiographical memory. In an interesting paper, Baumeister and Hastings (1997) offer evidence that shows how collective memory is or can be distorted (that is, collective self-deception) to create more positive images of the ingroup and more negative images of the outgroup. Collective self-deception processes to enhance group identity may range from the selection of particular memories to severe distortion of collective memory.

In short, besides being a socially constructed memory (Wertsch, 1997), collective memory is subject to change and manipulation (cf. Pennebaker *et al.*, 1997). It is therefore not surprising that no relation was found between aspects of collective memory and individual, social identity with Northern Irish students (Cairns *et al.*, 1998). Individual, social identity is not positively served by unstable collective memories, which often do not parallel personal memories or experiences (cf. Turner *et al.*, 1994).

The main question in this study pertains to the relationship between collective memory and personal memory with Dutch children and adolescents more than fifty years after the Second World War. One would expect that as a result of progressive collaboration among European countries and processes of integration within the context of the European Community the impact of collective memory on images of former enemies would have diminished (that is, in the present case the Germans).

Nevertheless, while more than fifty years have passed since the end of the Second World War, still every few years public controversies evolve concerning the attitude of Dutch youth towards their eastern neighbours, the Germans (for example, Peters, 1998; Peters and Schuyt, 1998). Some years ago, the following headline was published in one of the leading newspapers in the Netherlands: 'Pupils dislike and do not dislike Germans' (*Volkskrant*, 17 December 1997). In the article two recent studies were discussed which reported contradictory results. The first study, conducted by the Institute Clingendael (1997), demonstrated that Dutch secondary-school pupils possess a negative image of their eastern neighbours (that is, the Germans), do not want to live in Germany and when thinking of a warlike country think primarily of Germany. The second study, conducted by the European Platform for Dutch Education (1997) demonstrated, however, that Dutch secondary-school pupils consider Germans as a kind, pleasant, democratic and tolerant people. These contradictory findings, of course, resulted in heated discussions with respect to methodological aspects of the studies and coloured glasses of the investigators. While the Clingendael study was perceived as a reinforcement of stereotypes (that is, Germans are warlike, arrogant, totalitarian and so on), the Platform study was considered to be a manifestation of European unification (that is, Germans are democratic and tolerant of European citizens).

The evolving controversies, as a result of such contradictory findings, deal with processes involving reconciliation between the past and the present. That is, while it is accepted that older generations still may have vivid memories of the German occupation of the Netherlands during the Second World War, it is expected (or hoped) that younger generations are able to transcend these memories and subsequent antagonisms and to focus onto the future of an integrated Europe. The latter implies the necessity to co-operate and collaborate with all nations in Europe, including Germany. The findings of the previously discussed survey studies, however, indicate that depending on the type of question asked, the past still affects Dutch children's and adolescents' attitudes towards Germany. In addition, the findings suggest the presence of cross-generational processes of transfer of memories and knowledge about the Second World War. In this case, we expected that irrespective of educational processes (Peters and Schuyt, 1998), knowledge about the Second World War should be significantly higher as compared to knowledge about other situations in which the Netherlands have been involved in conflicts and wars.

For instance, in a recent study (Peters and Schuyt, 1998), three age cohorts of Dutch citizens (that is, $n = 200$; age ranges 20–40, 40–60 and older than 60 years) were asked to associate with the Second World War (that is, 'What do you think of first when you hear the concept of the Second World War?'). The findings show that in particular it is the younger age cohorts who associate the Second World War with the persecution of Jews (for example, anti-Semitism and the holocaust; 50 per cent and 40 per cent of the responses, respectively), Nazism and the Third Reich (for example, Hitler). The oldest age cohort consisting of people who actually experienced the war mentioned primarily personal experiences (that is, suffering, hunger, violence, and injustice; 50 per cent of the responses; see Figure 6.1). That is, with the inclusion of personal experiences of parents and grandparents, only 6 per cent and 12 per cent of the responses of the younger age cohorts referred to such experiences. The predominance of responses involving the persecution of Jews with the younger age cohorts is perceived as a product of educational processes rather than personal experiences (Peters and Schuyt, 1998).

While it is very plausible to assume that factual knowledge about conflicts and wars with the younger age cohort (that is, 20–40 year olds;

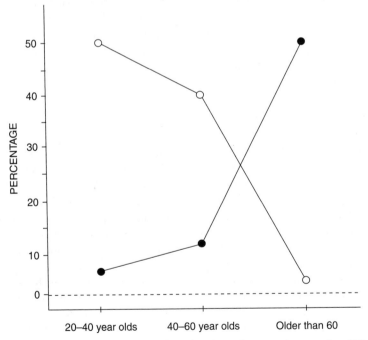

○ Persecution of the Jews
● Personal experiences, including those of (grand)parents

Figure 6.1 Proportion of responses for three age cohorts to the question: 'What do you think of first when you hear the concept of the Second World War?'

Source: Peters and Schuyt, 1998, p. 27.

Peters and Schuyt, 1998) is the result of educational processes, the age at which this knowledge and its detail is present may offer insights into processes other than educational processes. If collective memory plays a role in cross-generational transfer of (possibly emotionally-loaded) factual knowledge about conflicts and wars, then extensive factual knowledge should be present prior to the impact of educational processes (that is, with children and young adolescents).

The study

In our own study, (Hakvoort, 1996; Hakvoort and Oppenheimer, 1993, 1998) dealing with children's and adolescents' understanding of peace and war ($n = 216$; age range from 7 to 18 years), questions included were pertaining to the participants' factual knowledge about contemporary and past international conflicts and wars. The question of interest for the present study pertain to examples of past situations with 'no peace' in the Netherlands (Hakvoort, 1996, p. 157). When a particular situation of 'no peace' (that is, conflict or war) was given as a response, it was followed by the question 'what happened?' In the present study we will focus on the responses to this question with respect to the Second World War. The responses to each of the questions were scored only once in each response category for these questions (see Hakvoort, 1996).

Results

With respect to situations of 'no peace' in the Netherlands, a significant increase from the age of 8 years was observed for responses involving the 80-Years War ($\chi^2(9) = 144.42$, $p < .01$) and from the age of 7 the First World War ($\chi^2(10) = 216.77$, $p < .01$) and the Second World War ($\chi^2(10) = 603.86$, $p < .01$; see Figure 6.2). For all age groups, the frequency by which the Second World War was mentioned was larger than the frequency for the other two historical events combined. In short, at age 8 more than one third of the participants mentioned the Second World War as an example of a past situation of 'no peace' in the Netherlands. The finding that the First World War was also mentioned as an example of a situation of 'no peace' in the Netherlands (by more than 50 per cent of the 14- to 17-year-old participants) was surprising, because during the First World War the Netherlands were neutral and did not experience any direct hostile activities. In line with Peters and Schuyt (1998), we assume that this finding is the result of the educational

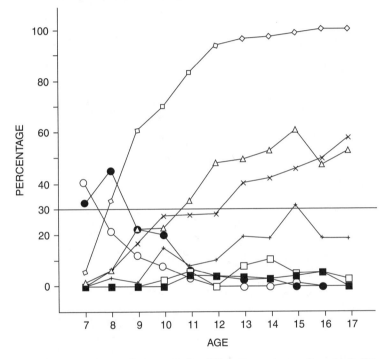

O   Do not know
●   General terms: Something happened in the past
□   Antiquity (i.e., Romans)
■   Middle Ages (i.e., sword fights)
+   War against France (Napoleon)
×   The 80-years war (against Spain)
△   First World War (1914–1918)
◇   Second World War (1940–1945)

Figure 6.2   Proportions of responses for different ages to question 5A-2: 'Situations with no Peace in the Netherlands'

process by which the effects of the 'Great War' are overgeneralised to include also the Netherlands.

The responses to the question 'what happened?' were scored in eight categories related to themes or particular events (that is, war against Germany; Hitler ruled Germany and the war; anti-Semitism and holocaust; rounding up of people to work for the Germans, torture and the winter of hunger; bombing of Rotterdam; resistance and underground

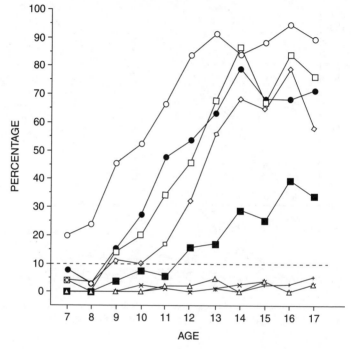

○ War against Germany
● Hitler ruled Germany and the war
□ Antisemitism and holocaust
■ Rounding up of people to work for the Germans; torture; hunger winter
+ Bombing of Rotterdam
× Resistance and underground organisations
△ Germany invades Russia
◇ The allied forces: America, England, France, and Russia

Figure 6.3 Proportions of responses for different ages to the question 'what happened?' when the Second World War was mentioned as a situation with 'no peace' in the Netherlands

organisations; Germany invades Russia; the invasion and allied forces: USA, England, France and Russia). With the exception of the themes referring to the bombing of Rotterdam, the resistance and the invasion of Russia, the other themes were mentioned significantly more with age with Chi-square values ranging from 49.24 for rounding up people and the winter of hunger to 483.06 for war against Germany ($p < .01$; see Figure 6.3). These data suggest that from the age of 8–9 years, Dutch children perceive the Second World War as the most important past situation of 'no peace' in the Netherlands and possess well-developed factual knowledge about events related to this war.

From personal to collective memory and vice versa

The findings of this study show that already from the age of 8–9 years children perceive the Second World War as the most important period of 'no peace' in the Netherlands and possess extensive knowledge about events that took place during this war. Since this knowledge is not based on personal experience, it must be the result of socialisation and educational processes. However, at the age of 8–9 years children will have followed only two to three years of formal education at elementary-school level. Consequently, educational processes alone cannot offer sufficient explanation for the predominance of the Second World War as a situation of 'no peace' in the Netherlands at such an early age. In accordance with our assumption, we assume that this finding is an indication of the presence and strength of cross-generational transfer processes of (negative) memories within a society (that is, the Netherlands) that has not known or experienced war for more than half a century. Personal memory is then socially constructed and informed by collective memory and cohort related. While the findings of Hakvoort (1996) coincide with those for the younger age cohorts of Peters and Schuyt (1998), they do not with those of the older age cohorts. For the older age cohort, personal experiences (for example, suffering) as a consequence of the Second World War have priority over factual knowledge in their memory.

These differences in knowledge about the Second World War between age cohorts illustrate the co-constructivist assumption (Winegar and Valsiner, 1992; Valsiner, 1998) that cultural messages (that is, knowledge) which are actively communicated by and among others, especially (grand)parents, are equally actively reassembled (reconstructed) by the recipient children, who are then joint constructors of the new (cultural) knowledge. That is, each age cohort will interpret cross-generationally transferred knowledge in accordance with the prevailing 'zeitgeist', the nature of the knowledge transferred and their own experiences. This theoretical approach assumes that collective memory is also subject to change over generations.

The consequent discrepancies between collective and personal memory may in part explain the contradictory findings of different surveys conducted in the Netherlands with respect to the attitudes of Dutch youth towards Germans. While on the personal experiential level the German people can be perceived as kind, democratic and tolerant (that is, I have many German friends), collective memory dictates a different image (that is, Germans are warlike, arrogant and so on). However, even if this distinction between personal and collective memory is correct, it does not explain the phenomena that can be observed when the Dutch national soccer team plays against the German national team (Kuper, 1998). Witnessing such an event does make one wonder whether the Second World War really did end in 1945.

The observed often vehement anti-German attitudes and feelings in different sections of the Dutch population and notably with youngsters cannot only be explained by the effects of cross-generational transfer of factual knowledge. Because of the ages involved, personal memory in the sense of autobiographical memory is not a plausible explanatory variable. Consequently, more is needed to understand these phenomena and in particular the processes by which factual knowledge is transformed into negative, emotionally loaded attitudes.

In an interview for the second German television network ZDF (10 January 1998), Prince Claus (husband of Queen Beatrix of the Netherlands), attempted to relativise the anti-German feelings of Dutch youth. According to Claus, one should perceive 'these feelings ironically, based on a cliché or stereotyped phrase, and always concerning "the bicycle" which was stolen by the Germans. Children tell, when asked why they do not like the Germans: "They stole my grandfather's bicycle." The story of the bicycle has become something like a national epos which is transferred from generation to generation' (verbatim from the interview).

What should be noted here is that it was possible for this 'story' to become something like a national epos, because the feelings related to the loss of a bicycle are understood, are experienced and are felt by each next generation as if they happened (and regularly do happen) today. Similarly, German army units when in the Netherlands (for example, during the yearly four-day marches) will never march in time, because 'I (read, "we") get sick when hearing marching Germans'. Specific remembered contents (that is, qualitative aspects of collective memory) are then meaningfully related to global activity contexts in which remembering takes place (Bangerter *et al.*, 1997). Within the context of the present study, it can be argued that thinking of Germans within the context of a survey and remembering that they stole grandfather's bicycle is ironic or trivial. But is it? The vehement anti-German attitudes and feelings prior, during and following a soccer match shows that past frustrations have not been processed, neither within the family nor in society.

While myths and stories may have their origin during the Second World War, they are not only related to contemporary experiences, by way of personal and autobiographical memory, but also via collective memory in a moral framework. By means of this framework the 'goodies' and the 'badies' or the 'victims' and 'victimizers' are specified. Collective memory is transformed into a collective moral interpretative framework by which past and contemporary events are evaluated, which in turn will regulate collective action and achievement (Bangerter *et al.*, 1997). And, of course, each group- or nation-related collective, moral interpretative framework is correct and the other by definition wrong (for example, the Palestinian *vs* the Israeli, Serbian *vs* Bosnian, Serbian *vs* Albanian, North Irish Catholic *vs* Protestant framework, and so on).

Fortunately, we are dealing here with only a survey and a soccer match, because these phenomena suggest that the past does not yet belong to the past and apparently the Germans have not yet been forgiven. In spite of the latter, the findings of the present study clearly illustrate the pervasive and long-term role of memory and collective memory, in particular, on the development of attitudes towards others. In addition, the observed effects of collective memory, by means of cross-generational transfer of knowledge from (grand)parents to children, are present at a much earlier age than hitherto assumed (Peters and Schuyt, 1998).

In our attempts to understand and solve ethnic conflicts and their origins, inclusion of the role of collective memory appears to be mandatory. Ways should be developed to break through the apparent cycle of 'negative' interpretative frameworks that are cross-generationally transferred. For this purpose, we propose to focus on personal (that is, autobiographical) memory as the link between collective memory and personal experiences and emotions. As Piaget (1948/1980) already noted targets of education processes should be that children discover by 'lived-in experience' the nature of the 'conflicts of reciprocity and the misunderstandings of all social intercourse.' Education processes should be extended 'in the direction of international exchanges or even of study groups that have international problems as their object' (p. 141). It is these *active* education processes, that have the stimulation and promotion of international life as their targets, that will result in real changes in the personal and shared general sociocultural structure and, hence, collective memory (Oppenheimer, 1997).

Part IV

Conflicting Memories and Conflict Resolution

7
History Teaching and the Perpetuation of Memories: the Northern Ireland Experience

Keith C. Barton and Alan McCully

Teaching history in a society that has experienced violent and on-going conflict, at least partially as a consequence of contested views of national identity, presents significant challenges for educators. This is particularly true in Northern Ireland, where the continued existence of two parallel educational systems often has been implicated in the perpetuation of community divisions, and where new directions in education are regularly promoted as important contributors to peace and reconciliation (Murray, Smith and Birthistle, 1997). This chapter examines the role of formal history instruction in Northern Ireland schools and points to some of the ways history teaching may help to overcome – or perpetuate – perceptions of community antagonism rooted in the past. In particular, we explore whether an emphasis on evidence-based inquiry and the avoidance of questions of identity, provides the most appropriate balance of historical approaches in a setting such as Northern Ireland.

One of the most notable features of the educational system in Northern Ireland is its segregated nature. Most schools are predominantly either Catholic or Protestant; those attended mainly by Protestants are known as 'controlled' schools and are under the direct management of regional education boards, while most Catholics attend 'maintained' schools administered by a council under the auspices of the Catholic Church. Although both are open to children of all denominations, in practice only a small proportion of students attend schools in which the majority is a different religion than themselves. This segregated system of schooling sometimes has been implicated in perpetuating community division; in particular, the practice of educating children in separate settings has been credited with encouraging group differences and loyalties, as well as with increasing mutual suspicion and ignorance

(Darby *et al.*, 1977; Murray, 1985; Gallagher, 1989). Responses to this segregation have included integrated schools (which currently enroll nearly four per cent of Northern Ireland students), systems for promoting cross-community contacts among students, and educational programmes aimed at increasing tolerance and respect for those from other traditions (Smith, 1999).

Our focus, however, is more directly on curricular and instructional issues, rather than the structure of schooling or interpersonal relations. Here, too, segregated schooling has been implicated in the perpetuation of group differences; some researchers assert that the two systems have emphasized different subjects, topics, or perspectives, particularly in history (see, Darby, 1976). Much store has been placed on the view that until the 1970s young people in Northern Ireland learned a selective version of the past 'in the streets' and that school history either failed to challenge this view or, worse, reinforced bias through the unconscious – and sometimes wilful – contributions of teachers. This assertion, however, is often made without convincing support; in fact, the empirical evidence for such a conclusion is sparse, and the data generally fragmentary and contradictory. (See, for example, Magee 1970; Darby, 1974; Barkley, 1976). In any event, overtly sectarian history teaching has not been common since at least the 1980s (Austin, 1985; Smith and Dunn, 1990), and since 1991 all schools have followed a common curriculum in history. Yet the question still remains whether the formal school curriculum – while not directly perpetuating the two communities' historical 'memories' – has a role to play in challenging such views and, if so, what that role may be.

Through the mandated cross-curricular themes of 'Cultural Heritage' and 'Education for Mutual Understanding' (EMU), schools in Northern Ireland are required to foster students' self-respect and respect for others, as well as to improve individual and community relationships, particularly through helping students understand and evaluate their common heritage and to examine aspects of culture that are distinct and diverse. History is often expected to play a critical role in such efforts, through engaging students in the investigation of past societies, evaluating evidence to reach conclusions and exploring controversial issues in an open-minded way. The relationship between studying the past and developing more tolerant perspectives in the present, however, is not a simple or straightforward process, especially in the emotionally charged atmosphere of Northern Ireland. The following accounts from the classroom experiences of one of the authors of this chapter illustrate some of the problems involved.

The first occurred several years ago as he sat at the back of a class of 14-year-olds in a controlled grammar school, supervising a student teacher. The lesson examined the impact of the Easter 1916 Rising (including the execution of its leaders under British martial law) on Irish politics in the next six years. The teacher successfully engaged the class using primary source material. Students were encouraged to seek understanding of reasons the protagonists in the rising acted as they did under the circumstances. In particular, they were asked to examine why Irish public opinion so quickly swung behind Sinn Fein in the aftermath of the executions and the attempts by the British government to introduce conscription into Ireland in the last months of the First World War.

A lively discussion ensued among a group of well-taught, articulate and bright students. In the course of this it became clear that a majority interpreted the responses of the British government as politically inept, thus contributing to the emergence of the Irish Republican Army and the desire for complete separation from Britain. These Protestant pupils – identifying with Britain today, and presumably critical of current nationalist positions – might have been expected to reject such arguments out of hand; but instead, they could be observed 'stepping out' of their own political positions to understand the meaning of events for people with very different perspectives. Here was an impressive lesson on a potentially controversial topic. But the student teacher chose to go further. In the remaining minutes he suggested that the class make comparisons with the contemporary violent Republican struggle (of the early 1990s) by asking whether there were similarities in the two sets of circumstances, and whether there was continuity in Republican actions from the 1920s to the present. The surprise for the observing tutor was not that the students rejected any justification for the current IRA campaign, but that most of them refused to engage with the exercise at all. In his field notes he observed 'an emotional wall ascend'. Students who previously were revelling in intellectual debate and imaginative speculation terminated the activity with impulsive finality, as if to say that there was no validity in the comparison.

The second classroom experience was a more recent one and sheds light on the links between past and present from a different angle. The co-author was working in a Controlled High School with a history teacher on *Speak Your Piece*, a project focusing on the handling of controversial issues (McCully, O'Doherty and Smith, 1999). The teacher, who had a strong relationship with his students, was conscious that several members of his class of 15-year-olds were coming into contact with paramilitary influences. He felt it appropriate to engage them in class activity that would give them opportunities to articulate and clarify their thinking. However, he was also determined that the work should be linked directly to their coursework on recent Irish history. A programme of work was devised to cover two 70-minute lessons. In the first, students were introduced to the emotive statements of two fictional television drama characters, one a Loyalist, the other a Republican, both claiming historical justification for extreme positions. They then examined which historical events from their previous studies might have been interpreted in ways to support contemporary positions in each of the two communities. Again, the work produced by the students reflected a grasp of the historical process and an understanding of differing perspectives and interpretations, and the class session indicated skilful practice on the part of the teacher. Yet students' reactions to the session were complex. They indicated a frustration that they were being taken to the brink of highly charged political issues that impacted on their every day lives but then, in the words of one student, being 'restrained by the need to observe the rules of history'. They requested that in the second session they be allowed to 'step out of the history classroom' to enable them to give vent to their views on contemporary issues.

These anecdotes raise three critical questions:

1. What contribution has history to play in helping young people to understand contemporary conflict?
2. Is the rational thinking encouraged through the enquiry approach of history easily transferable to emotionally charged contemporary situations?
3. Are there other approaches to history that might be more effective in challenging sectarian perspectives?

Teaching and learning history in Northern Ireland

History is no single entity, no monolith with an agreed-upon set of principles and practices. Rather, the past can be used to nurture a sense of individual, group, or national identity, provide moral examples, justify and legitimise the status quo, or empower marginalised groups as they struggle against that status quo or demand redress for historic injustices (Levstik and Barton, 2001). Yet many historians and history educators would consider each of these various approaches an *abuse* of the past; they would argue that proper history is a more rational endeavour, one that seeks to understand and explain the events of the past rather than to serve the ends of present-day social utility. (For particularly clear explanations of this perspective, see Lee, 1984, and Rogers, 1984.) Proponents of this 'rationalistic' approach do not necessarily deny that contemporary concerns shape the questions historians ask of the past, nor that modern perspectives influence their interpretations. They do assert, however, that history (and certainly history education in schools) must be centred on objective analysis of evidence and the construction of rational arguments, rather than oriented toward such 'popular' missions as the construction of identity or the mobilisation of social groups.

The rationalistic approach has been the dominant one in British schools, including those in Northern Ireland, for many years, and the teachers and students in the above examples clearly were familiar with analysis of historical explanations and interpretations. But these examples also show that perspectives developed outside the classroom cannot simply be wished away or ignored and they suggest that even the most careful academic analysis may not enable students to deal dispassionately with more emotionally charged issues. The old joke goes that incoming passengers to Belfast's International Airport are asked to fasten their seat belts . . . and then put their watches back three hundred years! Certainly, the resonance of past historical events is more overt to the observer in Northern Ireland than in many other places. Communities there remember such events through demonstration and symbolism in the form of marches, flags, regalia and wall murals, while politicians and community leaders make frequent references to perceived past triumphs or grievances in their exhortations to followers (Buckley and Kenney, 1995; McBride, 1997; Jarman, 1998). Understanding the complex relationships among popular and academic historical frameworks is particularly important in a setting such as Northern Ireland, where perceptions of historic events and processes continue to exert a significant influence on people's standpoints toward politics, religion and each other.

The idea that unionist and nationalist communities have distinct collective memories, accumulated through centuries of conflict, is an attractive one. Yet as Walker (1996) has demonstrated, much of that historical 'memory' was actually a creation of the highly charged political crisis surrounding the first Irish Home Rule bill in the mid-1880s, and trends established then characterise politics to the present. In particular, historical events are viewed as isolated incidents that signify victory or defeat, thus feeding triumphalism or fuelling grievance; they become 'a convenient quarry which provides ammunition to use against enemies in the present' (Stewart, 1977, p. 16). Because historical events are interpreted to satisfy contemporary needs and emotions, at best they draw on a highly selective version of the event and at worst perpetuate a mythical account that distorts or bears little relationship to available historical evidence. The prevalence in Northern Ireland of this kind of selective and self-serving history would seem to support the case of those who advocate a rationalistic, enquiry approach to the subject.

Unsurprisingly, with the onset of the most recent phase of the Irish Troubles in the late 1960s, the long established pattern of drawing on historical myth and half-truth to nourish entrenched political opinions was seen by commentators as a source of sectarianism and political intolerance. Educationalists argued that if historical myths on both sides were challenged, young people would be better informed and more resistant to community demagogues – that 'properly taught Irish history could be the basis of understanding' (Barkley, 1976, p. 12). In an influential paper, Magee (1970) outlined the challenges facing the history teacher with a desire to bring change. In doing so he anticipated future methodological developments in Northern Irish history teaching:

> If those of us who teach history can persuade our pupils to adopt a more critical attitude to what they hear and read, bring them to realise that there is generally more than one side to an argument; perhaps even prompt them to see that those from whom they differ are the products of their environment as they themselves are conditioned by their own – they will have rendered a great service to the community without sacrificing in any way the legitimate aims of history teaching (p. 21).

The details of the evolution and implementation of the Northern Ireland History Curriculum may be traced elsewhere (Gallagher and McCully, 1997; McCully, 1998; Phillips *et al.*, 1999). Suffice it to say that many of those committed to the thinking of the enquiry-based Schools Council History Project (pioneered first in England) became influential in the policymaking domain in the mid-1980s and afterward. The secondary examination syllabus introduced in 1987 closely followed this philosophy and the Northern Ireland Curriculum that emerged in 1991 consolidated this view of school history as a process of thinking modelled on the academic discipline. Briefly, the characteristics of the history programmes of study as they presently exist may be summarised as follows. Learning outcomes are defined within the rationalistic, enquiry model of history teaching. Pupils are encouraged to think critically about evidence presented to them, to see events from different perspectives and to reach conclusions based on the consideration of a range of interpretations. Irish history is at the core of the programmes but, to avoid introversion and to encourage multiple perspectives, it is placed in its wider contexts looking 'out from Ireland to Britain, Europe, and the wider world, or if more appropriate the reverse' (Department of Education Northern Ireland, 1990, p. 8). Pupils are encouraged to comprehend the complexity of cultural and political origins through studying successive waves of migratory groups to Ireland (Mesolithic settlers, early Celts, Vikings, Normans and English and Scots Planters). Particularly in the earlier years of schooling it is expected that common aspects of cultural heritage and experience, the stories of 'ordinary' people, be explored through local studies and aspects of social history. The exploration of crucial and contested events in Irish history, or those considered relevant to the evolution of the Irish conflict, is more evident in the later years. For example, in successive years of the secondary curriculum, students are asked to examine the growing English influence in Ireland from Norman times onwards, the Ulster Plantation and the Williamite Wars, the evolution of Unionism and Nationalism and the events that led to partition.

The history curriculum is also notable for two issues that are *not* explicitly addressed. First, there is no attempt to direct students in formulating their own identities in historical terms. The underlying assumption is that in a society where the expression of contested identities is a source of deep division, there can be no one 'national story', and history teaching has no role in transmitting any such story. The curriculum does gives prominence to the process of conquest and assimilation and suggests that the legacy of each group to the Irish landscape and culture should be traced – thus challenging simplistic notions of national primacy or purity, of 'them' and 'us', or 'We were here first' – but these challenges are only implicit; history teaching in Northern Ireland is not meant to provide a direct alternative for the formation of students' identity. Second, connections between historical events and contemporary issues are not given prominence. Controversial topics are largely omitted from history until the second year of secondary school, and even when students do begin to study the politically volatile events of the last four hundred years, they are not systematically expected to connect those events to the present or to consider parallels with contemporary issues. Individual teachers are free to explore such connections in their classes, and many do, but this approach remains very much a voluntary effort and one which a large portion of teachers would consider either risky or unnecessary. Again, the connection between past and present remains an implicit goal rather than an explicitly featured element of instruction.

Children's perspectives on history

The description above details the nature and purpose of the formal curriculum – that which has been planned by official educational bodies. But the representation of curricula in classrooms might or might not reflect the intentions of curriculum designers, and the ideas that are attended to and internalised by students are still further removed from official design. In seeking to understand the role of formal education, then, it is necessary to look beyond the design of the curriculum and to investigate both how history is represented in classrooms and how children themselves make sense of those representations. We have little evidence for the first issue, for there have been no recent studies of instructional patterns or curricular decisionmaking in history classrooms in Northern Ireland. However, research by one of the authors of this chapter does provide information on the second – how children understand the nature and purpose of history. This research, conducted in 1997, involved classroom observations in the primary grades, along with both formal and informal interviews with over 120 children, aged six to 12 (Barton, 2001). Students in the study were drawn from a variety of schools and social backgrounds and included those who attended maintained, controlled and integrated schools; who lived in areas with direct exposure to community conflict and in areas with little such experience; and who came from small and medium towns and villages with families from a variety of economic circumstances. While these findings may not be generalised as representative of 'typical' children in Northern Ireland – if such children exist – they nonetheless provide evidence of the views of a diverse population of children.

In interviews, children were shown a set of pictures from different times in history, asked to put them in chronological order and prompted to explain the reasons for their placements. They were then asked a series of questions about where they had learned about history and why they thought the subject was interesting and/or important. The choice of these methods reflect a trend over the past quarter-century in British and North American research on children's conceptual understanding away from the exclusive use of paper-and-pencil tests or surveys and toward open-ended interviews, often accompanied by concrete tasks or representational stimuli such as those used here. Open-ended interviews provide greater opportunities for probing children's responses in order to investigate their underlying assumptions and explanations, as well as the chance to explore novel or unanticipated questions, issues, or themes that arise during the discussions. In research on historical understanding, the use of visual sources has been particularly useful as a way of tapping into a wider range and depth of background knowledge than is generally revealed through oral or written tasks alone. Combining interviews with classroom observations, meanwhile, provides the chance to compare students' responses to classroom instruction and to inquire into topics, which have come up in class. As with most contemporary studies of conceptual understanding, the purpose of this research was not to identify an external standard of knowledge and then evaluate the extent to which children lived up to (or failed to live up to) that standard, but to give participants themselves the opportunity to describe and explain how they understood the topics under investigation.

Throughout these interviews, students demonstrated a great deal of consensus in their ideas about the nature and purpose of history. First, nearly all thought of themselves as historically conscious and aware individuals; they described themselves as interested in history and knowledgeable about its content (a description borne out by their high level of accuracy in placing the pictures from different time periods). A six-year-old girl, for example, explained, 'I'm very interested in olden day stuff, and it's interesting to go back, to go that far back . . . because it feels like you're going back and you're actually walking in those olden day streets, like in a time machine', while an eight-year-old boy noted, 'I think it's interesting because I like hearing about old people and how they lived and how they made houses and things like that'. Students also pointed to a common set of sources from which they had obtained their knowledge of history – noting especially relatives, historic sites (such as prehistoric remains, building ruins, history parks and museums) and the media. School was also an important source of information for many children, but even for those younger pupils who had encountered little or no history instruction at school, these other sources supplied them with a great deal of information about the past. And notably, most students had begun to associate historical knowledge with the use of evidence: When asked how people know what happened in the past, students frequently explained that conclusions in history are based on remains, artefacts, or other such sources of information. One nine-year-old girl, for example, noted that 'archaeologists find things from the past that tell us lots of things about it', and another observed, 'People find remains, and they started to study, and they started to find out what kind of life they had, the way they made their things.'

But perhaps most importantly, students consistently explained that studying history meant learning about how people lived in other times and places. They did not describe history in terms of narratives about particular people or events – in fact, they usually could not think of any such stories even when prompted – but rather in terms of the social and economic structure of other societies both in Ireland and beyond (such as the ancient Egyptians, Mesolithic people, the Victorians and so on). As one student put it, history is important 'to understand the way other people lived and went about their daily life'. The emphasis on *other people* was particularly salient: the more different a way of life was, the more interested in it students seemed to be. Rarely did they suggest that learning about their own country, heritage, culture, or background was especially interesting or important; rather they talked about their need to know about people who lived differently than they do today. A few even suggested that such curiosity is a basic human attribute; as one girl said, 'It's just interesting to know what it was like if we had been there [in the past], and people fifty years from now will be keen to know what it's like for us.'

These findings suggest that in some important ways, students' experiences with history in Northern Ireland are preparing them for the kinds of thinking envisioned by the formal curriculum. First, it was clear that sectarian stories of the region's past did not dominate these children's ideas about history. Although it is sometimes assumed that children in Northern Ireland learn sectarian history 'at their mother's knee', (Stewart, 1977, p. 16) and that this kind of history is firmly ensconced in their perception of the topic by the time they reach post-primary schooling, the students in this research almost never mentioned people or events related to Unionist or Nationalist versions of history, either during formal interviews or in informal conversations with the researcher. They sometimes talked about the Troubles in *contemporary* terms, but they did not link the topic specifically to *history*. Nor did they justify either the importance of history, or their own interest in it, on the basis of its role in communal identification or political conflict. At the very least, one can conclude that these children had ideas about history that extended beyond the sectarian representations found in popular culture and political debate in Northern Ireland.

Second, students' interest in learning about differences in lifestyles seems well suited to advance the kind of tolerance that is so much needed in Northern Ireland. These children had internalised the idea that history is about how people live – Victorian society, daily life during the Second World War, the way Mesolithic people met their basic needs and so on. This perspective accords well with the emphasis on common social experiences and shared aspects of cultural heritage promoted in the Northern Ireland Curriculum. Moreover, students' specific interest in people who are different than them may well provide the basis upon which a life-long commitment to diversity could be built. By helping children think of history as an outward-looking subject, rather than one focused on their own narrow interests, the curriculum appears to have accomplished an important goal. Finally, students' recognition that history is based on evidence corresponds closely to the intent of the formal curriculum and this might well provide them with the basis for developing more 'objective' conclusions about the past. The attention given to the role of historical evidence, and these children's developing understanding of its use, suggests that they may grow up with important intellectual resources for analysing and criticising received historical stories.

The results of this research, then, indicate important ways in which the curriculum that children in Northern Ireland are attending to and internalising matches the intent of the formal curriculum, and this correspondence should be highly encouraging to those who hope that education can play a role in addressing the uncritical transmission of sectarian historical 'memories'. But some significant questions remain concerning the extent to which primary education prepares students for the more extensive, more relevant and more emotionally charged history they will encounter as they move into early adolescence. The anecdotal accounts at the beginning of this chapter indicate that important issues in children's developing perspective on the past remain unresolved.

First, it is by no means clear that the evidence-based, outward-looking, social/cultural history that children study in primary school is effective in countering, replacing, or even influencing other historical perspectives to which they may be exposed. The children in the study described above may not have mentioned sectarian stories of the past while studying history at school, or even in interviews with the researcher, but that does not mean they are unfamiliar with them. There are few opportunities to bring up politicised historical topics when learning about Mesolithic peoples or the Vikings, and the pictures used in the research portrayed largely uncontroversial aspects of daily life – schools, cottages, antique cars and so on. Although students' responses may allow us to conclude that their understanding of the past is not *dominated* by politicised memories of historical events, such responses provide little information on whether such memories coexist with other kinds of knowledge. Researchers have noted the tendency of children to compartmentalise the information they obtain from differing sources: in science, for example, students often segregate school knowledge from their own, experience-based observations of natural phenomena. It may be that a similar process takes place among children in Northern Ireland – they might learn one kind of history at school (and from history parks, museums, and so on), while they are simultaneously learning a separate form of historical knowledge of the kind more often associated with sectarian memories and community conflict.

A second study, also conducted by one of the authors of this chapter, sheds some light on this issue. In that research, 40 secondary students were shown captioned pictures of historical events and asked to select those they considered the most important; they too were asked more general questions about history, such as what other people might think about the pictures, where they had learned about the past, and why they thought the subject was important enough to study at school (Barton, 1998). As with the study above, this task and the accompanying open-ended interviews were consistent with contemporary research into children's conceptual understanding, yet it provided greater opportunity to discuss events central to the histories of the two communities in Northern Ireland, for many of the pictures included politically volatile issues from the region's past – Bloody Sunday, the Battle of the Boyne, Penal Laws, the Enniskillen bombing and so on. It was clear from students' responses that they were indeed familiar with many such topics and that they had begun to pick up some of the basic details of Northern Ireland's community memories.

As noted above, the secondary curriculum, unlike that of primary schools, focuses directly on many of the major events that led to the political makeup of modern Northern Ireland. But it is important to note that the secondary pupils in this study had not learned about these events solely, or perhaps even primarily, from school. Students knew about many topics they had not yet encountered in the formal curriculum; they had learned about such topics from relatives, from peers and from the media. As one boy noted, 'Everybody's always talking about it.' Indeed, some students were consciously aware of the distinction between school history and that which they encountered from more informal sources. When one girl was asked how she knew so much about the events depicted in the research task, she said she had learned everything about them since coming to secondary school – she had not studied any history in primary school, she maintained, nor had she learned anything about it from any other source. The interviewer, in a tone of exaggerated surprise, asked if she really meant that everything she knew about history she had learned in just the last two years of school. She responded, somewhat self-consciously, 'Well, apart from the Catholic and Protestant stuff' – as though it were simply taken for granted that sectarian histories would be passed along outside of school. Similarly, one boy noted that school history was particularly useful because 'if you're taught history in school, then you get both sides of the view; if you're taught it outside of school, you're going, "Well, the Protestants do this and the Protestants do that, and this is why we're doing it", and, "The Catholics are bad people, the Catholics are doing this, and that's why they're doing it", and that's the whole story.'

These quotes suggest that some young adolescents recognize there is a set of school knowledge related to history, as well as a separate body of information deriving from other sources – and that there may be varying degrees of correspondence between the two. The extent to which students attempt to reconcile these potentially conflicting perspectives is still largely unknown, but one recent study suggests that the connection between histories in and out of school may be minimal. This study involved interviews and surveys with nearly 3,000 students, aged 10 to 14, and their teachers, across 51 schools in Northern Ireland during a three-year period (Harland *et al.*, 1999). Secondary students considered history to be among the least relevant in the school curriculum, whether considered in relation to their current lives, their future lives as adults, or their potential careers; the subject consistently outranked only music and Irish language in terms of relevance. Although this research is subject to a variety of interpretations, and although the wording of the questions may have influenced participants' responses, it nonetheless seems that students were unused to associating relevance with the study of history. Despite the broad cultural significance of history in Northern Ireland, then, and despite the commitment and innovative practice of many practitioners in the region, children appear to have little appreciation for the social significance of the subject. How can this be? How can history appear irrelevant in a place where historical events are the basis for political positions, parades, banners, gable wall paintings, even graffiti? Could it be that this perception derives from a failure to explicitly connect school history to the kind of history that children encounter in their lives outside school? And if so what can – or should – be done about it?

Where now for history teaching in Northern Ireland?

At the time of this writing, the Northern Ireland Curriculum is under review and initial indications are that significant change will result (Northern Ireland Council for the Curriculum, Examinations and Assessment, 2000). Emphasis is being placed on clarifying the curriculum's underlying values and improving its relevance and enjoyment for students. In line with developments in England, the review framework strongly advocates the introduction of 'education for citizenship', not only in history but throughout the curriculum; this is presented in the context of new political departures, 'to develop the capacity of young people to participate in a fair and inclusive society throughout their lifetime' (Northern Ireland Council for the Curriculum, Examinations and Assessment, 2000, p. 19). How this concern with citizenship might influence the study of history remains to be seen. In England, history educators' response to issues of citizenship education have been ambivalent: the advent of citizenship is seen as a threat to the subject's place in the curriculum, yet it also presents the opportunity to demonstrate history's relevance (Counsell, 1999). In Northern Ireland, given what has been outlined in this chapter, it seems crucial that the potential contribution of historical study to the contemporary dimensions of citizenship are thought through and, just as importantly, clearly and explicitly articulated. In effect, should history teaching restrain its contribution to providing a backdrop of knowledge to be drawn on in citizenship lessons? Or should it engage overtly in the pursuit of critical citizenship?

We believe that if the last question is answered affirmatively, the evidence presented in this chapter suggests two ways history teaching can more effectively contribute to education for citizenship. The first involves a reversal of the traditional relationship between the study of past and present. To date, the orthodoxy has been to study the past, then (perhaps) to project that learning to the present. The drawbacks of this are captured in the introductory anecdotes – students may be unprepared to make such connections, or they may consider historical methods too constraining for the highly charged issues they wish to confront. In effect, students' developing understanding of the nature and use of historical evidence may fail to transfer to consideration of more controversial topics. It is one thing to recognize that descriptions of Mesolithic people are based on remains uncovered through archaeological investigations, but it is quite another to apply such analytical techniques to more emotionally charged topics. Yet some secondary-level pupils in the research described above suggested that school history *should* encourage such analysis – they noted that learning history at school is important so that they will be able to detect statements not based on evidence, or so that they will be able to understand the perspectives of people who interpret historic events differently than they do. One Protestant student, for example, explained that without history, 'Your grandparents could just say, "This happened a long time ago", without proof – and history's the proof.' Similarly, a Catholic student noted that studying history 'gives us knowledge so that we wouldn't be one-sided against Protestants or like that'; another Catholic student agreed, noting, 'If we weren't learning about it, we would just be for our own opinions, and they could be wrong.' Only a few students, however, made such observations about the role of history in countering prejudice or unfounded opinions. How might history instruction more effectively encourage these kinds of connections?

Perhaps the relevance of history would be more apparent to young people if the *starting point* of study were their imperfect understanding of the historical dimension of contemporary issues. Seixas (1993) argues that beginning with students' own historical questions not only highlights the meaning and relevance of the subject but actually increases the scholarly authenticity of historical study – historians do; after all, begin their enquiries with questions they find interesting. That is not to suggest that students should, from the age of five, be encouraged to address only complex and controversial cultural and political issues. Rather, it may mean that whatever the historical topic chosen, the starting point could be contemporary representations of past events. The research discussed above demonstrates that children take considerable interest in, and learn from, various popular interpretations of history in a wide variety of informal settings – be they from television programmes, movies, advertisements, or theme and folk parks. And indeed, some of the most exciting work to emerge from the national curricula in the United Kingdom has been in the realm of interpretations; inspired by a model developed by McAleavy (1993), many teachers now use movies and other popular representations of historical figures and events as the basis for critical enquiry. We suggest that the history curriculum in Northern Ireland might be designed to more systematically follow this present-to-past-to-present model, in doing so it might draw, at intervals, on issues of real concern in students' communities as well as those derived from popular culture. In this way a process might be nurtured that helps students think rationally but also allows them to overcome the emotional dynamic, the 'wall', that impeded the students in the first anecdote.

A second way history might contribute to education for critical citizenship is through more explicit attention to questions of identity. In many countries, school history is closely tied to the development of a sense of common identity. In the United States, for example, children from an early age learn about the origin of their country as a political entity, the historical developments that have led to the current social and political structure of the nation, and the famous individuals who stand as enduring moral examples. The result is an overarching sense of Americanness that exists alongside other, more particular identifications (Barton and Levstik, 1998; Cornbleth, 1998). History becomes a way of creating, defining and debating who 'we' are. Of course, this kind of emphasis can also lead to serious abuses – questions of who we are often turn into strictures on who we are *not*, and US history has repeatedly been used to exclude members of various ethnic, religious, economic and even geographical populations. But the importance of American identity has led generation after generation of marginalised peoples to demand a place in the story of US history – to force their way into what 'counts' as American.

But as noted above, in the kind of rationalistic, evidence-based curriculum found in Northern Ireland, the creation of identity plays no formal role. The purpose of the curriculum, rather, is to provide young people with a foundation of historical skills and knowledge, from which they may draw, on their own initiative, in analysing or constructing a sense of identity. But by failing to address issues of identity more directly, history education in Northern Ireland may ultimately doom itself to irrelevance. Early adolescence is a time of strong pressure to identify with sectarian groups and with the historical perspectives that accompany such groups. And unlike primary children, several of the secondary students in the study above described history's importance in terms of the need to learn about one's own heritage, culture and background. One Catholic student, for example, explained, 'I think it's interesting and important to study your own culture so you know more about what happened in Ireland', while another noted, 'You should know what happened in your past'. Similarly, one Protestant student suggested that history is important 'to know your background, know your country's background', and another pointed out, 'It's important to know your past, know your heritage and that'. Again, these were not the most common responses students gave, but they suggest that at least some young adolescents are searching for personal meaning in the history they encounter at school and elsewhere.

Educators in Northern Ireland, then, might consider whether the disavowal of identity in the history curriculum has helped maintain separate communities with no shared sense of purpose and few resources for constructing any common notion of belonging. Rather than simply addressing historical topics that happen to include members of both communities (Victorian society, daily life during the Second World War), perhaps the curriculum could direct specific attention to what the people of Northern Ireland have in common, both now and in the past, so that the topic of identity itself becomes a topic of investigation. Perhaps, alongside studying perceived icons of the unionist or nationalist communities (such as William of Orange or Padraig Pearse), children could also learn about individuals who are worthy of admiration by both communities, or about those who have fought to overcome community divisions. If history is to provide students with a means for resisting sectarian appeals, teachers may need to address the topic of identity in much more explicit terms.

Conclusions

Returning to the young people in the opening anecdotes, both groups were enthused by the history they were encountering, and both demonstrated an impressive engagement with the rationalistic model of historical enquiry. Yet, in both cases there is a sense that this approach alone was not fully meeting their needs. In each incident an emotional reaction was present, fed by deeply held positions acquired through family and community, and in each case, students well versed in the 'rules' of the subject felt uncomfortable within themselves when the rational and the emotional confronted each other. We suggest that innovative planning and practice – through the use of contemporary historical representations and attention to elements of shared identity – can capitalise on the strengths of a rationalistic, inquiry-based approach while grappling more directly with the deeply felt personal and emotional aspects of history. These revisions will not be accomplished easily, and the challenge to teachers – both in being explicit about the values base within their own teaching, and in developing the skills necessary to handle emotionally charged issues in the classroom – should not be underestimated, nor should the possibility of repercussions from the community be discounted when controversial issues are raised. There also remains a 'fundamental tension' among teachers, between those who see history's role as being predominantly about the past, and those who wish to see students apply critical skills directly to contemporary issues and values (Gallagher, 1998; McCully, 1998). Changes in curricular and instructional patterns will require more than official edicts, they will require a process of consensus-building, as well as extensive support for teachers grappling with very difficult issues. But we believe that by beginning this process of rethinking the role of formal history instruction in Northern Ireland, the barriers between historical memories and historical understanding ultimately might be diminished.

8
Memories of Recent Conflict and Forgiveness in Northern Ireland[1]

Frances McLernon, Ed Cairns, Christopher Alan Lewis and Miles Hewstone

It is said that: 'The stupid neither forgive nor forget; the naive forgive and forget; the wise forgive but do not forget.' Sinn Féin President Gerry Adams to a meeting of the Sinn Féin Ard Comhairle, 24 November 1999

Introduction

In everyday discourse forgiving and forgetting are regarded as closely linked, sometimes, synonymous concepts. In this chapter we explore the relationship between forgiveness and memory in the context of the intergroup conflict in Northern Ireland. Much of the interest in forgiveness in the context of intergroup conflict has been inspired by the 'miracle' of South Africa's transition to democracy and in particular the role played in this process by the Truth and Reconciliation Commission (TRC). The TRC however, according to Asmal *et al.* (1996) did not lead to the forgetting of 'accusations and counter accusations, but more a settling of them through a process of evaluation – like the accountant's job of reconciling conflicting claims before closing a ledger book' (p. 46).

One thing is clear however, while forgiveness is under our own control, forgetting is not. Furthermore, while forgiving does not automatically lead to forgetting, there can be no forgiving if forgetting has already occurred. This is because some form of remembering is necessary if forgiveness is to take place. For these reasons forgiveness must not be confused with forgetting ... 'Genuine forgiveness cannot even begin to be considered until one recognizes the pain and consequences of the injury' (Enright and Coyle, 1994, p. 141). With this in mind this chapter will, after a brief history of the conflict in Northern Ireland, move to reviewing empirical evidence exploring social memories of the conflict in Northern Ireland and will then consider the possibility of intergroup forgiveness in the same context.

Background to the Northern Ireland conflict

Before considering what is known about the impact of conflict on memory and forgiving in Northern Ireland, it is necessary to review briefly the background to the political violence there. The conflict in Northern Ireland is most easily understood as a struggle between those who wish to see Northern Ireland remain part of the United Kingdom (Protestants/Unionists/Loyalists) and those who wish to see the reunification of the island of Ireland (Catholics/Nationalists/Republicans) underpinned by historical, religious, political, economic and psychological elements. Today it is estimated that 38 per cent of the Northern Irish population is Roman Catholic and 50 per cent is Protestant, with those not wishing to state a denomination comprising the rest of the population.

History

Although the conflict, in its modern form began around 1968, the conflict has in fact had a long history. Centuries before the 16th-century Protestant Reformation in Western Europe, the people of Ireland were in conflict with the English, due to England's control of the people and resources of Ireland. After the emergence of Protestantism in England, the controlling English swamped the Catholic faith in Ireland and the identity of the Irish people. In particular, the Plantation of Ulster introduced to the North of Ireland a community of foreigners (mainly Scots – hence the term Ulster-Scots) who spoke a different language and most of whom were Protestants in contrast to the native Irish who were Catholic. By the 18th century the colonists occupied 95 per cent of the land which they had confiscated from the natives and came to form a majority in Ulster in contrast to a Catholic majority in the south of the island of Ireland.

Years of oppression, on the part of the colonists and rebellion on the part of the native Irish, culminated in the Treaty of 1921. This partitioned the island into two sections: the predominantly Protestant six counties of the north, which remained an integral part of the United Kingdom, and the mainly Catholic 26 counties of the south which separated from the United Kingdom and became known as 'The Free State' (later the Republic of Ireland). After partition, Northern Ireland was ruled from Stormont, the seat of Northern Irish Government, but ultimately answerable to London. Since that time, spells of significant violence have occurred in Ireland with IRA campaigns in the 1920s, 1940s and 1950s, as some of the Catholic/Nationalist population, who saw partition as an attempt to maintain a Protestant majority, attempted to force the reunification of Ireland. The latest and most sustained period of violence began in the late 1960s, when claims by the Catholic population of Protestant discrimination against Catholics in the area of jobs, education, housing and local elections led to a civil rights campaign which quickly escalated into violence, resulting in the deployment of British troops to try to restore order. In 1972 the Stormont government was abolished and the province was governed by direct rule from London.

Recent violence

Over the last 30 years the violence in Northern Ireland has in fact been sporadic and confined to particular areas at any one time. Despite this most families have been touched in some way by what is colloquially called 'The Troubles'. With 3,000 plus deaths, the impact of the Troubles has been marked on the closely-knit urban and rural areas of Northern Ireland, an area with a population of only 1.7 million living in an area of just 32,000 square miles. Of the deaths, the vast majority (2,000 plus) have been civilians (including members of terrorist groups from both communities) while the remainder has been members of the security forces, that is, the police (RUC: Royal Ulster Constabulary), the British Army, and its associated locally recruited militia (UDR: Ulster Defense Regiment). By international standards the death rate in Northern Ireland could be seen as modest. On a pro rata basis, however, it is equivalent to 100,000 deaths in Britain, or 500,000 deaths in the US (O'Leary and McGarry, 1992). Nevertheless violence in Northern Ireland never reached the levels experienced in Lebanon or Bosnia and did not result, as some had predicted, in genocidal massacres.

In the 1990s a series of ceasefires by paramilitary groups on both sides led, eventually, to a political agreement known locally as 'the Good Friday Agreement'. This agreement received the support of 71 per cent of the Northern Irish electorate in a referendum which in turn led to the setting up of a local assembly and a power-sharing government, embracing all the major political parties. Despite rumours of its early demise the power-sharing government is still in place at the time of writing but it faces challenges both political and military. In particular dissidents in both communities maintain an almost daily litany of violence, both cross-community and intra-community, in the form of beatings, arson, pipe bombs and so on.

Intergroup memories of the recent conflict

According to Darby (1983, p. 13) 'dates from the past are fixed like beacons in the folklore and mythology of Irishmen'. Northern Ireland, therefore, makes a remarkable natural laboratory in which to study memory for recent conflict. In one of the first studies in this area in Northern Ireland, McKeever *et al.* (1993) asked participants to list as many incidents related to the troubles as possible. In addition they had to date and say who was responsible for a list of 14 incidents chosen by the researchers. McKeever et al. (1993) claimed there was a relationship between ethnic memory and ethnic-based social identity (see Devine-Wright this volume) when they speculated that better memory perform-ance by Catholics, in their study, might have resulted because Catholics as a minority group possess a more positive social identity. Therefore, they noted, it is important that future studies assess not only denomin-ational membership but also the extent to which individuals identify with their groups. The fact that McKeever *et al.* (1993) failed to do this, plus other weaknesses the authors themselves acknowledge, makes it important to explore these issues further.

Dating events

Cairns *et al.* (1998) attempted to do this by exploring the relationship between memory and social identity in the context of the Northern Irish conflict. Two samples of university students were tested in 1984 and in 1995. They were shown 12 short black and white video clips, which por-trayed a range of political events in Northern Ireland with an equal number of events of importance to both communities. The clips came from the period 1969 to 1980, with most concentrated in the early 1970s. Respondents had to date each event using a multiple-choice format.

The results provided only limited support for the claim (McKeever *et al.*, 1993) that Catholics, because they are a minority group, are more likely to remember events associated with their group's political past. In the 1984 sample only, was there evidence of a clear superiority for Catholics over Protestants, when asked to date Nationalist events. What the data did reveal was that Nationalist events (in contrast to Unionist events) were dated best in both years by both Catholics and Protestants. This was a surprising result given that one would not expect Protestants to remember Nationalist events best. As Wright and Gaskell (1992,

p. 287) have noted, in light of Social Identity Theory, one would predict that memories should remain vivid when they 'contribute to positively valued categorizations of both a personal and social nature and thus serve to increase self-esteem'. Given the importance of social identity in Northern Ireland (Cairns, 1982; Trew, 1992) this is a surprising result and deserves replication.

One possible explanation is that Nationalist events have simply received more publicity in the media. This raises the question of the source of these memories and undoubtedly one important source could be 'repeat broadcasts and retrospective programmes which fix certain representations in people's minds at the expense of others' (Bourdon, 1992, p. 545). Another interesting possibility is oral transmission from generation to generation. Both of these are issues that deserve further exploration. Either of these could explain how the young people involved in this study did so well at dating events that took place, in many cases, some years before they were born.

Memory for a negative event

Memory of course involves more than simply dating events. Cairns and Lewis (1999), therefore, explored correlates of collective memory for a traumatic event among residents of both Enniskillen, where in 1987[2] a bomb exploded injuring 63 people and killing 11, and 'Lowtown', a neighbouring town. It is important to note that the Enniskillen bomb was the work of the Provisional IRA, whom Protestants would see as their enemy. Further, it was targeted at an event which in Northern Ireland is seen as largely involving Protestants – Remembrance Sunday, the annual commemoration of the deaths of members of the British armed services. For this reason Cairns and Lewis (1999) predicted that Protestants would be more likely than Catholics to recall the Enniskillen bomb as a significant event some eight years later.

Interviews were carried out on the same day, on the streets of both Enniskillen and Lowtown in June 1995. Respondents were asked to recall two national or world events or changes that had taken place over the past 50 years that 'come to mind as important to you'. These questions were then repeated but this time with the emphasis on Northern Irish events or changes. As hypothesised more people from Enniskillen mentioned the Enniskillen bomb. Indeed apart from the ongoing IRA ceasefire, the Enniskillen bomb was the only single Northern Irish event considered to be important by at least 20 per cent of the respondents. Also more Protestants regarded the Enniskillen bomb as memorable and most of those Protestants came from Enniskillen. This means that, once more, there was no support for McKeever *et al.*'s (1993) idea that Catholics remember events related to the conflict better than Protestants because Catholics as a minority group 'maintain a higher sense of in-group identity'.

A better explanation for Cairns and Lewis's (1999) results is that when an event is consequential or important for a particular group, it is better remembered. This is what Brown and Kulik (1977) concluded when they found that the assassination of Martin Luther King was associated with a higher incidence of flashbulb memories among black North Americans, compared to white North Americans. Similarly, Gaskell and Wright (1997) found that respondents from higher social classes tended to report clearer memories of Mrs Thatcher's resignation.

Whatever the explanation for these phenomena the results of the present study highlight, but do not explain, the complex that is the possible relationship between politics, social identity and memory in a divided community such as Northern Ireland. At the very least, they emphasize the fact that 'we must be careful to locate the collective memories of groups in cultural and political space as well as in time' (Schuman and Reiger, 1992, p. 329).

Memory for a positive event

Recently a somewhat erratic peace process has been underway in Northern Ireland. Lewis and Cairns (1999) repeated their survey in Enniskillen and in a neighbouring town, 'Lowtown', three times in all, in June of each year between 1995 and 1997 as they attempted to trace the impact of various political events on Northern Irish residents' collective memories for the peace process. Using the methodology outlined above, they focused on memories for a major positive event related to the troubles, the first IRA ceasefire, which lasted from August 1994 to February 1996[3] and which heralded the beginning of the current Northern Irish peace process. Their prediction was that during the time of the ceasefire social identities were not particularly salient and that therefore Catholics and Protestant would represent that event in approximately the same way. However, as the ceasefire became more of a memory and as the political situation deteriorated, the salience of the cease fire for Catholics and Protestants would diverge, as would the two group's social representations of the ceasefire.

This is what happened. In June 1995, when the IRA ceasefire was still in tact and still a relatively novel event approximately 60 per cent of both Catholics and Protestants surveyed mentioned the ceasefire as an important Northern Irish event. In both 1996 and 1997, however, significantly more Catholics than Protestants mentioned the ceasefire. Respondents were also asked why they felt the event they mentioned was important. Lewis and Cairns (1999) reported that these responses could be classified into three main categories – because the ceasefire promised a 'better future'; because it was seen as a 'historic event'; or because it promised an 'improvement in security'. For example respondents who focused on the 'better future' theme often used the word 'hope' – 'hope for the children's future' or 'hope for peace in Ireland'. Those who saw the event as 'historic' said things such as 'a very important day' or 'a historic event' or 'a day we'd be able to look back on and remember'. Finally those who invoked the security aspect of the ceasefire said things like 'no more killings' or 'a return to normal day-to-day activities'.

In all three surveys, the most common response from Protestant respondents was that the ceasefire was important because of security considerations (with 'historic' next most popular). In 1995 and 1996 Catholics respondents were more likely to mention the historic nature of the event when asked why it was important with rather fewer mentioning the security aspect. This changed, however, in 1997, when security became the most popular response. Lastly, for both groups seeing the ceasefire as an event that had implications for the future, was the least popular suggestion at all three times.

Conclusion

Empirical research on memories of conflict is very much in its embryonic stage, with few studies having been published (Pennebaker *et al.*, 1997) and research on the memories of the Northern Irish Troubles is no different. Initial work has included the examination of the accuracy of dating events and asking the saliency of events connected with the Troubles. Subsequent research that has been undertaken has been contextualised within a Social Identity framework. This research has shown that the social memories and the salience of violent past events may be influenced by social identity.

Psychological aspects of forgiveness

Before beginning to examine evidence related to intergroup forgiveness in the context of the Northern Irish conflict, it is necessary to review some basic concepts. For example what exactly is forgiveness, what are its psychological aspects and how can one begin to measure forgiveness. In particular is it possible to measure intergroup forgiveness?

Empirical research in this area, from a psychological perspective, has undoubtedly been hindered by the fact that forgiveness is usually thought of as a largely theological term (Fitzgibbons, 1986; DiBlasio, 1992, 1993). While a growing amount of literature now exists in this area (see McCullough *et al.*, 2000) its usefulness in the present context is limited because, almost without exception, it focuses on interpersonal forgiveness. While work is proceeding at pace on interpersonal forgiveness, intergroup forgiveness remains a 'quandary' (Smedes, 1998) still to be understood. Unfortunately, as Pargament *et al.* (2000, p. 308) note

> There is no shortage of deep-seated social and political conflict. Mistrust, and hatred that represent powerful naturalistic laboratories for the study of forgiveness.

Definitions of forgiveness

According to McCullough *et al.* (2000) there is no clear agreement as to what forgiveness is but there is general agreement as to what forgiveness is not. It is not, for example pardoning, condoning, excusing, forgetting or denying. Hebl and Enright (1993) suggest that the most valuable definition of forgiveness is that postulated by North (1987). Based on North's (1987) definition, Robert Enright and those allied with his research connect the concept of forgiveness with the idea of mercy. Enright, a pioneer in the area of the empirical study of forgiveness has therefore defined forgiveness as the 'willingness to abandon one's right to resentment, negative judgement, and indifferent behaviour toward one who unjustly injured us, while fostering the undeserved qualities of compassion, generosity, and even love toward him or her' (Enright and The Human Development Study Group, 1991, p. 123).

An important debate in this area, which is pertinent to the content of this chapter, centres on the relationship between forgiveness and reconciliation. Enright and Zell (1989) argue that it is possible to forgive without reconciliation, whereas Power (1994) claims that forgiveness without reconciliation is not complete. Worthington (1998, p. 129), more reasonably claims that there are in fact four possible logical relationships between forgiveness and reconciliation (see Table 8.1). While there can be no argument that reconciliation and forgiveness may both take place (even if the causal relationship is not clear) what is perhaps most often debated is whether there can be reconciliation without forgiveness and/or forgiveness without reconciliation.

Table 8.1   Relationships between forgiveness and reconciliation

		Reconciliation	
		No	**Yes**
Forgiveness	No	Neither forgiveness nor reconciliation	Reconciliation without forgiveness
	Yes	Forgiveness without reconciliation	Reconciliation and forgiveness

Source: Worthington, 1998, p. 129.

Measuring forgiveness

Recent attempts to explore the psychological aspects of forgiveness have led to the creation of a number of measures of forgiveness, but only three have established validity and reliability (Sells and Hargrave, 1998). These are the Enright Forgiveness Inventory (EFI) (Subkoviak *et al.*, 1995), The Interpersonal Relationship Resolution Scale (IRRS) (Hargrave and Sells, 1997), and the Forgiveness of Self (FOS) and Forgiveness of Others (FOO) scales (Mauger *et al.*, 1992).

These and other measures have been used to investigate the forgiveness process and in particular the developmental aspects of forgiveness. Enright and The Human Development Study Group (1991) have described two phases in the forgiveness process, the interpersonal and the intrapersonal phases. In the interpersonal phase, the forgiver learns to perceive the injurer as a three-dimensional person, rather than a stereotypical wrongdoer. In the intrapersonal phase, the emphasis for the forgiver is on finding inner peace. This involves a succession of cognitive, emotive and behavioural steps that the forgiver must follow, regardless of the attitude of the offender. What is now needed, according to McCullough and Worthington (1994) is research to establish the role of individual differences in the forgiveness process, and to identify which factors helps or hinders the process.

The first to place forgiveness within a developmental framework was Piaget (1932/1965), who argued that the concept of forgiveness contains developmental features. However, Piaget's views have been criticized by Enright and the Human Development Study Group (1994) on the grounds that Piaget's main emphasis was on reciprocity. Enright's own theory is modelled on Kohlberg's (1984) stages of moral reasoning and has been used to provide evidence that the propensity to forgive has a developmental character which extends over the entire life span, with elderly people more likely to forgive than younger adults and younger adults more likely to forgive than adolescents (see Mullet and Girard, 2000).

Intergroup forgiveness in Northern Ireland

Given the evidence, noted above, that memory of the recent conflict is relatively salient and possibly socially divisive in present day Northern Ireland, the role of intergroup forgiveness in Northern Ireland becomes even more important. Stevens noted that at least in 1986, in Northern Ireland 'forgiveness and reconciliation have not been dominant values in politics and social life', yet he claims 'without forgiveness everything falls apart' (p. 72). This section will therefore attempt to examine the status of intergroup forgiveness in present day Northern Ireland, first by examining the discourse on forgiveness in the realms of politics and the Christian churches before moving on to summarise some empirical work which is underway in this area.

The salience of forgiveness in post-conflict Northern Ireland

Surprisingly, for a society that is struggling to overcome the effect of prolonged political violence and widespread personal suffering, intergroup forgiveness is *not* high on the agenda in Northern Ireland. After the euphoria that followed the overwhelming support for what has become known as the 'Good Friday Agreement', the realities to be faced in the acquisition of peace have become apparent. Most profound among these has been the need for survivors and their families to accept the early release of prisoners. In a belated move to appease victims the government-appointed Commissioner for Victims has proposed various forms of reparation, such as financial compensation, a physical memorial to the dead, or a day of remembrance be made for victims (Bloomfield, 1998).

Political statements on forgiveness

Few politicians in Northern Ireland appear to be prepared to risk alienating their electorate by speaking openly about the need to forgive. One reason for this could be that politicians who speak of forgiveness to their constituents risk intruding both upon personal grief and upon personal attitudes to religious belief. Second, attitudes and perceptions toward the need for forgiveness among their constituents undoubtedly differ. Some groups may feel that acts of violence have been a justifiable means to an end and that forgiveness is, therefore, not necessary.

Politicians from other nations, however, have been more forthcoming in their references to the need for forgiveness in Northern Ireland. In an address during the 1995 visit by then-president Bill Clinton to Belfast, he likened the conflict in Northern Ireland to the American Civil War when he said, 'We have all done wrong. No one can say his heart is altogether clean, and his hands altogether pure. Thus as we wish to be forgiven, let us forgive those who have sinned against us and ours. That was the beginning of America's reconciliation, and it must be the beginning of Northern Ireland's reconciliation.' Similarly, Senator Edward Kennedy in a visit to Londonderry/Derry in January 1998 urged 'The best way to ease these feelings (of tragedy) is to forgive and carry on – not to lash out in fury, but to reach out in trust and hope.'

Irish politicians, North and South, in contrast, tend to speak of reconciliation, but not of its (necessary) forerunner, forgiveness. In a joint statement issued in July 1997 by Bertie Ahern, then taoiseach, John Hume, the leader of the Social Democratic Labour Party, and Gerry Adams, the President of Sinn Fein, declared 'We are all committed to the achievement of lasting peace and reconciliation on this island, based on justice and equality.' The absence of any reference to possible routes to the psychological resolution of pain involved in this process render the politician's words profoundly impersonal for the people of Northern Ireland. Similarly, in May 2000 Peter Mandelson MP, then secretary of state for Northern Ireland, spoke of 'beginning the painstaking task of putting the past behind us' again without any suggestion as to how this was to be accomplished and without indicating whether or not forgiveness would be involved.

Exceptions exist, however, and private individuals from both sides of the religious divide in Northern Ireland have called for forgiveness in the face of great tragedy. Michael McGoldrick, whose 31-year-old son was shot by Protestant paramilitaries in July 1996, pleaded 'Bury your hate with my boy. Love one another. I can love the man that murdered my son.' And Gordon Wilson, whose daughter Marie, was killed in an IRA bomb attack in 1987 said: 'I bear no ill will. I bear no grudge. That will not bring her back.' For most survivors in Northern Ireland, however, the journey to forgiveness is arduous, and 'putting the past behind them' may not be a realistic part of the foreseeable future.

Christian church leaders

One might imagine that, unlike politicians, church leaders are not constrained by the need to woo their constituents. Sadly, this has not always been the case. In fact it has been acknowledged that the churches in Northern Ireland have in the past helped to sustain memories of grievance and injustice by defining their own identity primarily in opposition to other traditions (Faith and Politics Group, 1997). This is important because Northern Ireland is a particularly 'churched' part of the world where church leaders carry some weight in the community. On the other hand the main Churches have all officially condemned violence and there have been some individual church leaders who have attempted to facilitate and encourage an attitude that incorporates the recognition and acknowledgement of past wrongs and injustices by both sides.

For example, at a lecture in St Anne's Cathedral in Belfast in 1996, John Dunlop (Giffin *et al.*, 1996), a former moderator of the Presbyterian Church in Ireland, stated 'I believe that it is helpful for that part of the community to which one does not belong to hear some acknowledgement of responsibility being accepted for things that were wrong which caused them to be disadvantaged or to suffer. That admission might, in turn, help those who have suffered to offer forgiveness to those that made them suffer.' Furthermore, David Stevens, Secretary of the Irish Council of Churches, has suggested that the concept of forgiveness can be given political meaning only by acknowledging and accepting differences, rather than ignoring them, for if we avoid conflict, which is genuinely there, we go back to the way things were. (Stevens, 1986)

Empirical research on forgiveness in Northern Ireland

While this is a relatively new research area, a number of studies have recently been reported and are described in this section. For example, Roe *et al.* (1999) used questionnaires and semi-structured interviews to study a small number of adolescents ($n = 27$) from a high conflict area of Belfast, as well as their adult leaders ($n = 8$), who were taking part in an ongoing reconciliation project. The study focused on experiences of political violence, accepting responsibility for the violence of one's own community and forgiveness at the personal and intergroup levels.

Roe *et al.* (1999) report that while some of their young (15-year-old) participants 'argued for the importance of forgiveness; most . . . appeared to have little understanding of it' (p. 136) discussing it primarily in terms of putting political violence behind them. The leaders, on the other hand, spoke of their readiness to forgive suggesting that it followed on from empathy with the perpetrator.

Focus group study

In a more extensive study, a series of focus groups was carried out between June 1999 and February 2000, each involving between eight and 12 Northern Irish adults (McLernon *et al.*, 2000). Eight focus groups were carried out, each confined to participants from one of the following constituencies:

- Peace organisations (lay)
- Victims of violence
- Victim support organisations
- Community relations organisations (church-based)
- Ex-paramilitaries

The results of these group interviews can be summarised in terms of a series of themes, which were common to almost all groups. The themes involved defining forgiveness and exploring intergroup forgiveness in relation to justice issues, the public acknowledgement of wrongs, spirituality, the importance of remorse, the difference between individual forgiveness and intergroup forgiveness and the future of forgiveness in Northern Ireland.

What is forgiveness?

All groups agreed that forgiveness should not imply judgement, nor does it involve forgetting. In other words, people who cannot forgive should not be made to feel evil or unworthy because 'people have to want to forgive, for themselves and for their own sake, and not because somebody else says they should' (victim). The concept of forgiveness was described as a healing process, which involves accepting that the hurt has been committed, a process of self-help, and the cessation of anger, negative emotions and the desire for revenge. But it is more than all of these, as one woman who had lost a son and a sister in the Troubles explained

> I know that the people who did these things are probably alive now and enjoying the world. . . . But I don't begrudge those people that. I don't want them to be dead. . . . But that is not forgiveness. (victim)

For these attitudes to develop, it was felt that the injured party must try to develop some degree of empathy for the offender, and be able to understand some of the reasons behind the hurtful act.

Justice and the public acknowledgement of wrongs

One common theme was that forgiveness becomes easier if others (not necessarily the offenders) acknowledge and validate the pain of a hurtful act, and that lack of public acknowledgement of a wrong, in the context of Northern Ireland, has caused intense bitterness and lasting injury because so many people 'buried their heads in the sand, got on with their own lives and hoped it would go away without touching them' (Lay Peace Group Member). The process of criminal justice was perceived as not always conducive to forgiveness, since society must work for the greater good, and not just for the individual. This view was stated frequently in relation to the prisoner releases in Northern Ireland and caused a great deal of discussion and disagreement.

Forgiveness and spirituality

The majority of people in the groups felt that *true* forgiveness can only be achieved through spirituality and requires a declaration to God.

> When forgiveness is linked to a spiritual belief, that forgiveness is mutual. The Lord's Prayer says 'Forgive us our trespasses as we forgive those that trespass against us'. That is mutual forgiveness, and is an important part of forgiving. (victim)

Even then, forgiveness can only be achieved if God feels it is appropriate. Individuals should strive to forgive, but if God feels it is not appropriate, it will not happen. Furthermore, a small number of people suggested that forgivers should not seek punishment for wrongdoers. That is up to the law and to God. Through Christianity, it was stressed, individuals can learn to understand the wrongdoer and subsequently to find forgiveness easier.

The importance of remorse in the process of forgiveness

According to many of those interviewed, forgiveness is easier when remorse is shown by the perpetrator(s). Remorse can lead to acceptance of the grievance and of the offender's need to be forgiven. It was stressed, however, that this may not necessarily mean that the offender will be trusted again, a view which led many people to express the view that full forgiveness is not possible where trust does not exist. Only among the church-based peace group was it suggested that it was possible to forgive where remorse did not exist.

Forgiveness of individuals and of groups

Based on the link between forgiveness and trust, most people agreed that it is easier to forgive an individual than to forgive a group, because it is easier to place trust in an individual. Trusting a group means extending that trust to each individual member of the group and not all members may be represented by a spokesperson. Moreover, it was thought to be harder to forgive leaders of a group than its members. Some people in the victims' groups were hostile to the idea of forgiveness, since forgiving a group who had wronged them might imply that the wrongs which were done to them were justified.

> It would be like saying that you deserved all you got, you were just what they said you were, and they were right to do what they did. (victim)

Members from each of the two ex-paramilitary groups also questioned the value of forgiveness. Both groups felt that the actions of their own movements were fully justified at the time, therefore, they did not feel the need to ask for or to offer forgiveness.

The future of forgiveness in Northern Ireland

It was stressed by all groups that preaching forgiveness or trying to force its acceptance is likely to be counterproductive, but an act of remembrance (not necessarily a monument) would give others the opportunity to share the loss and may make forgiving easier through support and empathy. Acknowledgement that the violence is over for good may also help to promote forgiveness, which could assuage angry feelings becoming the basis of future action. The suggestion was made that some people may want to continue in the role of 'victim' 'because if you are not a victim you might be seen as a perpetrator'. These people could not therefore overtly forgive and thus risk the loss of the status of victim.

Correlates of intergroup forgiveness in Northern Ireland

One of the first major empirical studies in this area was carried out in June 1999 involving a survey of high school and university students in Northern Ireland (McLernon *et al.*, 1999). The aim of the study was to compare the correlates of forgiving in the context of an intergroup conflict with those already established in the literature, based on interpersonal forgiving, with particular respect to age and denomination.

Existing research shows gender to have little influence on the propensity to forgive. For example, studies by Girard and Mullet (1997), Enright *et al.* (1989) and Mullet *et al.* (1998) found little or no association between gender and the propensity to forgive. Conflicting evidence exists with regard to the influence of religious denomination on the willingness to forgive. In a study of the propensity to forgive among people in the United States differing in religion (Protestant, Catholic and Jewish), ethnicity (white, black and Hispanic) and gender, Gorsuch and Hao (1993) found that 'Protestants, as compared to Catholics, Jewish and no/other religious preference respondents, engaged in more forgiving responses' (Gorsuch and Hao, 1993, p. 345). By contrast, in Northern Ireland, there has been a suggestion in the literature that Protestants compared to Catholics have, as a group, been *less* tolerant toward outgroups in general, and that this extended to intergroup relations in Northern Ireland (Salters, 1970; Arthur, 1974; Russell, 1974; Fairleigh, 1975; Greer, 1985). This research, therefore, aimed to establish a preliminary assessment of the correlates of forgiveness among a small sample of Northern Irish students.

Participants completed the short-form of the GEFI (Group Enright Forgiveness Inventory described below). When those who had clearly not described an intergroup or ethnic conflict related incident, or had failed to complete the questionnaire, were excluded, a total of 169 participants remained. Of these 103 categorised themselves as Catholics and 69 Protestants. To facilitate further analyses the participants were divided into two age groups 17–20 years ($n=96$: X = 17.5 years), or 21–30 years ($n=73$: X = 22.6 years). The majority (82 per cent) of the participants were female.

The Group Enright Forgiveness Inventory (GEFI) is a 60-item questionnaire (Subkoviak *et al.*, 1995) based on the original Enright Forgiveness Inventory (EFI; Enright *et al.*, 1989), except that instructions were worded in such as way as to set the instrument in a context of intergroup rather than interpersonal forgiveness. To produce a short form of the Enright Forgiveness Inventory Intergroup version (GEFI short) 18 items were selected from Enright's original scale so as to include equal numbers of positive and negative items and equal numbers of items from the Affect, Behaviour and Cognition subscales. Each item was rated on a 1 to 6 scale and negative items were reverse scored. A mean item score was calculated for the GEFI (short) with a maximum possible score of 6 and a minimum score of 1. Before completing the short-form of the EFI participants were directed once more to think of an experience when 'your group' had been 'hurt by members of the other group'. They were then asked how deeply they had been hurt by the incident they had in mind and how long ago the incident had happened. Following completion of each version of the GEFI, participants were asked to indicate on a single, three-point scale ('not at all', 'trying to forgive', 'complete forgiveness') the extent to which they had 'forgiven the person(s)' 'they had described'. In addition participants were asked to provide their age, sex, and to indicate whether their 'religious or cultural background' was

Catholic or Protestant. Of those who reported an ethnic conflict related incident the majority (59 per cent) reported 'much' or 'a great deal of' hurt. For most of these participants (80 per cent) the event they recalled had occurred between one and two years ago.

The mean item total score on the GEFI (short) correlated positively with the single item forgiveness question (.63 $p < .05$) and Cronbach's alpha was .94, indicating a highly reliable scale. The mean score was 2.80, with scores ranging from 1.11 to 5.61. In order to investigate the relationship between denomination, gender, age and forgiveness, GEFI (short) mean total scores were subjected to a three-way analysis of variance (Age x Denomination x Gender) with Depth of Hurt and Time Since Event as co-variates. This analysis resulted in only one statistically significant main effect which was for Gender $F(1,159) = 5.77$ p. 05, with females scoring at a slightly higher level on the forgiveness measure (2.94) compared with males (2.52). In addition there was also one statistically significant interaction Age X Gender $F(1,159) = 4.63$ $P < .05$. There were no statistically significant differences due to denomination.

This study, therefore, failed to replicate the work of Enright *et al.* (1996) and Girard and Mullet (1997) who suggested that younger people are generally less forgiving than middle-aged or older people. Furthermore, the suggestion that Northern Irish Protestants are less forgiving of the outgroup than Northern Irish Catholics was not confirmed in this context. Finally, previous research has consistently reported a definite lack of gender differences in relations to willingness to forgive. This finding was not replicated, as demonstrated by the greater propensity of females, particularly those in the older age group, to forgive.

In a further study with university students as respondents, Cairns *et al.* (2001) explored the degree to which intergroup forgiveness is related to levels of religiosity, and/or the degree to which individuals have been hurt by events related to the Northern Irish political violence and attitudes towards the 'offending' group. This time the measure of intergroup forgiveness consisted of questions developed from the focus group responses noted above, such as 'My community can only forgive members of the other community when they have apologised for past violence.' Religiosity was measured using the seven-item Francis Scale of Attitudes toward Christianity (Francis, 1992), which asked questions such as 'I think going to church is a waste of time' or 'God helps me lead a better life'. Also measured was level of victimhood and outgroup attitudes (using a 'thermometer' scale).

Again there were no denominational differences in intergroup forgiveness, which in turn was not related to religiosity or personal levels of suffering as a result of the political violence. Instead willing-ness to forgive the other community in Northern Ireland was related, for both Catholics and Protestants, to overall attitudes towards the outgroup, while for Protestants gender also was a significant correlate.

What the data gathered so far do suggest however, is that neither age nor group affiliation in Northern Ireland are important correlates in the development of forgiveness of the outgroup; on the other hand, gender may play a significant role in the propensity to forgive. Surprisingly, given the comments of the participants in the focus groups noted above concerning the close relationship between spirituality and propensity to forgive, no empirical evidence was found to support this relationship. Both these studies indicate the need for further research into the concept of forgiveness in Northern Ireland, based on more representative samples.

Conclusions

After thirty years of virtually continuous political violence, preceded, some would argue, by hundreds of years of conflict, Northern Ireland has reached a peace settlement of a sort. We, however, think that if this peace settlement is to take root and blossom into something, which can stand the frosts of time, it will need to go one step further than simply bringing the parties together. This chapter has suggested that one impediment to such progress is the fact that memories, of both the current conflict and conflicts from the past, are alive and well and living in Northern Irish society. In particular the research noted above has suggested that from the recent conflict memories that record the victimisation of the Catholic/Nationalist community are particularly prominent. Even in the minds of Protestant respondents, violent acts in which Catholics were the victims are much more readily recalled. Incidentally, a similar phenomenon has been noted among Catholic and Protestant Irish Americans (Roe, 2002).

This could prove to be a stumbling block to long-term peace as each side tries to establish its pre-eminent claim to victimhood. In particular this suggests that if the historical cycle of revenge is to be brought to an end, then the whole question of forgiveness will have to be moved further up the agenda. At the moment the research reviewed here would suggest that this is unlikely to be an immediate prospect. Nevertheless the importance of forgiveness at an intergroup level must not be neglected. If this is to be achieved the ground work must be laid now.

The critical nature of such forgiveness on a social and political level has also been emphasized by the noted theologian Donald Shriver, who describes the concept as 'a future-oriented social transaction' (Shriver, 1998, p. 133). Furthermore, according to Couper (1998, p. 130) 'the result of neglecting forgiveness... in both our interpersonal and national lives will be a nation and a people distanced, divided, vengeful and unforgiving'. Observations such as these are justification for attempting to find ways of encouraging the development of forgiveness among those who have suffered in Northern Ireland. If this is not done, as Smedes (1998, p. 343) notes, 'the parity of pain' will remain forever elusive, resulting in an 'endless cycle of revenge'.

Notes

1. We gratefully acknowledge a grant from the Templeton Foundation to Ed Cairns and Miles Hewstone which supported part of the work reported here.
2. The Remembrance Day explosion occurred in Enniskillen on Sunday 8 November 1987.
3. On 9 February 1996 the IRA planted a huge bomb in London's Docklands. It killed two, injured more than 100 and caused more than £85m of damage. The ceasefire had lasted 17 months. A second ceasefire was declared on 20 July 1997.

9
Symbolic Closure through Memory, Reparation and Revenge in post-Conflict Societies

Brandon Hamber and Richard A. Wilson

> We are meant to be a part of the process of the healing of our nation, of our people, all of us, since every South African has to some extent or other been traumatised. We are a wounded people.... We all stand in need of healing. (Archbishop Desmond Tutu in his opening address to the South African Truth and Reconciliation Commission on 16 December 1995)

The South African Truth and Reconciliation Commission (TRC)[1] has become the paradigmatic international model of how to 'work through' a violent past and in so doing, to 'heal the nation'. Increasingly it is being argued that countries, which have undergone large-scale conflict such as Bosnia, Rwanda and Northern Ireland, need to set up similar truth commissions. A countrywide process of revealing and confirming past wrongs is said to facilitate a common and shared memory, and in so doing create a sense of unity and reconciliation. By having this shared memory of the past, and a common identity as a traumatised people, the country can, at least ideally, move on to a future in which the same mistakes will not be repeated.

Yet the idea of dealing with the past through a national truth commission ascribes a collective identity to a nation, and assumes that nations have psyches that experience traumas in a similar way to individuals[2]. This act of 'psychologising the nation' mistakenly implies that the pursuit of national unity is a unitary and coherent process, and that individual and national processes of dealing with the past are largely concurrent and equivalent.

This chapter assesses the psychological impact on victims of the nation-building discourse of truth commissions. It asks to what degree does a nation undergo a uniform and collective truth-telling experience?

What are the consequences for individual subjectivities of asserting that nations have psyches or collective consciences? This chapter argues that psychologising the nation can be an ideology for subordinating diverse individual needs to the political expediency of national unity and reconciliation. Truth commissions aim to construct memory as a unified, static and collective *object*, not as a political practice, or as a struggle over the representation of the past that will continue to be vigorously contested after their existence.

The discussion draws attention to a range of post-conflict societies (or those in some sort of political transition) and explores the many divergences between individual psychological processes and national processes of remembering such as truth commissions. We conclude that the nation-building discourse of truth commissions homogenise disparate individual memories to create an official version, and in so doing they repress other forms of psychological closure motivated by less ennobled (although no less real) emotions of anger and vengeance. Claims to heal the collective unconscious of the nation, therefore, mask how truth commissions both lift an authoritarian regime of denial and public silence, as well as create a new regime of forgetting which represses other memories and forms of psychological closure.

Juxtaposing national and individual trauma

Nations do not have collective psyches, which can be healed, nor do whole nations suffer post-traumatic stress disorder and to assert otherwise is to psychologise an abstract entity, which exists primarily in the minds of nation-building politicians. Nevertheless, it is remarkable how widely accepted this nationalist language is in the literature on truth commissions and post-communist truth-telling. It is almost as if, because nationalist discourse is contained within human rights talk then it cannot be in any way misguided or destructive. However, the mythology of nation building can have damaging consequences for individual survivors who are seen as 'out of step' with a putative collective conscience. Michael Ignatieff challenges the notion of national psyches when he writes:

> We tend to vest our nations with conscience, identities and memories as if they were individuals. It is problematic enough to vest an individual with a single identity: our inner lives are like battlegrounds over which uneasy truces reign; the identity of a nation is additionally fissured by region, ethnicity, class and education. (1998, p. 169)

Instead of reconstructing the national psyche and healing the nation, Ignatieff argues that truth commissions can only provide a frame for public discourse and public memory. They can help to create a new public space in which debate and discussion on the past occurs. Beyond this they can do little, although they can be useful if they present the past as an irresolvable argument that is to be continually debated. This is not wholly open-ended, as they must also define the acceptable limits of the argument over *what happened to whom* and reduce the range of permissible historical revisionism. Within the context of public discourse, the past is subject to infinite debate where memory is not a fixed object, but the social practice that constitutes narratives on the past.

At the level of the subject, victims' expectations and desires can converge with the efforts of national truth commissions, which can legitimate the multiplicity of voices that make up the national debate on the past. The legitimating function of this new framing of history is important because during the authoritarian era such narratives are regularly silenced and deformed by the media, the courts and public institutions. Truth commissions and other processes to establish new truths (for example, commissions of enquiry) can create public spaces in which survivors can articulate their individual narratives. Their voices are heard often for the first time by a national audience, many of whom previously claimed they did not know about the violent past. After the extensive media coverage of a truth commission, the argument that atrocities did not occur can never again be made – the range of licit truths (and lies) is, in this way, irrevocably narrowed.

Yet if we look hard, we start to see cracks appearing between the national and individual representation of trauma, if only because there is a 'truth that can be known only by those on the inside' (Ignatieff, 1998, p. 175) and that the truth itself is highly personalised. Michael Lapsley (1997, p. 46), priest and facilitator of the *Healing the Memory Workshops*, in South Africa, argues that 'memory can be healed' by individuals. To this end individuals need to talk about *their* distinctive pasts, put their memories on the table, open them up, clean them out and in so doing facilitate healing. Apart from his rather outdated 'suitcase' metaphor of memory, Lapsley does capture the uniqueness of individual acts of remembering, and the need for a diversity of memory processes outside of national commissions.

The *Healing the Memory Workshops* are independent of the South African TRC and provide a structured forum in which individuals can constitute a new identity by gazing upon the past in a highly personalised way. The South African TRC in itself did provide some of these functions through its hearings process, and was a psychologically healing process insofar as it provided a space for memory work to occur. It was also useful in that it created the context and new legitimate space for endeavours such as Lapsley's workshops. Nevertheless, recent history from Latin America teaches us that the establishment of a truth commission in itself is not enough to meet the psychological needs of individuals – they may be necessary first steps toward individual psychological healing but they are generally not sufficient in themselves (see Hamber, 1998a).

Survivors and the victims for whom they grieve both inhabit a liminal space, which is both part of society but removed from society; it could be called an experience of 'the living dead'. This space is characterised by uncertainty and doubt, and is caused, according to Freud, by survivors' experiences of the uncanny. Survivors' needs for closure and symbolic reintegration, (that is, an end to a state of uncertainty and liminal status) may work in different ways to those enshrined within national commissions. Truth commissions can assert an oversimplistic view of what it takes to move on from the past. Importantly, it should not be assumed too easily, as the banners displayed by the TRC did, that 'Revealing is Healing' (Hamber, 2001, p. 136). Hayes writes, 'Just revealing, is not just healing. It depends on how we reveal, the context of the revealing, and what it is that we are revealing.' (Hayes, 1998, p. 43) Thus, remembering, in itself, is not necessarily a directly redemptive and liberating practice, and is only one of many possible routes to symbolic closure for survivors. By 'closure' we mean a situation where the trauma is no longer seen as unfinished business, requiring, for instance a compulsion to take revenge. Grief and loss no longer plague the individual consciously or unconsciously, and the victim lives not in a state somewhere between denial and obsession, where the loss is to a large degree accepted and incorporated into the functioning of everyday life.

Furthermore commissions, since they are often transitory and last at best only a few years, may seek forms of closure, which are only partial. Truth commissions often operate on a time frame which is highly curtailed and limited, and which requires a premature process of dealing with the past from survivors of atrocities for whom the process of grieving often lasts a lifetime. 'Truth' in the sense of speaking about the past and having one's version recognized is but one of the many possible forms of closure for the individual. Processes aimed at closure are also inherently contradictory in their nature. Reparations provided through truth commission processes or after formal enquiries, for example, can aid closure but can also be viewed as problematical by some victims who may be uncomfortable with accepting what they perceive as 'blood money'. Arguably, revenge could also serve the function of closure for the individual; a possibility wholly excluded and deemed outside the acceptable range of discourse of the South African TRC. Equally, revenge could also serve as a way of perpetuating violence and in so doing trap the individual in the liminal space.

The rest of this chapter addresses how truth commissions seek symbolic closure and how the limited procedures adopted converge or diverge with survivors' individual agendas. We will argue that truth commissions (and other projects to rewrite the official version of the past) and individuals proceed along different temporal continuums when dealing with violence and trauma. This chapter shows how different processes embodied in individual trauma work, national history making and reparations offered by truth commissions. These interact and shape one another, and at times are mutually reinforcing while at other times they are disharmonious and incongruous.

The meaning of reparations and acknowledgement[3]

> Another arena of societal struggles over memory centres on the physical markers of past violence and repression. Monuments and museums, plaques and other markers are some of the ways in which governments as well as social actors try to embody memories. Other social forces, meanwhile, try to erase and transform these physical markers, as if by changing the shape and function of a place one can banish it from memory. (Jelin, 1998, p. 26)

Reparations are one of the main means by which truth commissions and similar processes seek to achieve national and individual reconciliation, and they result in common psychological consequences in each case. Psychologically speaking, the so-called symbolic acts of reparation[4] such as reburials, and material acts of reparation such as payments, serve the same end. Both these forms of reparation can, although not necessarily, play an important role in processes of opening space for bereavement, addressing trauma and ritualising symbolic closure. They acknowledge and recognize the individual's suffering and place it within a new officially sanctioned history of trauma. Symbolic representations of the trauma, particularly if the symbols are personalised, can concretise a traumatic event and help reattribute responsibility. The latter stage is important because labelling responsibility can appropriately redirect blame towards perpetrators and relieve the moral ambiguity and guilt survivors often feel.

Reparations, symbolic or otherwise, can serve as focal points in the grieving process, and this can aid recovery by allowing individuals to focus exclusively on their grief. Survivors often unconsciously turn to institutions such as truth commissions, the criminal justice system or community/traditional justice processes as a context in which they externalise their grief and seek to come to terms with it. The symbols of public or collective ritual, and material reparations in some instances, can mark the point of moving onto a new phase and represent an individual's mastery over the past. On a macro level extensive social processes like truth commissions can represent a new willingness by the state or civil society institutions to exhume the buried issues of the past. This can occur metaphorically or literally, as when truth commissions recover the hidden physical remains of the disappeared.

Unfortunately, no matter how well meaning, all reparations strategies and governmental commissions face the same, albeit obvious, intractable problem. Acknowledgement, apology, recognition, material assistance, a perpetrator's confession and even exhuming the bodies/bones of the 'missing' can never bring back the dead or be guaranteed to converge with, and ameliorate, all the levels of psychological pain suffered by a survivor. Memory work revisits the past as an alienated tourist, and its attempts at recovery are constantly undermined by both the fractured nature of lived memory and the irrecoverability of time. The trauma and accompanying senses of injustice, anger and hurt, which lie in the depths of the actor's psyche, are both immeasurable and ineffable. Furthermore, recovery from trauma is obstructed by the unlikelihood of justice in many societies in transition. This is typified by the South African TRC's amnesty process that grants indemnity from civil and criminal proceedings to perpetrators who confess to political crimes; and more dramatically where blanket amnesties have been granted to perpetrators as occurred in Chile, Argentina, Brazil, Guatemala and a number of African countries.

Thus reparation (and all action undertaken by a truth commission) has ambivalent psychological consequences for survivors – public acknowledgement of social truths and monetary compensation are valuable contributions, but they can never wholly meet all the psychological needs of the survivors, as these are disparate, inchoate and contradictory. The result is that in the aftermath of large-scale political violence, we should expect to have to live with the unsatisfied demands (for their own versions of truth, justice, compensation and so on) of survivors for a long time. Truth commissions, with their focus on speaking about and writing a revised account of the past, are at best only the beginning of a set of linked processes, which may lead to symbolic closure for some individuals.

Liminality and reintegration

To better understand the impact of nation-state attempts at reconciliation through reparations, truth commission reports and the like, we have to return and look more closely at survivors' experiences of trauma caused by political violence. Trauma and violence shatter individual cognitive assumptions about the self and the world. Severe forms of trauma shatter the cognitive assumptions of personal invulnerability, viewing oneself positively and that the world is a meaningful and comprehensible place (Janoff-Bulman, 1985).

Trauma often results in confusion, and an inability to fully understand the causes of one's suffering. This 'bafflement' grows out of a negative encounter with the authoritarian state, which deforms rationality and foments personal and social chaos and an attendant fragmenting of the self (Neal, 1998, p. 6). As a result of trauma and a state-sponsored regime of denial, basic questions are raised and remain unanswered, such as, how and why did the event happen and what is going to happen next? (Neal, 1998, p. 201) The confusion and bafflement following a trauma, and the shattering of cognitive assumptions about the world, are exacerbated when the markers of the past that give it its coherence, such as the existence and compassion of loved ones, are destroyed or rendered invisible. This is particularly the case with regard to political disappearance that thrusts an inordinate amount of unanswered (and technically unanswerable) questions upon the survivor. The personal perplexity and incoherence of the trauma is extreme in the case of political disappearances.

Suarez-Orozco (1991) has written about such issues with respect to Argentina, and he documents how disappearances and the lack of bodies to be buried creates an ontological uncertainty among survivors and a psychological experience of what Freud termed the *uncanny*. This notion captures the common difficulties experienced by survivors who must mourn without a corpse: 'The uncanny feeds on uncertainty (Is he/she alive? Is he/she dead?)' (Suarez-Orozco, 1991, p. 491). As a result, in Argentina, mummification took on epidemic proportions following disappearances, where the bedrooms and offices of the disappeared were kept as they were at the time of the disappearance, while the living waited for their return (Suarez-Orozco, 1991, p. 490). Similarly, in Brazil some families even refuse to move house in case their missing relatives finally come home.[5] In Northern Ireland, some of the families of the disappeared[6] have not cleaned out the rooms of their missing relatives, despite the fact that the last political disappearance happened in the early 1980s.[7]

Both the survivor and the dead inhabit a symbolically liminal social space. Both are part of society but removed from society. This is captured in the words of a relative of the disappeared in Northern Ireland, when he says, 'We have been left hanging in space. There are people who know exactly where the disappeared are. Why doesn't somebody tell us where they are?'[8] In South Africa, survivors and the families of victims reiterate the same haunting cry, 'If they can just show us the bones of my child, where did they leave the bones of my child?'[9] The full horror of the liminal space is most poignantly captured by Mathilde Mellibovsky in a book entitled *A Circle of Love Around Death*, about the mothers of the disappeared in Argentina. She writes:

> I do not imagine hell as beds with shackles where the condemned must lie, but rather as a couple of easy chairs in which one can sit comfortably and wait for the postman to bring news – which will never come. (in Bronkhorst, 1995, p. 113)

Experiences of the *uncanny* can be exacerbated by the responses of government officials. Relatives of those arrested or disappeared, particularly in Latin America, Eastern Europe and South Africa, would search in local jails, police stations and morgues, but would often receive little information. In many cases, relatives looking for the disappeared were given a run around by authorities from one police station to another. Authorities would deny any knowledge of their fate and leave writs of *habeas corpus* unanswered. As Malin (1994, p. 197) writes of the uncertainty generated in the Latin American context:

> In denying knowledge or responsibility for the disappearances, the state created a system in which their victims seemed to have never existed at all. *Habeus corpus* does not work for the simple reason that there is 'no corpus'. No *cuerpo*. No body.

In South Africa, the police often told families that their children had left the country to join the liberation movement armed forces in exile.

This was, in some cases, true – but in others was a cover up for a security force disappearance and murder. This left many families in an *uncanny* space in which they believed (or at least hoped) that their loved ones were in exile and would return once liberation was achieved. Joyce Mtimkulu, who lived in hope for eight years that her son was in exile, captures the uncertain feelings around this. She says:

> The release of Mandela to me was the loss of my son because he should have come back with others ... that hope that everybody is coming back home, the other people got happy about that, but to us it was the moment of tears because our son never came back. (see note 9)

In many cases in Latin America, the security forces, in a Kafkaesque twist, would seize and destroy all identification papers of their victim and then deny that they had ever existed. Security police and the military intentionally promoted the unreality of death by making the victim's body vanish and then wiping away any official record of the victim's existence.[10] This eradication of the identity of the victim would leave survivors in a state of profound ontological insecurity.

Political disappearances around the world appear to have different gender effects. Most commonly, it is the female relatives of victims who are most vocal about being forced into a liminal space along with their relatives. Ramphele (1996) has analysed in detail how in South Africa widowhood places women into a liminal phase and a state of ambiguity that is symbolically marked. Political widows became the embodiment of social memory about the fallen hero and social ambiguity is inscribed onto their bodies during this state. In Sotho and Tswana communities, the body of the widow is marked in ways which express a fear of ritual dangers: her head is shaved, her body is smeared with charcoal and herbs and her face is covered with a black veil (Pauw, 1990). Occasionally a widow wears her clothes inside out, or only one shoe. She does not eat off everyday utensils and must stay out of the public arena. Silence becomes a marker of liminal status.

Unfortunately, however, the reality is that the material symbol (usually the body) that is necessary for moving out of the liminal space is seldom recovered after large-scale political violence. In these cases in South Africa, the truth commission became the next best (or the least worst) option, as it attempted to at least corroborate some information about what happened to disappeared individuals.

Public testimony and symbolic closure

How does testifying at hearings relate to feelings of the *uncanny* and liminality? Speaking at public hearings like those of the South African TRC can break an enforced silence and represent a point of closure and transition in the grieving process, through interacting with the national symbolic process of the TRC. The widow, in Ramphele's sense, leaves behind her grieving phase, shedding the symbols of her liminality. In its reparations policy (which may include personal monetary reparation and symbolic forms like tombstones or monuments), the TRC creates possibilities for the internalisation of loss and Freud's work of mourning (*trauerarbeit*) that does not exist through legal channels.[11] Without a corpse or a conviction it was often not possible to get compensation legally, but through the TRC it was much easier to obtain a finding (recognition of loss or suffering) and to obtain reparations (symbolic compensation for the loss).

One case which demonstrates a survivor's experience of uncertainty and her quest to resolve liminality through legal and TRC channels is that of Susan van der Merwe of Potchefstroom, a teacher and mother of five. Susan van der Merwe was married to a white farmer who went missing at Buffelsdrift, at the border post between South Africa and Botswana on 1 November 1978. Susan van der Merwe reported at the TRC hearings in Klerksdorp in September 1996 the same kinds of deep uncertainty as documented by Suarez-Orozco for victims in Argentina, 'my whole life was then an uncertainty ... and this uncertainty hung over us like a dark cloud. It left such an immense, indescribable feeling of a vacuum that you cannot explain it to anyone else. One's life, your whole life is incomplete.'[12] The uncertainty surrounding her husband's disappearance was worse than knowing that he was dead and placed the family in a liminal state. The two children at university were 'deeply disturbed' and failed their term exams. This state of liminality was material and financial, as well as psychological. Since Susan van der Merwe had no official evidence of her husband's death, she could not conduct financial transactions and she was not able to secure loans to buy a house or pay for her children's university costs. She said:

> At the beginning of 1979, the two children wanted to go and reregister at the university but the bank manager informed me that I did not have any security. The circumstances were that I was completely dependent on my husband. He ran on the financial matters ... It never occurred to me that because of the way in which my husband

had died, that if there were any funds available from him, that it would have been taken away from me because we were not married in community of property. (see note 11)

Prior to the TRC the case was investigated by the security police and four years later, in 1982, the Supreme Court established the events around the farmer's disappearance. Through the evidence of a police informer 'Mr X', the court heard how four *Umkhonto we Sizwe* (MK)[13] combatants had been walking along the road to Thabazimbi, when van der Merwe stopped and offered them a lift to the next town. Once in the car, the MK cadres pulled out guns and forced the farmer to drive in the opposite direction and they used his car to transport goods. They then walked Mr van der Merwe out into the bush and executed him and drove his car to the border. One MK cadre led police to the scene, but the body was never found.

For the family of the farmer, the court case resolved only some of their questions. 'After these findings, the Supreme Court certified my husband as dead, and this left my children in another vacuum of uncertainty. Why was such a horrendous deed done to my husband, which cost him his life? For what purpose, what were they hoping to achieve by that?' (see note 11) Susan van der Merwe never got the answers to those questions from her husband's killers, yet, despite opposition from her conservative white community in the West Rand, she explicitly stated that speaking in public in itself was important to her. She needed to present her story and wrestle with its inconsistencies publicly and also to affirm her renunciation of a past of radicalised violence.

In the case of Susan van der Merwe, and many others like it, we see how the pursuit of truth through the courts and TRC became a way of addressing loss publicly. According to Suarez-Orozco (1991), by pursuing their crusade for justice, the *Madres of the Plaza de Mayo*[14] similarly internalised their loss. Thus national institutional processes (such as truth commissions and the justice system) are, at least in certain ways, closely bound up with individual psychological processes. The TRC in South Africa, at least to some degree, became a mode of psychological repair, where denial could be superseded and both work of mourning (transition out of uncertainty and liminality) and narrative fetishism (teleologising and attaching transcendental meaning to loss) could take place. Both are ways in which individuals reconstruct their social identities through forging a meaningful and coherent narrative in the wake of trauma. The TRC thus became a mechanism through which ideological rationalisations for loss could be internalised. Suffering became meaningful by associating it with the teleology of the liberation struggle and the universal redemption of reconciliation.

In some instances even more minimal forms of recognition by the TRC can be useful and move the individual toward closure. Sandra Peake, co-ordinator of the WAVE Counselling Centre in Belfast, says it is only over the last year – as the peace process has moved forward – that some of the families of the disappeared in Northern Ireland have started to clean out the rooms of their missing relatives and get rid of their clothes. She feels that this subtle change has come about because of the moves toward peace and the recognition in 1995, and onwards, that there are in fact disappeared persons in Northern Ireland (see note 6).

However, based on our comparative analysis of several countries, it is evident that for most people more is needed than simple recognition and acknowledgement. The body itself, and the process of grieving around it, is of significance in most cultures. In Northern Ireland it is common for the families of the disappeared to stress the importance of a 'proper and decent Christian burial'.[15] The rituals that take place around the bodily remains aid closure and, without the body, closure seems all the more improbable. In this regard, Sandra Peake points out the importance of the Irish wake and the ritual significance of sitting up all night with the corpse (see note 6). If this is not possible because the body is truly gone, she says, the only other strategy that can bring some closure for the relatives is the revealing of the facts about the disappearance and why the person was taken in the first place. This stresses again that a truth recovery process (for example, the South Africa TRC, a formal inquiry, and so on) remains the only, albeit limited, hope for having some questions answered.[16]

Reparations and the liminality of the dead

In the absence of the body and without information, as is the case in so many post-conflict societies, can symbolic processes of closure take place? The projection of liminality of the subject onto a reified image of the deceased in South Africa provides unexpected answers to this question. In South African townships, research has commonly found that survivors projected their own liminality onto an image of those killed violently or disappeared.[17]

Although not a political incident, the case of Two-Bob Mpofu demonstrates the link between violent endings and the liminal dead in South Africa. In this case, which received national press coverage, the people of Msogwaba near Nelspruit in South Africa were, according to reports, being haunted by a man who was stabbed to death by his girlfriend in 1993. The ghost of the deceased, Two-Bob Mpofu, was seen walking around the streets and assaulting passers-by. One man, Thami Mlaba, reported that he was kidnapped by the ghost, assaulted and dumped in the graveyard. The dead man's relatives were particularly prey to his vengeance. The ghost attacked his sister, Nomajele Mpofu, in her home and chased her out of the house. Even a local policeman, Vusi Magagula of the Criminal Investigations Department, claimed to have been assaulted, 'I fired several shots at the ghost and emptied my gun, but nothing happened. So I ran away.'[18]

A similar phenomenon is also observed in cases of political murder, such as the Sebokeng Night Vigil massacre of 1991, which resulted from a fratricidal war between militarised youth of the rival African National Congress (ANC) and Inkatha Freedom Party (IFP). Margaret Nangalembe is the mother of the murdered ANC comrade Christopher Nangalembe who was allegedly killed by his IFP adversary (and former childhood friend) Victor Kheswa. Nangalembe's night vigil was attacked, allegedly by members of Kheswa's heavily armed gang, who threw hand grenades and fired into the crowd with AK-47s. Forty-two mourners attending the vigil were killed.[19] At the end of an author interview with Margaret Nangalembe, she broke down and implored, 'Why don't people come around to my house like before? They avoid it. They say that the dead are walking around in this house, and in the garden.'[20]

For Margaret Nangalembe, going to the TRC, testifying in public and receiving reparations was an inchoate attempt to symbolically lay the ghosts of the Sebokeng Night Vigil Massacre to rest. Experiences of liminality demand symbolic recognition, at some level, through public testimony, a memorial or reparations. All reparations (including monetary compensation) are like tombstones – a way of materialising the dead, a way of shifting from the 'liminal unknown to the liminal known' (Ramphele, 1996, p. 111). Reparations are, therefore, a material representation and fixation of memory work, recognition of the experience of liminality and its objectification in the external world.

Material reparations and compensation serve the same psychological ends as symbolic acts. They are both attempts to ritually create symbolic closure. Financial reparations are often mistakenly viewed and spoken about by policymakers and victims alike, as a form of concrete assistance that is different (and certainly more substantial) than symbolic acts such as the erection of tombstones or the naming of streets after the dead. However, the reality is that seldom will the sums of money granted ever equal the actual amount of money lost over the

years when a breadwinner is killed and it is questionable whether
the low levels of material reparations offered will dramatically change the
life of the recipients. In the South Africa case, material reparation is
merely another form of symbolic reparation, albeit particularly wel-
comed by the destitute survivors for whom any amount of money
is appreciated.

When the living receive payment for offences against the dead (and
forsake revenge), this can, in some cases, solidify and resolve the dead
who were previously seen as wandering like undead ghosts. Reparations
(and processes of remembering and commemoration) stabilise the ghosts,
they domesticate and tame them by representing the compensation for
their death.

Reparations seem to be one key strategy survivors pursue in order to
address their overwhelming feelings of uncertainty. In his essay *The Gift*,
Marcel Mauss asserts that presentations are 'total social movements'
that are at the same time economic, juridical, moral and psychological
phenomena, where 'the law of things remains bound up with the law of
persons' (Mauss, 1988, p. 2). Material things transferred between people
are not inert but contain a spirit of obligation and a part of the giver,
that is, 'to give something is to give a part of oneself' (Mauss, 1988, p. 10).
The objects exchanged are never completely separate from the people
that exchange them and the social context of the exchange, and thus
the act of exchange is replete with rights and duties. Thus, objects are
embedded in a social grammar of loss, liminality, closure and responsibility. To this end genuine reparation, and the process of healing, we
assert, does not occur through the delivery of the object (for example,
a pension, a monument and so on) but through the process that takes
place around the object.

Mauss is drawing our attention to something very important in the
transfer of material objects between people, and that is how persons
and things become symbolically equalized and inter-exchangeable.
There seems to be an unconscious principle of the transmutability of
people and things being played out when the state gives reparations to
families of the dead and disappeared. Mauss' discussion of the *hau*, or
the 'spirit of the gift' is relevant here, where the *hau* of reparations is
compensation for the spirit of the deceased. The spirit of the dead person
and the spirit of the material reparations become exchanged in the
transaction between the state and the survivor. The state's obligation to
pay reparations results from the duty to repay victims for their sacrifice
(in terms of suffering and loss) to the liberation and the construction of
the new political order. Victims gave the gifts of their own spirits to 'the

community' and the obligation of the new state is to return the gift in the form of reparations to their families.

The darker side of closure

The unconscious associations around reparations are not without their darker connotations, as Mauss has recognized, 'The gift is something that must be recognised and that is, at the same time, dangerous to accept' (Mauss, 1988, p. 58). Reparations place survivors in double-bind situations. Reparations can constitute closure and the final acceptance of loss, but they also can create difficulties for survivors. Some of the *Madres of the Plaza de Mayo* in Argentina are opposed to monetary reparations, since to accept reparation is to acknowledge death.[21] This stands in sharp contrast to the constant rallying cry of the *Madres* in Argentina, which is 'those who were taken from us alive should be returned to us alive'. Accepting reparations implies giving up hope that the disappeared would return alive. Similarly, in Brazil, a process of naming streets after the missing (and killed) under the Brazilian dictatorship (1964–85) has been greeted with ambivalent responses. Some families have been against it because they believe that naming the street concretises the death of their missing relatives. These families appear to still live in hope (or denial) that their children will return and have therefore refused to attend the inauguration of the streets named after their loved ones (see note 4). This refusal also links to feelings of betrayal. Suarez-Orozco argues this is the case for the *Madres* in Argentina, when he writes:

> The Mothers argue that any such bureaucratic intervention requires them to psychologically become their children's executioners: they would first need to psychologically kill and bury their children before proceeding with the legal route. And this is too costly, much too guilt inducing. It is as if giving up hope is betraying their children (Suarez-Orozco, 1991, p. 496).

Perhaps part of their refusal may also involve wanting others to experience the frustration they have felt. They are determined to offer constant reminders that, in reality, there is nothing that can ever be done to replace their missing loved ones. Yet part of the refusal also relates to the way in which governments often seek closure on the past more readily than individuals. For survivors, the state's desire to build a new post-conflict society often means sloughing off the past too easily and asking survivors to engage in a premature closure before all the psychological processes around truth and recompense are fully internalised.

The *Madres* did not accept the sacrifice of their children or husbands for the new civilian order. They refused to be embodied symbols of the contrast between the old repressive regime and the new benevolent political order. This is read as a vehement rejection of the post-authoritarian regime. This is one reason why government officials and the Argentinean press came to vilify the *Madres*, who, over the years, have changed from being the 'Mothers of the Nation' to *Las Locas* or the 'Crazy Little Old Ladies' of the *Plaza de Mayo*. The recalcitrant *Madres* were demonised as they no longer embodied the state's vision of a reconciled nation. They persisted in remaining ambiguous when politicians such as former Argentinian President Carlos Menem demanded unity, certainty and closure to bolster a post-authoritarian nation-building project.

Similarly, despite decades having passed since the dictatorship in Brazil, the continuous demands of the *Comissão de Familiares de Mortos e Desaparecidos Políticos* (Commission for the Family Members of the Persons Killed or Disappeared for Political Reasons) for the truth before compensation, and their refusal to see the new law[22] as the final stop, has made them unpopular. The government and even some previously sympathetic members of society now refer to the group as 'dinosaurs' (Hamber, 1997). They, and the *Madres*, are seen as imprisoned in the past, as hostages to their own memory and, therefore, obstructions to the process of selective forgetting advocated by reconciling national political leaders.

The rise and fall of social movements such as the *Madres* indicates that drawing closure around past violations is an inherently contradictory process that can be expected to take decades. This is the lesson of the French obsession with the war crimes trial of Maurice Papon in 1997, or the rejoicing of many Chileans after the arrest of General Pinochet in a London clinic in late October 1998. Clearly, how to address a history of mass violations is not an issue that will simply be resolved by a two-year truth commission, or when reparations are granted. Reparations and symbolic acts are useful markers in the first stages of recognizing and dealing with formerly silenced memory. However, although reparations may well be necessary (and a good starting point) on an individual level, they will never be sufficient. Resolution depends on how individuals personally engage in 'trauma work' at their own idiosyncratic pace.

On a psychological level, for a survivor to react in an overly forgiving way toward perpetrators, or to simply 'let bygones be bygones' in the words of former South African state president F.W. de Klerk, is highly improbable in the short-term, and even over decades in some cases (Hamber, 1998a, p. 68). The South African TRC has been a catalyst for successful resolution of the past for some individuals.[23] However, by the time reparations are granted (still outstanding at the time of writing), most survivors will not have completed their trauma work and be willing to adhere to nationally defined prerogatives of remembering and forgetting. It is critical that victims are not expected, either implicitly or explicitly, to forgive the perpetrators, or forget about the past because some form of reparation (or a comprehensive report on the nature and extent of past violations) has been made.

When reparations are granted before the survivor is psychologically ready, any form of reparation can be expected to leave the survivor feeling dissatisfied. When survivors or families of victims disparagingly talk of reparations as a form of blood money (as some do in Chile, Brazil, Argentina and Northern Ireland), this is because the national process of 'reconciliation' does not coincide with the individual psychological process. Reparations and the truth about what happened must be linked, because without this link any form of reparation runs the danger of being seen by the survivors as a governmental strategy to close the chapter on the past prematurely and leave the secrets of the past hidden. Reparations without truth make survivors feel that reparations are being used to buy their silence and put a stop to their continuing quest for truth and justice.

The long-term and individualised nature of coming to terms with the past is captured by the words of Joyce Mtimkulu, whose son went missing in Port Elizabeth, South Africa in the 1990s. Through the TRC a version of the truth has been revealed. The perpetrators have confessed that her son was tortured, shot, his body burnt and his remains thrown into the Fish river. Despite the emergence of a fairly coherent version of the truth, inconsistencies still exist in the stories of the security police killers, and Mtimkulu remains dissatisfied with what has taken place. After testifying at the hearing and hearing the killers confess, she says:

> I have not forgiven them, why must I forgive them when they don't want to tell the truth, and the beauty of this is that they are not asking for forgiveness from us, the people who have lost their beloved ones. They are asking forgiveness from the government, they did nothing to the government, what they did; they did to us. (See note 8)

Ignatieff concludes in this case, 'Joyce speaks with words of anger, words of grief, truth is not enough, the time for forgiveness has not yet come, the time for reconciliation is in the future.' (1997)

Revenge and punishment as forms of closure

> We are concerned that the commissioners [*of the South African TRC*] are critical of efforts to bring to book those who perpetrated crimes against humanity. They think justice is of less value than their reconciliation showbiz and avalanche of tears.[24]

To effectively deal with the impact of large-scale political violence, we need to fully comprehend its variegated impact on individuals. National politicians cannot expect individuals to accept their agenda and time schedule for dealing with the past. In particular, they cannot be expected to abandon demands for justice as a form of redress necessary for ending liminality in some cases. This was demonstrated during the Azanian People's Organisation (AZAPO) and the survivors' families of high profile murder cases (Biko, Mxenge and Ribeiro) constitutional challenge in 1996. They challenged section 20(7) of the National Unity and Reconciliation Act, which permitted the TRC to grant amnesty according to certain criteria laid down in the Act. They contested the amnesty provision because, if amnesty is granted, the survivors are denied a right to criminal or civil action against the perpetrator.[25] The Constitutional Court dismissed this constitutional challenge in 1996,[26] which finally laid aside victims' demands for legal retribution and prosecution for those who were granted amnesty in South Africa.

Although the foregoing of formal justice in South Africa may have been necessary to ensure peace, this national process can run counter to the individual psychological healing process and asks another sacrifice from the victims. This is captured in the words of Archbishop Tutu when he says:

> If the security forces had thought that they were going to be up for the high jump we would not have had a negotiated settlement, that is the price that had to be paid, and yes, the victims and survivors are probably asked a second time and to be willing – if this high price had not been paid this country would have gone up in flames.[27]

Indeed the price for the survivors has been high – but how do survivors, given the loss that they have suffered, process this? At the time of significant loss most people enter into a number of invisible pacts with themselves. Sometimes this can be a vow to avenge the death of a loved one, either through formal punishment or personal vengeance. This vow is made, not due to sadistic pleasure, but rather as a way of respecting the person who has died, to make their death and memory meaningful. Individuals also often vow that nothing will ever replace what has been lost.

Revenge, or inflicting of harm in response to perceived harm or injustice (see Stuckless and Goranson, 1994, pp. 803–11) is, according to Michael Ignatieff, commonly regarded as a low and unworthy emotion because its deep moral hold on people is rarely understood (Ignatieff, 1998, p. 188). Ignatieff recognizes that revenge is a profound moral desire to keep faith with the dead, to honour their memory by taking up their cause where they left off. To this end, revenge keeps faith between generations and the violence that follows is a ritual form of respect for the community's dead. For Ignatieff, therein lies the legitimacy of revenge.

Nietzsche is one of the few philosophers to have asserted the centrality of revenge in the pursuit of justice, 'The spirit of revenge: my friends, that up to now, has been mankind's chief concern: and where there was suffering, there was always supposed to be punishment.' (Nietzsche, 1969, p. 162) Practically the whole of the rest of western philosophy and jurisprudence has followed Kant and Hegel in denouncing revenge and distinguishing rational law and justice from revenge. The South African TRC has, in the interests of national reconciliation, muted feelings of vengeance and replaced them with what it calls a more restorative model.[28] As a result of national imperatives, survivors have generally felt inhibited in expressing their legitimate rage and anger and demanding just retribution. Erich Fromm feels that vengeance (revenge) is in some senses a magical act and, like punishment for a crime, it can serve the function of magically expunging the perpetrators' act (Fromm, 1984, p. 364). Fromm links vengeance directly to reparation; vengeance is said to be a magical reparation. In this way, like reparations, we contend that revenge and punishment (and perhaps the fantasies thereof) can also be a way to lay the ghosts of the violently killed to rest and end the liminal status of the victim and survivor.

Furthermore, if the desire for vengeance grips the survivor, then accepting paltry reparations can also be experienced by the survivor as a disrespectful act that betrays the loss they have endured or the memory of those killed. In essence, rituals of respect (such as retribution through the courts) and remembering can be broken by reparations, just as they can in some cases serve as a symbol of mending.

The difficulties of coming to terms with the aftermath of political trauma for the individual have to be acknowledged. Coming to terms with the past can only be eased by recognizing as legitimate the multiple and contradictory agendas which exist among a heterogeneous community of survivors. The demands of some survivors for retributive justice need to be seen as just as legitimate a path to 'reconciliation' as forgiveness. Public and private space needs to be made to enable them to rework their diverse memories of past conflicts and feelings of anger. Contained, yet legitimate, revenge and punishment feelings are obviously more desirable than acted-out fantasies.

A state-led process of substantial and personalised symbolic, material and collective reparations also needs to be set in motion. This did not occur in the South African context, where reparations were very low on the list of priorities of national politicians, and a compensation scheme for the majority of victims had not been established at the time of writing, over a year after the TRC's report was published. In January 2000, the Mbeki government stated its intention to offer only token compensation of a few hundred pound (Rands, 2000), instead of the £15,000 which the TRC recommended should be given to 22,000 victims of apartheid. Duma Khumalo spoke for many victims when he protested bitterly, 'We have been betrayed. The previous government gave the killers golden handshakes and the present government gave them amnesty. [But] the victims have been left empty handed.' ('Apartheid Victims Reject Handouts', *Guardian*. 3 January 2000)

Conclusion: where dwell the vast hosts of the dead?

His soul had approached the region where dwell the vast hosts of the dead. He was conscious of, but could not apprehend, their wayward and flickering existence. His own identity was fading into a grey impalpable world: the solid world itself which these dead had one time reared and lived in was dissolving and dwindling (James Joyce in his short story entitled *The Dead*).

The process of breaking a regime of denial, addressing and recognizing repressed memories, compensating for loss, and ultimately arriving at some type of closure and reintegration of liminal subjects, works at different levels; that is, individuals, truth commissions and criminal prosecutions. There are different motivations at these different levels and they proceed at different paces. There is not a single process of dealing with the past that restores the 'national psyche' to good health. We have rejected the idea of the collective as an extrapolation of the individual as a myth of nation-building. Instead, we have drawn attention to the disjunctures, as well as the convergences, between individual responses and national institutions. National processes such as truth commissions (although by no means the only process) can provide a useful framework in which new rituals or spaces can be provided for the enactment of closure.

Strategies such as truth commissions, Fiona Ross argues, are performances of memory that create a framework of explanation (Ross, 1997, p. 9). Further, Ross quotes Jack Kugelmas' formulation that memory is a process of both remembering and forgetting. Facts need a narrative framework in order to be rendered meaningful and take their place in a shared account of the past. Where there is no accessible literature of destruction, performing rituals are a means to bridge what he calls the 'fundamental discontinuities of life'. To this end, Ross argues that through the South African TRC:

> South Africa is currently witnessing a process of shifting a new framework of description and definition into place, creating, if not a cohesive narrative of past pain, then at least the beginnings of a framework within which moralities can be placed and debated.... The framework is contested. Indeed, that is the strength of the commission's process.... It gives visible and tangible shape to the past, providing, shall we say, a ritual context within which the past can be examined and placed on record – at least in part. (1997, p. 10)

Governmental strategies like truth commissions can create the public space for survivors to begin the process of working through a violent and conflicted history. Of course they are also not the only means. For any strategy for dealing with the past to be successful, an ongoing space has to be provided for survivors to express both their grief and their rage, as they struggle to come to terms with the inherent ambivalences of the psychological and emotional impact of their loss – a loss that reparation and even the truth can only partially acknowledge. It is how the individual processes the symbolic meaning of the ritual, the reparation or a national process such as a truth commission that is critical. For this reason, making space for the legitimate complaints and opposition of survivors should be seen as an integral component of dealing with the past. These spaces can take the form of private spaces (for example, counselling, culturally appropriate mechanisms for story-telling and sharing, and so on) and the ongoing use of public space (for example, media, exhibitions, theatre, and so on).

At a national level, this means recognizing publicly that the past is a site of struggle, not a fixed object to which all members of the nation must identify. As Antze and Lambek write, 'Memory becomes a locus of struggle over the boundary between the individual and the collective or between distinct interest groups in which power becomes the operative factor' (1996, p. 98). In this context, the analysis of trauma work in post-conflict situations involves the charting of the dynamic between national appropriations of memory and individual resistance and acquiescence.

In addition, the calls for punishment of perpetrators (even when this is not pragmatically possible), or the impossible demands of survivors like those of the *Madres*, need to be understood as rituals of closure in themselves. These calls can re-establish the discontinuities in time for the survivor; that is, they survived, their loved ones did not and will not ever appear again. In post-conflict societies, angry calls for justice and revenge persist until the process of trauma work and reintegration is resolved. The rituals which national polities put into place both hinder and promote individual psychological processes of recovery. Recognizing the diversity of responses to suffering (including anger and vengeance) ensures that the demanding and inherently ambivalent psychological processes of grieving the dead are not wholly appropriated by post-conflict societies using narrow Christian and human rights discourses of reconciliation and nation-building.

Truth commissions do not heal the nation, restore the collective psyche or categorically deal with the past. Their value is much more limited and constrained, and lies in creating a public space in which publicly telling subjective truths, which are but one form of closure among many, may occur. They may also cause further psychological trauma when individuals (such as widows) are treated as the social embodiment of the nation, and are expected to advance at the same pace as the state institutions which are created in their name, but which are primarily pursuing a national political agenda.

Notes

1. Space does not permit a thorough discussion of the nature, mandate and structure of the Truth and Reconciliation Commission. For more detail, see Simpson and van Zyl (1995); Asmal *et al.* (1996); Burton (1998); Hamber and

Kibble (1999); Wilson (2000). For the full mandate of the TRC, see the full text of the *Promotion of National Unity Act*, No. 34 of 1995, at *http://www. truth.org.za/legal/act9534. htm.*

2. Tina Rosenberg (1995, p. 24) writes of the need for official acknowledgement, 'If the whole nation is suffering from post-traumatic stress disorder, this process would be appropriate for the whole nation.'

3. For a more detailed discussion of the reparations issue in South Africa, see Hamber (2000). Also see the TRC's Reparation and Rehabilitation Policy in the *TRC Final Report*, Volume 5, Chapter 5.

4. Within this chapter we use the TRC's definition of reparation, which can include measures in the form of compensation, an *ex gratia* payment, restitution, rehabilitation or recognition. To this end our notion of reparation is very broad and not only includes monetary compensation but also incorporates a range of other reparation strategies. These include the need for symbolic reparations (for example, erecting headstones, the building of memorials and so on), legal and administrative interventions (for example, expunging criminal records or the issuing of declarations of death), as well as community reparations (such as programmes for better access to health).

5. Cecilia Coimbra from *Grupo Tortura Nunca Mais* (Rio de Janeiro), Interview with Brandon Hamber, December 1996, Rio de Janeiro. For a fuller discussion on the families in Brazil, see Hamber (1997).

6. There are more than 20 bodies unaccounted for in Northern Ireland, most said to be Catholics killed by the Republican groups and the (Provisional) Irish Republican Army or the IRA. The IRA has acknowledged that 12 of the people abducted and killed between 1972 and 1980 were activities committed under its command. See the *Irish Times*, 26 June 1998, front page.

7. Sandra Peake, Co-ordinator of the WAVE Counselling Centre, Interview with Brandon Hamber, 27 October 1998, Belfast.

8. William McKinney, *The News Letter*, 14 August 1998, p. 2. William McKinney's son, Brian, disappeared in 1978 after being abducted by Republicans in West Belfast.

9. Joyce Mtimkulu, Interview with Michael Ignatieff, 'Getting Away with Murder', *Special Correspondent Programme* (1997) BBC2. Joyce Mtimkulu is the mother of Siphiwo, who went missing in South Africa a decade and a half ago.

10. For a study of these events in Argentina, see Malin (1994).

11. For a discussion of Freud, *trauerarbeit* and the history of the Holocaust, see Santner (1992).

12. Susan van der Merwe, Testimony at the TRC hearings, Klerksdorp, 23 September 1996.

13. The military wing of the African National Congress (ANC).

14. The *Madres* emerged as an important democratising social movement during Argentina's military dictatorship of the late 1980s. These mothers of the disappeared began by marching around the *Plaza de Mayo* in Buenos Aires, demanding the return of their sons and daughters taken by the military's death squads.

15. See comments by the families of the disappeared in the *Irish Times*, 31 August 1998, p. 6; *The News Letter*, 14 August 1998, p. 6; the *Irish Times*, 26 June 1998, front page; and the statement issued on behalf of the relatives of the disappeared on 7 September 1998.

16. For a discussion on the importance of truth in the Northern Ireland context, see Hamber (1998b) and Rolston (1996).
17. This was confirmed by interviews conducted by Richard Wilson in the Vaal townships of Sebokeng, Sharpeville and Boipatong, from 1996 to 1998.
18. 'Stabbed man's ghost haunts our village', report Eric Mashaba and Sylvester Lukhele, *Sunday Times*, 29 September 1993.
19. Newspaper reports are inconclusive on the exact number of people killed in the incident. Reports range from 39 to 46 fatalities; 42 is the figure used by the Nangalembe family and is, therefore, the number used in this chapter.
20. Margaret Nangalembe, interview with Richard Wilson, 29 November 1996, Sebokeng, South Africa.
21. In Argentina two main groups exist. The *Madres de la Plaza de Mayo* reject all government attempts to investigate the truth and only want justice. This group split with the *Madres de la Plaza de Mayo – Linea Fundadora* in 1986. The *Madres de la Plaza de Mayo – Linea Fundadora*, despite initially being against all investigations and truth recovery processes, now work with the government in investigating disappearances (for example, exhumations) and accept the reparations offered; See Hamber (1997).
22. The issue of compensation has only recently been thrust into main focus when the government agreed in 1995 to compensate the families of the murdered and 'disappeared', in some cases two decades after the 'disappearances'. The Brazilian Congress approved the bill in September 1995. The government officially acknowledged 136 names of disappeared persons. The number of those considered dead or disappeared is still contested by some of the families of victims in Brazil. The onus is however on the families to prove the government was responsible. The group sees this as the government's final attempt to buy their silence and close the book on the past, without revealing the true facts of what happened during the military dictatorship.
23. For a discussion of several cases where there has been forgiveness between victim and perpetrator in South Africa, see Frost (1998) as well as the *TRC Final Report*, Volume 5, Chapter 5: 'Reconciliation'.
24. Azanian People's Organisation (AZAPO) chair in Guateng, Lybon Mabaso, telling a Johannesburg news conference that the TRC was defeating the ends of justice by attempting to stop the attorney general from pursuing apartheid-era human rights offenders. In 'The Truth as it was Told', *Weekly Mail and Guardian*, 23 December 1997.
25. *Azanian People's Organisation (AZAPO) and Others v. the President of the Republic of South Africa* (25 July 1996). CCT 17/96, Constitutional Court.
26. In sum, the judgment largely argues that amnesty was necessary and pragmatic to ensure democracy in South Africa, and that hopes for large-scale prosecution were not viable given the inefficiencies of the court system. It argues that the TRC offered at least potentially some truth and reparations to a greater number of survivors than the courts would have. The courts would have offered this to fewer people although the civil claims would have undoubtedly been larger than the reparations that may be made available through the TRC. Despite the upholding of the amnesty provisions, the judgment makes it clear that because perpetrators will be granted amnesty, those found to be victims are entitled to 'individually nuanced'

reparations. Nonetheless, the judgment makes an important rejoinder to this argument, that is, the state can take into consideration the available resources, the claims of all victims and the competing demands of the government when deciding what reparation policies to implement. See *South African Journal of Human Rights*, *13*(2), which has published several papers dealing with this ruling.

27. Archbishop Desmond Tutu, interview with Michael Ignatieff, 'Getting Away with Murder', *Special Correspondent Programme*, (1997) BBC2.

28. To some degree, the TRC can be said to embody restorative justice principles at a national level, however, it is argued that it does not wholly embody the principles of restorative justice at an individual level. This is because victims in the TRC scenario still do have the individual capacity to affect the outcome of the amnesty process and that reparation is made from the state. There is no obligation on the perpetrator to make direct amends or offer restitution to the victim in the TRC model; see Hamber and Kibble (1999).

Part V
Conclusion

10

Memories in Conflict: Review and a Look to the Future

Mícheál D. Roe and Ed Cairns

The impetus for this collaborative project on memories in conflict emerged in 1995 in a working group of psychologists addressing peace and conflict issues under the auspices of the Committee for the Psychological Study of Peace of the International Union of Psychological Science, and the Initiative on Conflict Resolution and Ethnicity, of the United Nations University and the University of Ulster. We were meeting in post-apartheid South Africa a year following the remarkable election of Nelson Mandela to that country's presidency. It was a time of great anticipation, even exuberance (that South Africa won the world cup in rugby that year only added to the sense of shared optimism). It was also a time of continuing intergroup violence, particularly between the predominantly Zulu Inkatha and the predominantly Xhosa ANC. The East Rand area of Johannesburg was a battleground, for example. During this period of national transition and hope, the persistence of violence fuelled by ethnic memories of competing interests and conflict was sobering.

Most of this working group regathered in 1998 for an international symposium at the 24th International Congress of Applied Psychology in San Francisco. Here early drafts of a number of the chapters in this book were presented and discussed. In the three years since the South Africa meeting, intergroup conflicts continued in Bosnia-Herzegovina, Croatia, Kosovo, Indonesia and East Timor, Rwanda, Burundi, Zaire, Algeria, Sri Lanka, Israel/Palestine and so on. It was actually during that 1998 international congress that the horrific Omagh bomb exploded in Northern Ireland – the single most lethal act of terrorism in thirty years of political violence there.

Today, intergroup conflicts around the world have not lessened. Our understanding of their origin, maintenance and resistance to amelioration has advanced, but our efforts at conflict resolution at best have been marginally effective and in only a handful of settings.

The chapters in this book provide tentative, but rich insights into understanding the role of social memories in fomenting and possibly resolving intergroup conflict. They reflect a variety of personal experiences with conflict from a variety of world views and national settings. Before attempting to highlight these insights it is worth noting that the various chapters are based on different methodologies and modes of analysis. For example Bar-Tal, Devine-Wright, and Hamber and Wilson provide theoretical examinations of memories in conflict, with Bar-Tal particularly influenced by the Israeli–Palestinian context, Devine-Wright – the Northern Irish context, and Hamber and Wilson – the South African context. Qualitative techniques were used in Barton and McCully's open-ended interviews of Northern Irish children prompted by pictures from different events in history. Mellor and Bretherton, also qualitatively content analysed responses from in-depth interviews of their Australian Aboriginal participants and from the more structured responses of their white university subjects. In contrast, Oppenheimer and Hakvoort applied quantitative content analytic and statistical techniques to responses from Dutch children and adolescents. Finally, a combination of qualitative and quantitative techniques was utilised by McLernon, Cairns, Lewis and Hewstone, and by Roe. McLernon *et al.* applied qualitative content analysis to oral data from focus groups of Northern Irish adults, as well as using quantitative survey and psychometric scales of forgiveness and of religiosity with their high school and university participants. Similarly Roe applied qualitative content analysis to oral data from Cowlitz Indian elders, and quantitative survey and attitude scales to elicit responses from the general membership of the Cowlitz Indian tribe.

In spite of the variety of methodologies and cultural settings, a number of consistent themes emerged from these chapters. These themes, which will be discussed below, are as follows: (1) content of social memories and their origin, maintenance, and transmission; (2) roles of social identity; (3) social status of *victim*; (4) social status of *perpetrator*; and (5) conflict resolution.

Social memories

Content

It is clear that social memories are often distinct from, even in conflict with, 'official' recorded history, with recorded history itself reflecting a particular social construction often in line with a dominant culture's values and priorities (Mellor and Bretherton, in this volume). These memories often serve political functions, whether they originate from dominant or minority groups (see Devine-Wright, Chapter 2). Perhaps most importantly several chapters illustrate that social memories are often associated with emotion-laden events (Bar-Tal), with strong emotions increasing the likelihood that memories will be formed, as in the case of 'flashbulb memories' (Devine-Wright; McLernon *et al.*).

In addition social memories are located in moral interpretive frameworks in which the content may coexist at odds with personal experience. In the context of conflict, this framework often is negative, with victims and perpetrators specified (Oppenheimer and Hakvoort, Chapter 6). If the conflict is long-term, the memories include themes related to a society's one-sided and selective beliefs about the conflict, delegitimisation of the opponent, claims of self-victimisation, and patriotism (Bar-Tal). It should be noted that Bar-Tal's 'patriotism' here could be more specifically described as an 'ethnocentric patriotism' or 'nationalism' since it implies a sense of ingroup superiority and outgroup enmity (see Druckman, 2001).

Origin, maintenance and transmission

A clear theme running through many chapters is that social memories must be located in cultural and political space and time; that is, they are dependent on social identities and the salience of the identities at time of the relevant event (McLernon *et al.* Chapter 8). They are formed and transmitted via informal socialisation processes in family and community (Barton and McCully; Oppenheimer and Hakvoort; Roe), intentional teaching and review (Roe), and/or formal education (Barton and McCully; Oppenheimer and Hakvoort). There is the possibility of critical developmental periods for forming social memories within each generation (Devine-Wright) and such memories are transmitted at an early age (Oppenheimer and Hakvoort). This latter finding in particular is in line with Verbeek and de Waal's (2001) examination of 'peacemaking' among preschool children (see also Hakvoort and Hagglund, 2001; and McLernon and Cairns, 2001).

One intriguing suggestion is that in continuous conflict, the core of social memories is relived and renewed by each generation (Mellor and Bretherton, Chapter 3; Roe, Chapter 4; Bar-Tal, Chapter 5). This process though is not rote memory, but a 'co-constructivist' one – assembled by one generation and reassembled by recipient generations (Oppenheimer and Hakvoort). Interestingly, this reassembling may actually involve the insertion of new content from the past. Walker (1996), for example, argues that Northern Irish social memories associated with the 1690 Battle of the Boyne are not three hundred years old, but was initiated for specific political purposes in the late nineteenth century.

An interesting variation of this 'reliving' in each generation is presented in the chapters by Mellor and Bretherton and Roe. These authors discussed indigenous peoples' non-linear view of time, where past and present coexist in some form. Under these circumstances, 'memory' is too static a concept, since social memories of the past are experienced in the present as well, and as such facilitate their maintenance.

Finally, in a way this book helps to illustrate how concrete markers or cyclical experiences support 'active remembering' processes (Devine-Wright). These include participating in commemorations or cultural traditions (Devine-Wright; Roe; Bar-Tal), and designating memorials or environmental referents (Devine-Wright; Bar-Tal). Aboriginal lands or 'place' fill a similar role for indigenous peoples (Mellor and Bretherton; Roe).

Roles of social identity

The role of social identity is touched on in almost every chapter. In particular social identities are presented as setting ingroup–outgroup boundaries, including those inherent in patriotism and nationalism (Devine-Wright; Bar-Tal), and in influencing what social memories are formed and maintained (Devine-Wright; McLernon *et al.*). Arguing from the other direction with indigenous peoples, social memories can be significant in maintaining social identities (Mellor and Bretherton; Roe). Differing social identities are of course associated with differing views of history and such differences contribute to continuing conflict between groups (Mellor and Betherton). In contrast, Barton and McCully claim that formal education can reveal shared histories, lead to shared social identities, and as a consequence reduce intergroup conflicts.

Finally, there is the encouraging suggestion that victims of political violence can reconstruct social identities through the work of truth commissions (Hamber and Wilson). In contrast, nation-builders in post-conflict societies are motivated to ascribe an artificial collective or social identity to a nation, and assuming that a nation possesses such a collective identity may have negative consequences for psychological healing of traumatised individuals (Hamber and Wilson).

Social status of *victim*

A number of authors discussed how *victim* and *perpetrator* not only describe actual experiences in conflicts; they also describe ascribed social roles, which may be independent of experience. It is not uncommon for groups in conflict (that is, sharing the same history) both to claim victimhood and both to accuse the other of victimiser (Bar-Tal; Oppenheimer and Hakvoort). In turn this sense of shared victimisation in social memory can be seen as elements promoting group cohesion (Devine-Wright; Roe).

Despite this, several chapters illustrate that victims of intergroup violence exist in a 'liminal space'; that is, the victims are both part of and removed from society, and their lives are characterised by uncertainty and doubt. These victims are in need of 'closure', where the trauma is no longer seen as unfinished business (Hamber and Wilson). The lack of acknowledgement of victims by perpetrators or others even within one's own community hinders reconciliation (McLernon *et al.*; Mellor and Bretherton), and such *unacknowledgement*, particularly in settings of continuous conflict, makes it very difficult for victims even to contemplate intergroup forgiveness (McLernon *et al.*).

Social status of *perpetrator*

As with victims, perpetrators may be identified through ascription processes associated with social memories (Bar-Tal; Oppenheimer and Hakvoort). For example, perpetrators may use social memories to legitimise, motivate and idealise their acts of violence and the power they wield (Devine-Wright; McLernon *et al.*).

An important insight into the role of revenge is offered by several of the authors who note that by delegitimising perpetrators, victims believe they are justified in becoming perpetrators themselves and a cycle of revenge results (Bar-Tal; McLernon *et al.*). Seeking revenge may be conceptualised as faithfulness to oneself and to victims, even as honouring of victims. Under such a conceptualisation, revenge is seen as an ethical or moral act (Bar-Tal; Hamber and Wilson).

Revenge also may be sought to protect personal or group self esteem (Bar-Tal; Devine-Wright), and it may define one avenue for bringing psychological closure and ending the liminal status of victims and survivors. Under these circumstances, and in contrast to reparations resulting in forsaking revenge (Hamber and Wilson), revenge fulfils the role of reparation (Hamber and Wilson).

Conflict resolution

Throughout this volume a variety of processes are presented which implicate memory in the facilitation of conflict resolution. The first of these relates to formal peace processes in the political arena. Even if conflict persists, setting peace processes into effect can move a victim away from liminal status (Hamber and Wilson). Truth commissions in particular may provide a frame for public discourse and public memory (that is, a public space) (Hamber and Wilson), corroborate information and place limits on historical revisionism (Hamber and Wilson), and for some individuals, provide one mode for psychological repair (Hamber and Wilson). On the other hand Hamber and Wilson believe that truth commissions are not necessarily effective in healing psychological trauma. Victims of violence are often on different timetables than truth commissions, and they possess multiple and contradictory agenda (Hamber and Wilson). Even concrete reparations may result in ambivalent psychological consequences for traumatised persons (Hamber and Wilson; see also Roe).

In seeking peace, according to several authors, there are roles for superordinate social identities and shared histories between conflicting groups (Barton and McCully), particularly where conflict results from a lack of agreement on what constitutes history (Mellor and Bretherton). This may involve the need to relinquish past constructions of history used to legitimate actions in conflict, and adopt new constructions in tune with changing societal contexts (Devine-Wright). This relinquishing, it is suggested, will break the cycle of negative interpretive frameworks that are cross-generationally transferred (Oppenheimer and Hakvoort).

In addition there are roles for 'active educational processes' in general (Barton and McCully; Oppenheimer and Hakvoort), and history education in particular to challenge myths and directly to address emotionally laden contemporary events and questions of social identity (Barton and McCully). Education as intervention into conflict fits within the broader call for peace education or education for social responsibility in which the status quo is challenged, empathy for and knowledge of other cultures (groups) is promoted, and non-violence is emphasized in conflict resolution (for example, Dyal and McKenzie-Mohr, 1992; La Farge, 1992).

Finally, several chapters explore the challenge of understanding intergroup as well as interpersonal forgiveness, for personal healing of victims, for breaking cycles of revenge, and for intergroup and interpersonal reconciliation (McLernon *et al.*). Such forgiveness, we learn however, must not be forced on victims as an expectation, nor should it be expected to lead to forgetting (Mellor and Bretherton; Hamber and Wilson; McLernon *et al.*).

Synthesis/future

Settings of intergroup conflict are filled with confusion, mixed motivations and instabilities, so it is not surprising that this book clearly reveals the apparent paradox or conflicting goals that exist. For example, social identities and social memories may fill paradoxical roles; they may hinder or facilitate peacemaking processes, or both, *and* simultaneously. While focusing on group distinctives, that may sustain or exacerbate conflict, it may also empower groups to maintain cohesiveness and to continue to function until conflict resolution is achieved. Peacemaking processes which acknowledge, even value, such distinctives rather than mask or attempt to eliminate them, ultimately may be more effective, since groups in conflict rarely desire to deny their group allegiances. For example, in response to the annual tumult surrounding marches of the Orange Order in Northern Ireland, a leading Orangeman argued for respecting the different cultures: 'The future for this country is one of mutual respect and tolerance which has to be practiced and not just preached'. ('Parades body in pledge on march culture', *Belfast Telegraph*, 28 June 2001)

In a similar vein, individual trauma work, national history making and reparations offered by truth commissions, may mutually reinforce each other under some circumstances; however, under other circumstances they can be disharmonious, incongruous, even counterproductive. Or take the question of, seeking revenge, which we have learned often perpetuates cycles of conflict. However, it also can be conceptualised as an ethical or moral response of faithfulness and respect, and as such could possibly bring psychological closure and end the liminal status of victims and survivors. Finally, forgiveness is considered a positive human response to violence, which brings personal healing and decreases conflict. Intergroup forgiveness as an intervention into intergroup conflict, however, may be perceived as very difficult, or even irrelevant. From the perspective of perpetrators who view their actions as justified by furthering political causes, seeking or receiving forgiveness is viewed as unnecessary, even counterproductive. Under some circumstances, granting forgiveness and risking loss of victim status as a result may actually raise suspicion in others that the grantor is a perpetrator.

Looking to the future, an obvious approach to peacemaking is to attempt to find shared social identities by recognizing shared histories. One message we can take from the chapters in the present volume is that, while this is a theoretically sound approach, such a strategy is difficult to achieve in practice. One reason is that over many years it is likely that a selective form of remembering will have occurred, with the result that all semblance of a collective past will have been obliterated from the collective memory. Further, this very act of remembering the past, often through glorifying one's own group's triumphs, will, because of its exclusivity, give the impression to the opposing group that its claims to collective rights and a unique identity have been ignored (Connerton, 1989). In addition, it appears that often the desire to start with a clean slate is held by the group that was in power, while those who saw themselves as the disenfranchised consider peace as a chance not only for reparation, but also to adopt their own selective view of the past. Under such circumstances, it may take many generations to adopt a shared history. In the short-term as Asmal *et al.* (1996) noted when speaking from experience in South Africa, reconciliation is not the 'escapist flight from the facts or the arrival at a jerry-built consensus', instead it involves recognizing 'unwelcome truths in order to harmonize incommensurable world views' (p. 46). Such world views inevitably include views of the past.

In 1910, William James noted that what was needed to replace the culture of war so prevalent then (as it is today) was 'a moral equivalent of war'. A major difficulty in replacing a culture of war with a culture of peace appears to revolve around the perception that war is an active state, while peace is a passive one; and this contrast in perceptions has its origin early in childhood (Hakvoort and Oppenheimer, 1993). In the context of the present volume it is only too apparent that collective memories almost inevitably are memories of war or intergroup struggle, and that there are very seldom memories of peace or heroic acts to achieve peace – except when 'peace' is seen in the context of victory. Indeed in societies like Northern Ireland, where the history of intergroup struggle has been punctuated with periods of relative peace, the collective memory is such that it portrays a history of continuous violence. In turn this means that how we think and talk about conflict is crucial in shaping what we do to settle these conflicts. The media, therefore, has an important role in influencing intergroup attitudes and stereotypes, particularly stereotypes of victims and perpetrators (Staub,

1999; Ross, 2000) through its treatment both of the recent past and the historical past. While the media does act largely to reinforce existing attitudes it does have a role in cultivating basic assumptions about the nature of society. In particular the media may have an important role if not in forming, at least in triggering, collective memories. What Bartlett observed in 1932 is still relevant today.

> In perceiving, in imaging, in remembering proper and in constructive work, the passing fashion of the group, the social catchword, the prevailing approved general interest, the persistent social custom and intuition set the stage and direct action. (p. 244)

Unfortunately, too often the media is used in this way as a catalyst for conflict, as for example in Rwanda or the Balkans. The media, however, can fill a role in constructing a more peaceful society. In particular they can act as a challenge to certain constructions of the past and, because of their role in determining both what groups remember and how they remember, the media can help trigger memories of more peaceful times and/or times of shared identity for groups in conflict.

This active/passive perception of war and peace is often referred to as *negative* peace; that is, that state which exists in the absence of conflict (for example, Barash, 1991). When the UN General Assembly declared the year 2000 as the International Year for the Culture of Peace, it was focused on the implementation of *positive* peace. Positive peace is active and proactive. Its core includes social justice, human rights, nonviolence, inclusiveness, civil society, formal and informal peace education, and sustainability of global resources (Wessells *et al.*, 2001). A culture of peace becomes rather complicated when addressing social memories and intergroup conflict, for it juxtaposes nonviolence and civil society with inclusiveness, and inclusiveness includes 'respect for difference, participation by different groups, meeting identity needs, [and] cultural sensitivity' (Wessells *et al.*, 2001, p. 351). These descriptors imply that social identity and associated collective memories not only will be, but also should be maintained, returning us to that paradox and challenge noted at the beginning of this section.

Finally, we believe that the principal lesson the contributions in this volume teach us is that societies torn apart by ethnic conflict must, at some stage, face up to the past especially if they wish to deal with conflict in the long term. Falconer (1988) posited a three-part model to address social memories of pain and unatoned violence, and to break cycles of conflict and revenge. According to Falconer, reconciliation of memories involves a process of: (1) accepting responsibility for past actions of one's own community; (2) seeking and granting intergroup forgiveness; and (3) appropriating the history of the other community to learn from its experiences. Forgiveness is essential. 'Through this process of forgiveness both [communities] are empowered to be and to enter a new relationship which is able to embrace the memories of the hurt and alienation' (Falconer, 1988, 95). While we do not underestimate the difficulty of this task, we are convinced that *collectively* accepting responsibility, and collectively seeking and granting forgiveness are necessary, because past hurts and traumas appear not to disappear readily with the passage of time. Only a determined effort on the part of society to deal with the past can end the cycles of revenge and ensure lasting peace. On the other hand, we return again to that paradox and challenge – forgiveness as intervention is not likely to be considered, as long as social identities are perceived to be threatened. Forgiveness by its very nature is counter to group distinctiveness. In the forgiveness process, those who forgive must look beyond violent acts to the humanity they share with their victimisers and recognize the inherent equality between them. Ultimately in forgiveness, the *cognitive* operation of *identity*, as presented by Enright *et al.* (1994), threatens the *social identity* operation of *distinctiveness*, and as such likely will not receive widespread welcome in settings of intergroup violence. That is, until there is a decrease in the investment in, or greater certainty in the persistence and valuing of, each group's identity and social memories (see Roe *et al.*, 1999). Of the two, we consider the latter to be the more viable route to peace.

References

25 Code of Federal Regulations, Section 83.1 (1978, revised April 1985).

Aizpurua, J.P.S. (1992) 'Adjustment to Modernity' in J.H. Elliot (ed.), *The Hispanic World* (pp. 97–128). London: Thames and Hudson.

Almog, O. (1992) 'Israeli war memorials: A semi-logical analysis' Master thesis submitted to Tel-Aviv University, Tel Aviv, Israel.

Alonso, A. (1988) 'The Effects of Truth: Re-Presentations of the Past and the Imagining of Community' *Journal of Historical Sociology*, 1, 33–57.

Anderson, B. (1983) *Imagined Communities: The rise of the modern state*. London: Verso.

Anderson, J.R. and L.J. Schooler (1991) 'Reflections of the environment in memory' *Psychological Science*, 2, 396–408.

Antze, P. and M. Lambek (eds) (1996) *Tense past: Cultural essays in trauma and memory*. London: Routledge.

Arthur, A. (1974) *'Attitude change and neuroticism among Northern Irish children participating in joint-faith holidays'* Queen's University of Belfast, M.Sc. Thesis.

Ascherson, N. (1995) *Black Sea*. London: Jonathan Cape.

Asmal, K., L. Asmal and Roberts, R.S. (1996) *Reconciliation through truth: A reckoning of Apartheid's criminal governance*. Cape Town: David Roberts Publishers.

Austin, R. (ed.) (1985) *History in schools: Essays on history teaching in the classroom*. Coleraine, Northern Ireland: University of Ulster.

Azaryahu, M. (1995) *State cults: Celebrating independence and commemorating the fallen in Israel 1948–1956*. Beer Sheva: Ben-Gurion University of the Negev Press (in Hebrew).

Babey, S.H., S. Queller and S.B. Klein (1998) 'The role of expectancy violating behaviors in the representation of trait knowledge: A summary-plus-exception model of social memory' *Social Cognition*, 16, 287–339.

Bandura, A. (1982) 'Self-efficacy mechanism in human agency' *American Psychologist*, 37, 122–47.

Bangerter, A., M. Von Cranach and C. Arn (1997) 'Collective remembering in the communicative regulation of group action: A functional approach' *Journal of Language and Social Psychology*, 16, 365–88.

Barash, D.P. (1991) *Introduction to peace studies*. Belmont, CA: Wadsworth.

Barkley, J. (1976) *Do myths influence people? Irish history: Fact or fiction?* Belfast: The Central Churches Committee for Community Work.

Bar-Tal, D. (1988) 'Delegitimizing relations between Israeli Jews and Palestinians: A social psychological analysis' in J. Hoffman (ed.), *Arab-Jewish relations in Israel: A quest in human understanding* (pp. 217–48). Bristol, Indiana: Wyndham Hall Press.

Bar-Tal, D. (1989) 'Delegitimization: The extreme case of stereotyping and prejudice' in D. Bar-Tal, C. Graumann, A.W. Kruglanski and W. Stroebe (eds), *Stereotyping and prejudice: Changing conceptions* (pp. 169–88). New York: Springer-Verlag.

Bar-Tal, D. (1990a) 'Causes and consequences of delegitimization: Models of conflict and ethnocentrism' *Journal of Social Issues*, 46(1), 65–81.

Bar-Tal, D. (1990b) 'Israeli-Palestinian conflict: A cognitive analysis' *International Journal of Intercultural Relations*, 14, 7–29.

Bar-Tal, D. (1993) 'Patriotism as fundamental beliefs of group members' *Politics and the Individual*, 3, 45–62.

Bar-Tal, D. (1998) 'Shared beliefs in a society' *International Journal of Conflict Management*, 9, 22–50.

Bar-Tal, D. (2000) *Societal beliefs of ethos*. Thousand Oakes, CA: Sage.

Barthes, R. (1957/1972) *Mythologies*. New York: The Noonday Press.

Bartlett, F.C. (1932/1995) *Remembering: A study in experimental social psychology*. Cambridge: Cambridge University Press.

Barton, K.C. (1998) *'Best not to forget them: Positionality and students' ideas about historical significance in Northern Ireland'* paper presented at the annual meeting of the American Educational research Association, April, San Diego.

Barton, K.C. (2001) 'You'd be wanting to know about the past: Social contexts of children's historical understanding in Northern Ireland and the United States' *Comparative Education*, 37, 89–106.

Barton, K.C. and L.S. Levstik (1998) 'It wasn't a good part of history: National identity and ambiguity in students' explanations of historical significance' *Teachers College Record*, 99, 478–513.

Baumeister, R.F. and S. Hastings (1997) 'Distortions of collective memory: How groups flatter and deceive themselves' in J.W. Pennebaker, D. Paez and B. Rime (eds), *Collective memory of political events: Social psychological perspectives* (pp. 277–93). Mahwah, NJ: Erlbaum.

Beckham, S.D. (1997) *Petition for federal acknowledgment, Cowlitz Tribe, State of Washington: Criteria 54.7(a)–(g)*. Supplemented by exhibits, enrolment files and oversize items, submitted to the Branch of Acknowledgment and Research, Bureau of Indian Affairs, Washington DC, Cowlitz Indian Tribe, Longview, WA.

Beckham, S.D. (1987) *'Without statutory authority: The termination of the Chinook and Cowlitz Tribes'* paper presented at the Eightieth Annual Meeting of the American Historical Association, Pacific Coast Branch, August.

Beer, F.A. (1981) *Peace against war: The ecology of international violence*. San Francisco: W.H. Freeman and Company.

Ben-Amos, A. (1993) 'Monuments and memory in French nationalism' *History and Memory*, 5, 50–81.

Berlin, I. (1979) 'Nationalism: Past Neglect and Present Power' *Partisan review*, 46, 344–61.

Berry, J.W. (1980) 'Acculturation as varieties of adaptation' in A.M. Padilla (ed.), *Acculturation: Theory, models, and some new findings* (pp. 9–25). Boulder, CO: Westview Press.

Berry, J.W. (1984) 'Cultural relations in plural societies: Alternatives to segregation and their socio-psychological implications' in N. Miller and M.B. Brewer (eds), *Groups in conflict: The psychology of desegregation* (pp. 11–27). Orlando, FL: Academic Press.

Berry, J.W. (1997) 'Immigration, Acculturation, and Adaptation' *Applied Psychology: An International Review*, 46, 5–68.

Berry, J.W. (1994) *Cross-cultural health psychology*. Keynote address presented at the 23rd International Congress of Applied Psychology, July, Madrid, Spain.

Billig, M. (1995) *Banal nationalism*. London: Sage.

Bloomfield, Sir Kenneth (1998) 'We will remember them' Report of the Northern Ireland Victims Commission, Sir Kenneth Bloomfield, KCB.

Bourdon, J. (1992) 'Television and political memory' *Media, Culture and Society*, 14, 541–60.

Boutros-Ghali, B. (1992) *An agenda for peace*. New York: United Nations.

Bowyer-Bell, J. (1978) *A Time of Terror*. Basic Books: USA.

Branch of Acknowledgment and Research (1997) 'Summary status of acknowledgment cases' Technical report, Bureau of Indian Affairs, Department of Interior, Government of the United States, 13 February.

Breakwell, G.M. (1986) *Coping with threatened identities*. London: Methuen.

Breakwell, G.M. (1994a) 'The Echo of Power: A Framework for Social Psychological Research' *The Psychologist*, February, 65–72.

Breakwell, G.M. (1994b) 'Identity processes and social changes' in G.M. Breakwell and E. Lyons (eds), *Changing European identities: Social psychological analyses of social change* (pp. 13–27). Oxford: Butterworth-Heinemann.

Brecher, M. (1984) 'International crises, protracted conflicts' *International Interactions*, 11, 237–98.

Bretherton, D. and D. Mellor (1998) 'Reconciliation between Black and White Australia: The role of memory' in E. Cairns (Chair), *The role of memories in ethnic conflict*. Symposium conducted at the 24th International Congress of Applied Psychology, August, San Francisco, CA.

Bronkhorst, D. (1995) *Truth and reconciliation: Obstacles and opportunities for human rights*. Amsterdam: Amnesty International.

Brown, M.E. (1997) 'Causes and Implications of Ethnic Conflict' in M. Guibernau and J. Rex (eds), *The Ethnicity Reader: Nationalism, Multiculturalism and Migration* (pp. 80–100). Cambridge: Polity Press.

Brown, R. and J. Kulik (1977) 'Flashbulb memories' *Cognition*, 5, 73–99.

Bruner, J. (1994) 'The remembered self' in U. Neisser and R. Fivush (eds), *The remembering self. Construction and accuracy in the self narrative* (pp. 41–54). Cambridge: Cambridge University Press.

Buckley, A.D. and M.C. Kenney (1995) *Negotiating identity: Rhetoric, metaphor, and social drama in Northern Ireland*. Washington DC: Smithsonian Institution Press.

Burton, J.W. (1969) *Conflict and communication*. London: Macmillan.

Burton, M. (1998) 'The South African Truth and Reconciliation Commission: Looking back, moving forward – revisiting conflicts, striving for peace' in B. Hamber (ed.), *Past imperfect: Dealing with the past in Northern Ireland and societies in transition*, (pp. 13–24). Derry/Londonderry: University of Ulster – INCORE.

Butler, T. (ed.) (1989) *Memory: History, Culture and the Mind*. Oxford: Basil Blackwell.

Cairns, E. (1982) 'Intergroup conflict in Northern Ireland' in H. Tajfel (ed.), *Social Identity and Intergroup Relations* (pp. 277–97). Cambridge: Cambridge University Press.

Cairns, E., C.A. Lewis, O. Mumcu and N. Waddell (1998) 'Memories of recent ethnic conflict and the relationship to social identity' *Peace and Conflict: Journal of Peace Psychology*, 4, 13–22.

Cairns, E. and C.A. Lewis (1999) 'Collective memory, political violence and mental health in Northern Ireland' *British Journal of Psychology*, 90, 25–33.

Cairns, E., F. McClernon, C.A. Lewis and M. Hewstone (2001) 'Correlates of Intergroup Forgiveness in Northern Ireland' The British Psychological Society Northern Ireland Branch Annual Conference, Cavan, 11–13 May.

Capps, W.H. (ed.) (1976) *Seeing with a native eye.* New York: Harper and Row.

Chirot, D. (2001) 'Theories of Nationalism and Ethnic Conflict: An Introduction' in D. Chirot and M. Seligman (eds), *Ethnopolitical Warfare: Causes, Consequences, and Possible Solutions* (pp. 3–27). American Psychological Association: Washington, DC.

Clark, N.K., G.M. Stephenson and B.H. Kniveton (1990) 'Social Remembering: Quantitative aspects of individual and collaborative remembering by police officers and students' *British Journal of Social Psychology*, 81, 73–94.

Cohen, A.P. (1975) *The Management of Myths: The Politics of Legitimation.* Newfoundland, Canada: Newfoundland Social and Economic Studies 14: University of Newfoundland.

Cohen, A.P. (1985) *The Symbolic Construction of Community.* London: Tavistock.

Cohen, P.S. (1969) 'Theories of Myth' *Man*, 4, 337–53.

Connerton, P. (1989) *How societies remember.* Cambridge: Cambridge University Press.

Cornbleth, C. (1998) An American curriculum? *Teachers College Record*, 99, 622–46.

Coser, L. (1956) *The functions of social conflict.* New York: Free Press.

Coser, L.A. (1992) 'The Revival of the Sociology of Culture: The case of Collective Memory' *Sociological Forum*, 7, 365–73.

Counsell, C. (1999) 'Editorial' *Teaching History*, 96, 2.

Couper, D. (1998) 'Forgiveness in the community: Views from an episcopal priest and former chief of police' in R.D. Enright and J. North (eds), *Exploring Forgiveness* (pp. 121–30). Wisconsin: University of Wisconsin Press.

Csikszentmihalyi, M. and E. Rochberg-Halton (1981) *The Meaning of Things: a study of domestic symbols and the self.* Cambridge: Cambridge University Press.

Darby, J. (1974) 'History in the schools' *Community Forum*, 4 (2), 37–42.

Darby, J. (1976) *Conflict in Northern Ireland: The development of a polarized community.* Dublin: Gill and Macmillan.

Darby, J. (1983) *Northern Ireland. The Background to the Conflict.* Belfast: Appletree Press.

Darby, J., D. Murray, D. Batts, S. Dunn, S. Farren and J. Harris (1977). *Education and community in Northern Ireland: Schools Apart?* Coleraine, Northern Ireland: New University of Ulster.

Department of Education Northern Ireland (1990) 'Proposals for History in the Northern Ireland Curriculum' Belfast: Northern Ireland Curriculum Council.

Devine-Wright, P. (1999) '*Tracing the hand of history: the role of social memories in the Northern Ireland conflict*' unpublished doctoral dissertation, Department of Psychology, University of Surrey, Guildford.

Devine-Wright, P. (2001a) 'History and identity in Northern Ireland – an exploratory investigation of the role of historical commemorations in contexts of conflict' *Peace and Conflict: Journal of Peace Psychology*, 297–315.

Devine-Wright, P. (2001b) 'Identity, memory and the social status of groups in Northern Ireland: Relating processes of social remembering with beliefs about the structure of society' *Irish Journal of Psychology*, 22 (2), 1–21.

Devine-Wright, P. and E. Lyons (1997) 'Remembering Pasts and Representing Places: The Construction of National Identities in Ireland' *Journal of Environmental Psychology*, 17, 33–45.

DiBlasio, F.A. (1992) 'Forgiveness in psychotherapy: Comparison of older and younger therapists' *Journal of Psychology and Christianity*, 11, 181–7.

DiBlasio, F.A. (1993) 'The role of social workers' religious beliefs in helping family members forgive' *Families in Society*, 74, 163–70.

Doise, W. (1986) *Levels of Explanation in Social Psychology*. Cambridge: Cambridge University Press.

Donagan, A. (1979) *The theory of morality*. Chicago: University of Chicago Press.

Douglas, M. (1986) *How Institutions Think*. London: Routledge and Keegan Paul.

Druckman, D. (2001) 'Nationalism and war: A social-psychological perspective' in D.J. Christie, R.V. Wagner and D.D. Winter (eds), *Peace, conflict, and violence: Peace psychology for the 21st century* (pp. 49–65). Upper Saddle River, NJ: Prentice Hall.

Durkheim, E. (1912/1947) *The Elementary Forms of Religious Life*. New York: The Free Press.

Dyal, J.A. and D. McKenzie-Mohr (1992) 'Psychological contributions to education for social responsibility' in S. Staub and P. Green (eds), *Psychology and social responsibility: Facing global challenges* (pp. 366–80). New York: New York University Press.

Edwards, D. and Middleton, D. (1987) 'Conversation and Remembering: Bartlett revisited' *Applied Cognitive Psychology*, 1, 77–92.

Eisenstadt, S.N. (1973) *The Israeli society: Background, development and problems (2nd edn)*. Jerusalem: Magnes Press (in Hebrew).

Eldridge, A.F. (1979) *Images of conflict*. New York: St. Martin's Press – now Palgrave Macmillan.

Eliade, M. (1963) *Myth and Reality*. New York: Harper and Row.

Enright, R.D., M.J. Santos and R. Al-Mabuk (1989) 'The adolescent as forgiver' *Journal of Adolescence*, 12, 95–110.

Enright, R.D. and R.L. Zell (1989) 'Problems encountered when we forgive one another' *Journal of Psychology and Christianity*, 8, 52–60.

Enright, R.D. and The Human Development Study Group (1991) 'The Moral Development of Forgiveness' in W. Kurtines and J. Gerwitz (eds), *Moral Behaviour and Development* (Vol. 1) (pp. 123–52). Hillsdale, NJ: Erlbaum.

Enright, R.D. and C.T. Coyle (1994) 'Researching the process model of forgiveness within psychological interventions' in E.L. Worthington (ed.), *Dimensions of Forgiveness: Psychological Research and Theological Perspectives* (pp. 139–61). Radno, PA: Templeton Foundation Press.

Enright, R.D. and The Human Development Study Group (1994) 'Piaget on the Moral Development of Forgiveness: Identity or Reciprocity?' *Human Development*, 37, 63–80.

Enright, R.D. and The Human Development Study Group (1996) 'Counselling within the forgiveness triad: On forgiving, receiving forgiveness, and self-forgiveness' *Counselling and Values*, 40, 107–26.

Erikson, E.H. (1968) *Identity: Youth and Crisis*. New York: Norton.

Essed, P. (1990) *Everyday racism: Reports from women of two cultures*. Claremont, Ca: Hunter House Inc.

Essed, P. (1991) *Understanding everyday racism: An interdisciplinary theory.* Newbury Park, Ca.: Sage Publications.

Fairleigh, J. (1975) 'Personality and social factors in religious prejudice' in Fairleigh *et al.*, *Sectarianism – Roads to Reconciliation.* Papers read at the 22nd Annual Summer School of the Social Study conference, St. Augustine's College, Dungarvan, 3–10 August (Dublin: Three Candles).

Faith and Politics Group (1997) *New Pathways: Developing a peace process in Northern Ireland.* Belfast: Community Relations Council.

Falconer, A.D. (1988) 'The reconciling power of forgiveness' in A.D. Falconer (ed.), *Reconciling memories* (pp. 84–98). Blackrock, Co. Dublin: Columba Press.

Falconer, A.D. (ed.). (1988) *Reconciling Memories.* Dublin: The Columba Press.

Feagin, J.R. and M.P. Sikes (1994) *Living with racism: The black middle-class experience.* Boston: Beacon Press.

Feldman, F. (1992) *Confrontations with the reaper: A philosophical study of the nature and value of death.* New York: Oxford University Press.

Fennell, D. (1993) *Heresy.* Belfast, Northern Ireland: Blackstaff Press.

Finch, J. (1993) '"It's great to have someone to talk to": Ethics and politics of interviewing women' in M. Hammersley (ed.), *Social research: Philosophy, politics and practice* (pp. 166–80). Milton Keynes: Open University Press.

Finkenauer, C., L. Gisle and O. Luminet (1997) 'When Individual Memories are Socially Shaped: Flashbulb Memories of Sociopolitical Events' in J.W. Pennebaker, D. Paez and B. Rimé (eds), *Collective Memory of Political Events: Social Psychological Perspectives* (pp. 191–207). New Jersey: Lawrence Erlbaum Associates.

Fitzgibbons, R.P. (1986) 'The cognitive and emotional uses of forgiveness in the treatment of anger' *Psychotherapy*, 23, 629–33.

Fitzpatrick, D.A. (1986) 'We are Cowlitz: Traditional and emergent ethnicity' Doctoral dissertation, University of Washington, Seattle, WA, on file with University Microfilms International, Ann Arbor, MI.

Fowler, D.D. (1972) *In a sacred manner we live: Photographs of the North American Indian by Edward S. Curtis.* New York: Weathervane Books.

Fox, R. (1994) 'Nationalism: Hymns ancient and modern' *The National Interest*, 35, 51–7.

Francis, L.J. (1992) 'Reliability and validity of a short measure of attitude towards Christianity among nine to eleven-year-old pupils in England' *Collected Original Resources in Education*, 16, 1, fiche 3, A02.

Frazer, J.G. (1918) *Folklore in the Old Testament*, Volume 1. London: Macmillan.

Frijda, N.H. (1997) 'Commemorating' in J.W. Pennebaker, D. Paez and B. Rimé (eds), *Collective memory of political events: Social psychological perspectives* (pp. 103–27). Mahwah, NJ: Lawrence Erlbaum and Associates.

Frisch, M. (1989) 'American History and the Structures of Collective Memory: A modest exercise in Empirical Iconography'. *Journal of American History*, 75 (March), 1130–55.

Fromm, E. (1984) *The anatomy of human destructiveness.* Great Britain: Penguin Books.

Frost, B. (1998) *Struggling to forgive: Nelson Mandela and South Africa's search for reconciliation.* Great Britain: HarperCollins Publishers.

Gallagher, A.M. (1989) *Majority minority review 1: Education and religion in Northern Ireland.* Coleraine, Northern Ireland: University of Ulster.

Gallagher, C. (1998) 'The future of history: A plea for relevance?' paper given to the Schools History Project Conference, Leeds, April.

Gallagher, C. and A. McCully (1997) 'The contribution of curriculum enquiry projects to educational policies in Northern Ireland' internal paper UNESCO Centre, School of Education, University of Ulster, Coleraine.

Galnoor, I. (1982) *Steering the polity: Communication and politics in Israel.* Beverly Hills, CA: Sage.

Galtung, J. (1969) 'Conflict as a way of life' in H. Freeman (ed.), *Progress in mental health.* London: Churchill.

Gaskell, G.D. and D.B. Wright (1997) 'Group Differences in Memory for a Political Event' in J.W. Pennebaker, D. Paez and B. Rime (eds), *Collective Memory of Political Events: Social Psychological Perspectives* (pp. 175–89). Mahwah, NJ: Lawrence Erlbaum.

Gellner, E. (1983) *Nations and Nationalism.* Oxford: Blackwell.

Giddens, A. (1985) *The Nation State and Violence.* Cambridge: Polity Press.

Giffin, V., E. McDonagh, J. Dunlop, J. McMaster and G. Smyth (1996) 'Brokenness, forgiveness, healing and peace' lectures delivered in St Anne's Cathedral, Belfast, Lent.

Gillis, J.R. (ed.) (1994) *Commemorations: The Politics of National Identity.* Princeton, N.J.: Princeton University Press.

Girard, M. and E. Mullet (1997) 'Forgiveness in adolescents, young, middle-aged and older adults'. *Journal of Adult Development,* 4 (4), 209–20.

Gochman, C. and Z. Maoz (1984) 'Militarized interstate disputes, 1816–1976: Procedures, patterns and insights' *Journal of Conflict Resolution,* 28, 585–616.

Goertz, G. and P. Diehl (1992) 'The empirical importance of enduring rivalries' *International Interactions,* 18, 151–63.

Gorsuch, R.L. and J.Y. Hao (1993) 'Forgiveness: An exploratory factor analysis and its relationship to religious variables' *Review of Religious Research,* 34, 333–47.

Gover, K. (2000) Final determination to acknowledge the Cowlitz Indian Tribe. *Federal Register,* 65 (34), 18 February, 8436–8.

Graumann, C. (1983) 'On Multiple Identities' *International Social Science Journal,* 35, 309–21.

Graves, R. (1955) *The Greek Myths, Volume 1.* Harmondsworth: Penguin.

Greer, J. (1985) 'Visiting the other side in Northern Ireland: Openness and attitudes to religion among Catholic and Protestant adolescents' *Journal for the Scientific Study of Religion,* 24 (3), 275–92.

Grundy, K.W. and M.A. Weinstein (1974) *The ideologies of violence.* Columbus, Ohio: Charles E. Merrill.

Haebich, A. (2000) *Broken circles: Fragmenting indigenous families 1800–2000.* Perth, Western Australia: Fremantle Art Centre Press.

Hakvoort, I. (1996) 'Conceptualization of peace and war from childhood through adolescence: A social-cognitive approach' Doctoral Dissertation. Amsterdam: University of Amsterdam, Faculteit der Psychologie.

Hakvoort, I. and L. Oppenheimer (1993) 'Children and adolescents' conceptions of peace, war and strategies to attain peace: A Dutch case study' *Journal of Peace Research,* 30 (1), 65–77.

Hakvoort, I. and Oppenheimer, L. (1998) 'Understanding peace and war: A review of developmental psychology research' *Developmental Review,* 18, 353–89.

Hakvoort, I. and Hagglund, S. (2001) 'Concepts of peace and war as described by Dutch and Swedish girls and boys' *Peace and Conflict: Journal of Peace Psychology*, 7 (1), 29–44.

Halbwachs, M. (1925) *Les Cadres Sociaux de la Memoire*, p. 404. Paris: F. Alcan.

Halbwachs, M. (1941) *La Topographie legendaire des evangiles en terre sainte*. Paris: Presses Universitaires.

Halbwachs, M. (1950/1968) *Le memoire collective*. Paris: Presses Universitaire de France.

Halbwachs, M. (1950/1980) *The Collective Memory*. New York: Harper and Row.

Halbwachs, M. (1992) *On collective memory*. Chicago: University of Chicago Press.

Halliday, W. (ed). (1915) *Propatria: A book of patriotic verse*. London: J.M. Dent and Sons.

Hamber, B. (1997) 'Living with the legacy of impunity: Lessons for South Africa about truth, justice and crime in Brazil' *Unisa Latin American Report*, 13 (2), 4–16. Pretoria: Unisa Centre for Latin American Studies, University of South Africa.

Hamber, B. (1998a) 'The Burdens of truth: An evaluation of the psychological support services initiatives undertaken by the South African Truth and Reconciliation Commission' *American Imago*, 55 (1), Spring, 9–28.

Hamber, B. (ed.) (1998b) *Past Imperfect: Dealing with the past in Northern Ireland and societies in transition*. Derry/Londonderry: University of Ulster – INCORE.

Hamber, B. (2000) 'Repairing the irreparable: Dealing with double-binds of making reparations for crimes of the past' *Ethnicity and Health*, 5 (3/4), 215–26.

Hamber, B. (2001) 'Does the truth heal? A psychological perspective on the political strategies for dealing with the legacy of political violence' in N. Biggar (ed.), *Burying the past: Making peace and doing justice after civil conflict* (pp. 131–48). Washington: George Town University Press.

Hamber, B. and S. Kibble (1999) 'From truth to transformation: South Africa's Truth and Reconciliation Commission' briefing paper. London: Catholic Institute for International Relations (CIIR).

Handelman, D. (1990) *Models and mirrors: Towards an anthropology of public events*. Cambridge: Cambridge University Press.

Hargrave, T.D. and J.N. Sells (1997) 'The development of a forgiveness scale' *Journal of Marital and Family Therapy*, 23, 41–63.

Harland, J., M. Ashworth, R. Bower, S. Hogarth, A. Montgomery and H. Moor (1999) 'Real curriculum: At the start of Key Stage 3' Report Two from the Northern Ireland Curriculum Cohort Study. Berkshire, England: National Foundation for Educational Research.

Hayes, G. (1998) 'We suffer our memories: Thinking about the past, healing and reconciliation'. *American Imago*, 55 (1), 29–50.

Hebl, J.H. and R.D. Enright (1993) 'Forgiveness as a psychotherapeutic goal with elderly females' *Psychotherapy*, 30 (4), 658–67.

Helms, J.E. (1990) *Black and white racial identity: Theory research and practice*. New York: Greenwood Press.

Helms, J.E. (1995) 'An update on Helms' white and people of color racial identity models' in J.A.G. Penetrate, J.A.M. Cassias, L.A. Suzuki and C.A. Alexander (eds), *Handbook of multicultural counseling* (pp. 181–98). Thousand Oaks, CA: Sage.

Hilton, D.J., H.P. Erb, M. Dermot and D.J. Molian (1996) 'Social Representations of History and Attitudes to European Unification in Britain, France and

Germany' in G.M. Breakwell and E. Lyons (eds) *Changing European Identities: Social Psychological Analyses of Social Change* (pp. 275–95). Oxford: Butterworth Heinemann.

Ho, D.Y. (1985) 'Psychological aspects of slavery and colonialism' *Bulletin of the Hong Kong Psychological Society*, 115, 337–42.

Hobsbawm, E. (1983) 'Introduction: Inventing Traditions' in E. Hobsbawm and T. Ranger (eds) *The Invention of Tradition* (pp. 1–14). Cambridge University Press: Cambridge.

Hobsbawm, E. (1990) *Nations and Nationalism since 1780*. Cambridge: Cambridge University Press.

Hobsbawm, E. and T. Ranger (eds) (1983) *The Invention of Tradition*. Cambridge University Press: Cambridge.

hooks, B. (1993) *Sisters of the yam: Black women and self-recovery*. Toronto: Between the Lines.

Horowitz, D.L. (1985) *Ethnic Groups in Conflict*. Berkeley, London: University of California Press.

Human Rights and Equal Opportunity Commission (1997a) *Bringing them home: National Inquiry into the separation of Aboriginal and Torres Strait Islander children from their families*. Canberra: Australian Government Publishing Service.

Human Rights and Equal Opportunity Commission (1997b) *Bringing them home: A guide to the findings and recommendations of the National Inquiry into the separation of Aboriginal and Torres Strait Islander children from their families*. Sydney: Human Rights and Equal Opportunity Commission.

Human Rights and Equal Opportunity Commission (1999) 'Real curriculum: At the start of Key Stage 3' Report Two from the Northern Ireland Curriculum Cohort Study. Berkshire, England: National Foundation for Educational Research.

Hunter, J.A., M. Stringer and R.P. Watson (1991) 'Ingroup violence and intergroup attributions' *British Journal of Social Psychology*, 30, 261–6.

Ignatieff, M. (1984) 'Soviet war memorials', History Workshop, issue 17, 157–63.

Ignatieff, M. (1993) *Blood and Belonging: Journeys into the New Nationalism*. London: BBC/Chatto & Windus.

Ignatieff, M. (1997) 'Narration in the documentary Getting Away with Murder' *Special Correspondent Programme*, BBC2.

Ignatieff, M. (1998) *The warrior's honor: Ethnic war and the modern conscience*. London: Chatto & Windus.

Inouye, D. (1989) Indian Federal Acknowledgment Administrative Procedures Act. *Congressional Record--Senate*, S2846, 16 March.

Irwin, J. (1979) 'The Cowlitz way a round of life' *Cowlitz Historical Quarterly*, 21 (1), 5–24.

Irwin-Zarecka, I. (1993) 'In search of Usable Pasts' *Society*, 30, 32–6.

Irwin-Zarecka, I. (1994) *Frames of Remembrance*. New Jersey: Transaction.

Jackson, A. (1992) 'Unionist Myths 1912–1985' *Past and Present*, 136, 164–85.

Jacobi, M. and D. Stokols (1983) 'The Role of Tradition in Group-Environment Relations' in N.R. Feimer and E.S. Geller (eds) *Environmental Psychology: Directions and Perspectives* (pp. 157–90). New York: Praeger.

James, W. (1910) 'The moral equivalent of war. International conciliation' reprinted in *Peace and Conflict: Journal of Peace Psychology*, 1, 17–26 (1995).

Janoff-Bulman, R. (1985) 'The aftermath of victimisation: Rebuilding shattered assumptions' in C.R. Figley (ed.), *Trauma and its wake* (pp. 15–36). NY: Brunner Mazel Publishers.

Jarman, N. (1998) *Material conflicts: Parades and visual displays in Northern Ireland.* New York: Berg.

Jelin, E. (1998) 'The minefields of memory' *NACLA Report on the Americas, Report on Memory*, 33 (2).

Johnson, C., S.H. Ratwik and T.J. Sawyer (1987) 'The evocative significance of kin terms in patriotic speech' in V. Reynolds, V. Falger and I. Vine (eds), *The sociobiology of ethnocentrism: Evolutionary dimensions of xenophobia, discrimination, racism and nationalism* (pp. 157–74). London: Croom Helm.

Johnson, G.R. (1997) 'The evolutionary roots of patriotism' in D. Bar-Tal and E. Staub (eds), *Patriotism in the lives of individuals and nations* (pp. 45–90). Chicago: Nelson-Hall.

Johnston, N. (1994) 'Sculpting Heroic Histories: celebrating the centenary of the 1798 rebellion in Ireland' *Transactions of the Institute of British Geographers*, 19, 78–93.

Joyce, J. (1987) *Dubliners*. Grafton Books: London.

Jung, C.G. (1969) *The structure and dynamics of the psyche*, 2nd edn. Princetown, NJ: Princeton University Press.

Kammen, M. (1991) *Mystic chords of memory: The transformation of tradition in American culture*. NY: Knopf.

Katz, D. (1960) 'The functional approach to the study of attitudes' *Public Opinion Quarterly*, 24, 163–204.

Kleinig, J. (1991) *Valuing life*. Princeton: Princeton University Press.

Kohlberg, L. (1984) *Essays in Moral Development: Vol. II. The Psychology of Moral Development: Moral Stages Their Nature and Validity*. San Francisco: Harper & Row.

Kriesberg, L. (1993) 'Intractable conflicts' *Peace Review*, 5, 417–21.

Kriesberg, L. (1998) 'Intractable conflicts' in E. Weiner (ed.), *The handbook of interethnic coexistence* (pp. 332–42). New York: Continuum.

Kuper, S. (1998) *Football against the enemy*. London: Phoenix.

La Farge, P. (1992) 'Teaching social responsibility in the schools' in S. Staub and P. Green (eds), *Psychology and social responsibility: Facing global challenges* (pp. 345–65). New York: New York University Press.

Lame Deer and R. Erdoes (1972) *Lame Deer seeker of visions*. New York: Simon & Schuster.

Lapsley, M. (1997) Healing the memory: Cutting the cord between victim and perpetrator – Interview with Father Michael Lapsley by Hannes Siebert. *Track Two*, 6 (3 and 4), p. 46.

Larsen, S.F. (1988) 'Remembering without experiencing: Memory for reported events' in U. Neisser and E. Winograd (eds), *Remembering Reconsidered: Ecological and traditional approaches to the study of memory* (pp. 326–55). Cambridge: Cambridge University Press.

Lee, P.J. (1984) 'Why learn history?' in A.K. Dickinson, P.J. Lee and P.J. Rogers (eds), *Learning history* (pp. 1–19). London: Heinemann Educational Books.

Lerner, M. (1980) *The belief in just world*. New York: Plenum.

Levinger, E. (1993) *War memorials in Israel*. Tel Aviv: Hakibbutz Hameuchad (in Hebrew).

Levi-Strauss, C. (1958) *Anthropologie structurale*. Paris: Plon.

Levi-Strauss, C. (1966) *The Savage Mind*. London: Weidenfeld & Nicolson.

Levstik, L.S. and K.C. Barton (2001) 'Committing acts of history: Mediated action, humanistic education, and participatory democracy' in W. Stanley (ed.), *Critical issues in social studies research for the 21st century*. Greenwich, CT: Information Age Publishing.

Lewis, C.A. and E. Cairns (1999) 'The impact of peace on the memories of the troubles'. The British Psychological Society Annual Conference, Belfast, Northern Ireland, 8–11 April, *Proceedings of the British Psychological Society*, 7 (2), 129.

Liebman, C.S. and E. Don-Yehiya (1983) *Civil religion in Israel: Traditional Judaism and political culture in the Jewish State*. Berkeley: University of California Press.

Lipstadt, D.E. (1993) *Denying the Holocaust: the growing assault on truth and memory*. Oxford: Maxwell Macmillan International.

Liu, J.H., M.S. Wilson, J. McClure and E. Ripowai Higgins (1999) 'Social Identity and the perception of history: cultural representations of Aotearoa/New Zealand'. *European Journal of Social Psychology*, 29, 1021–47.

Lynch, K. (1972) *What time is this place?* London: MIT Press.

Lyons, E.L. (1993) 'Coping with Social Change: Processes of Social Memory in the Reconstruction of Identities' paper presented at Changing European Identities: Social Psychological analyses of Social Change, Conference at Farnham Castle, Surrey, UK, 7–9 May.

Lyons, E.L. (1996) 'Coping with Social Change: Processes of Social Memory in the Reconstruction of Identities' in G.M. Breakwell and E. Lyons (eds), *Changing European Identities: Social psychological analyses of social change* (pp. 31–9). Oxford: Butterworth-Heinemann.

Mack, J. (1983) 'Nationalism and the Self' *Psychohistory Review*, 11, 47–69.

Magee, J. (1970) 'The teaching of Irish history in Irish schools' *The Northern Teacher*, 10 (1), 15–21.

Maier, C. (1988) *The unmasterable past: history, holocaust, and German national identity*. London: Harvard University Press.

Malin, A. (1994) 'Mothers who won't disappear' *Human Rights Quarterly*, 16 (1), 187–213.

Malinowski, B. (1948) 'Myth in primitive psychology' in *Magic, science and religion and other essays*. Boston: Beacon Press.

Mannheim, K. (1925/1952) 'The Problem of Generations' in *Essays on the Sociology of Knowledge*. London: Routledge and Kegan Paul.

Mauger, P.A., T. Freeman, A.G. McBride, J.E. Perry, D.C. Grove and K.E. McKinney (1992) 'The measurement of forgiveness: Preliminary research' *Journal of Psychology and Christianity*, 11, 170–80.

Mauss, M. (1998) *The gift: Forms and functions of exchange in archaic societies*. London: Routledge.

McAleavy, A. (1993) 'Using the attainment targets in Key Stage 3: AT2, Interpretations of History' *Teaching History*, 72, 14–17.

McBride, I. (1997) *The siege of Derry in Ulster Protestant mythology*. Dublin: Four Courts Press.

McConahay, J.B. and J.C. Hough Jr (1976) 'Symbolic racism' *Journal of Social Issues*, 32 (2), 22–45.

McCullough, M.E. and E.L. Worthington Jr (1994) 'Models of interpersonal forgiveness and their applications to counseling: Review and critique'. *Counseling and Values*, 39, 2–14.

McCullough, M.E., K.I. Pargament and C.E. Thoresen (eds). (2000) *Forgiveness: Theory, Research, and Practice*. New York: Guilford.

McCully, A. (1998) *The teaching of history in a divided community*. Strasbourg, France: Council of Europe.

McCully, A., M. O'Doherty and P. Smith (1999) 'The Speak Your Piece project: Exploring controversial issues in Northern Ireland' in L.R. Forcey and I.M. Harris (eds), *Peacebuilding for adolescents: Strategies for educators and community leaders* (pp. 119–38). New York: Peter Lang.

McFarlane, G. (1986) 'Violence in rural Northern Ireland: Social scientific models, folk explanations and local variation' in D. Riches (ed.), *The anthropology of violence* (pp. 184–203). Oxford: Basil Blackwell.

McKeever, C.F., S. Joseph and J. McCormack (1993) 'Memory of Northern Irish Catholics and Protestants for Violent Incidents and their Explanations for the 1981 Hunger Strike'. *Psychological Reports*, 73, 463–6.

McLernon, F., E. Cairns and M. Hewstone (1999) 'Northern Ireland: A time to forgive?' British Psychological Society Annual Conference, London, December.

McLernon, F., E. Cairns and M. Hewstone (2002) 'Views on forgiveness in Northern Ireland'. *Peace Review*, 14 (3), 285–90.

McLernon, F. and E. Cairns (2001) 'Impact of political violence on images of war and peace in the drawings of primary school children'. *Peace and Conflict: Journal of Peace Psychology*, 7 (1), 45–57.

Mead, G.H. (1938) *The Philosophy of the Act*. Chicago: Chicago University Press.

Mellor, D. (1998) 'Experiences of racism by Aboriginal Australians and Vietnamese immigrants' unpublished PhD thesis, University of Melbourne.

Mellor, D., D. Bretherton and L. Firth (2000) 'Everyday racism in Australia: The experience of Aboriginal Australians' paper presented at XXVII International Congress of Psychology, Stockholm, 23–28 July.

Middleton, D. and D. Edwards (1990) *Collective Memory*. London: Sage Publications.

Mitchell, C.R. (1981) *The structure of international conflict*. London: Macmillan.

Montville, J.V. (1993) 'The Healing Function in Political Conflict Resolution' in D.J.D. Sandole and H. van der Merwe (eds), *Conflict Resolution Theory and Practice: Integration and Application* (pp. 112–27). Manchester: Manchester University Press.

Montville, J.V. (1993). 'The Healing Function in Political Conflict' in D. Sandole and H. van der Merwe (eds), *Conflict Resolution: Theory and Practice* (pp. 112–28). Manchester: Manchester University Press.

Moscovici, S. (1988) 'Notes toward a description of social representations' *European Journal of Psychology*, 18, 211–50.

Mosse, G.L. (1990) *Fallen soldiers: Reshaping the memory of the world wars*. New York: Oxford University Press.

Mullet, E. and M. Girard (2000) 'Developmental and Cognitive points of view on forgiveness' in M.E. McCullough, K. Pargament and C.E. Thoresen (eds), *Forgiveness: Theory, Research and Practice* (pp. 111–32). New York: Guilford Press.

Mullet, E., A. Houdbine, S. Laumonier and M. Girard (1998) 'Forgivingness: Factor structure in a sample of young, middle-aged and elderly adults' *European Psychologist*, 3 (4), 1–9.

Munroe, R.L. and R.H. Munroe (1986) 'Field work in cross-cultural psychology' in W.J. Lonner and J.W. Berry (eds), *Field methods in cross-cultural research* (pp. 111–36). Beverly Hills, CA: Sage.

Murray, D. (1985) *Worlds apart: Segregated schools in Northern Ireland*. Belfast, Northern Ireland: Appletree Press.

Murray, D., A. Smith and U. Birthistle (1997) *Education in Ireland: A comparison of the education systems in Northern Ireland the Republic of Ireland*. Limerick, Ireland: Irish Peace Institute Research Centre, University of Limerick.

Nabokov, P. (ed.) (1991) *Native American testimony: A chronicle of Indian-White relations from prophecy to the present. 1492–1992*. New York: Viking Penguin.

Neal, A.G. (1998) *National trauma and collective memory: Major events in the American century*. New York and London: M.E. Sharpe.

Nietzsche, F. (1969) *Thus spoke Zarathustra*. London: Penguin.

Nora, P. (1989) 'Between Memory and History' *Les Lieux de Memoire. Representations*, 26, 7.

North, J. (1987) 'Wrongdoing and Forgiveness' *Philosophy*, 62, 499–508.

Northern Ireland Council for the Curriculum, Examinations and Assessment (2000). *Northern Ireland curriculum review phase 1 consultation*, Belfast.

O'Leary, B. and J. McGarry (1992) 'Auditing the Antagonism' in B. O'Leary and J. McGarry (eds), *The Politics of Antagonism: Understanding Northern Ireland Politics* (pp. 8–53). London: Athlone Press.

Oberschall, A. (ed.) (2001) *Ethnopolitical warfare: Causes, consequences and possible solutions* (pp. 119–50). Washington DC: American Psychological Association.

Olick, J.K. and J. Robbins (1998) 'Social Memory Studies: From Collective Memory to the Historical Sociology of Mnemonic Practices'. *Annual Review of Sociology*, 24, 105–40.

Oppenheimer, L. (1997) 'Obiettivi dell'educazione prosociale alla pace: L'istituzione della pace (Targets for prosocial behavior towards peace: The institution of peace)' *Terapia del Comportamento*, 14, 85–99.

Osgood, R.E. and R.W. Tucker (1967) *Force, order and justice*. Baltimore: John Hopkins Press.

Overing, J. (1997) 'The Role of Myth: An Anthropological perspective or The Reality of the Really Made-Up' in G. Hosking and G. Schopflin (eds) *Myths and Nationhood* (pp. 1–18). London, Hurst and Co.

Pareek, U. and T.V. Rao (1980) 'Cross-cultural surveys and interviewing' in H.C. Triandis and J.W. Berry (eds), *Handbook of cross-cultural Psychology methodology: volume 2* (pp. 127–79). Boston: Allyn and Bacon.

Pargament, K.I., M.E. McCullough and C.E. Thoresen (2000) 'The Frontiers of Forgiveness: Seven directions for psychological research and practice' in M.E. McCullough, K.I. Pargament and C.E. Thoresen (eds), *Forgiveness: Theory, Research, and Practice* (pp. 1–14). New York: Guilford Press.

Pauw, B.A. (1990) 'Widows and rituals: Danger in Sotho and Tswana communities' *African Studies*, 49 (2), 75–99.

Pennebaker, J.W. (1992) *On the Creation and Maintenance of Collective Memories*. Unpublished manuscript.

Pennebaker, J.W. and B.L. Banasik (1997) 'History as Social Psychology' in J.W. Pennebaker, D. Paez and B. Rimé (eds), *Collective memory of political events: Social psychological perspectives* (pp. 3–19). Mahwah, NJ: Lawrence Erlbaum and Associates.

Pennebaker, J.W., D. Paez and B. Rimé (eds) (1997) *Collective memory of political events: Social psychological perspectives*. Mahwah, NJ: Erlbaum.

Peters, S. (1998) 'Mythische waas rond oorlog moet verdwijnen (Mythical air surrounding the war has to disappear)'. *Historisch Nieuwsblad*, 7 (3), 18–23.

Peters, S. and M. Schuyt (1998) 'Weinig kennis, veel moralisme (Little knowledge, much moralism)' *Historisch Nieuwsblad*, 7 (3), 24–7.

Phillips, R., P. Goalen, A. McCully and S. Wood (1999) 'Four histories, one nation? History teaching, nationhood and a British identity' *Compare*, 29, 153–69.

Piaget, J. (1932/1965) *The Moral Judgement of the Child*. London: Routlege and Kegan Paul.

Piaget, J. (1948/1980) 'Le droit à l'éducation dans le monde actuel (The right to education in the present world)' in J. Piaget (ed.), *To understand is to invent: The future of education* (pp. 128–42). Hammondsworth, Middlesex, UK: Penguin.

Picard, R.G. (1991) 'How violence is justified in Sinn Fein's An Phoblacht' *Journal of Communication*, 41, Autumn, 90–103.

Poole, M.A. (1995) 'The spatial distribution of political violence in Northern Ireland. An update to 1993' in A. O'Day (ed.) *Terrorism's laboratory: The case of Northern Ireland* (pp. 27–45). Aldershot: Dartmouth.

Pope, K.S. (1996) 'Memory, abuse and science: questioning claims about the false memory syndrome epidemic' *American Psychologist*, 51, 957–74.

Power, F.C. (1994) 'Commentary' *Human Development*, 37, 81–5.

Procedures for establishing that an American Indian group exists as an Indian tribe. Final rule. 25 CFR Part 83. (1994, 25 February). *Federal Register*.

Proceedings of the Commission to Hold Treaties with the Indian Tribes of Washington Territory. Council with the Upper and Lower Chehalis, Lower Chinook, Cowlitz and Quinaiutl Indians. 20 February to 2 March 1855.

Purkhardt, S.C. (1993) *Transforming Social Representations: A social psychology of common sense and science*. London: Routledge.

Ramphele, M. (1996) 'Political widowhood in South Africa: The embodiment of ambiguity' *Daedalus*, 125 (1), 99–117.

Ray, V.F. (1982) *Expert testimony in Congressional Hearings on the judgment of the Cowlitz claims case*, Docket 118, 7 December.

Ray, V.F. (1966) *Handbook of Cowlitz Indians*. Seattle, WA: Northwest Copy Company.

Redfield, R., R. Linton and M.T. Herskovits (1936) 'Memorandum for the study of acculturation' *American Anthropologist*, 38, 149–52.

Reykowski, J. (1982) 'Social motivation' *Annual Review of Psychology*, 33, 123–54.

Richardson, L.F. (1960) *Statistics of dead quarrels*. Pittsburgh: Boxwood and Quadrangle.

Roblin, C.E. (1919) *Schedule of unenrolled Indians in western Washington*. RG 75: Records of the Bureau of Indian Affairs, National Archives, Washington DC.

Roe, M.D. (1991) 'Tribal identity and continuity in the Cowlitz modern community, Study 1: Cowlitz tribal leadership' Technical report submitted to the Cowlitz Tribal Council, Longview, WA. Document submitted to the Branch of

Acknowledgement and Research, Bureau of Indian Affairs, Department of Interior, Washington DC.

Roe, M.D. (1992) 'Cowlitz modern community. Study 2: General tribal membership' Technical report submitted to the Cowlitz Tribal Council, Longview, WA. Document submitted to the Branch of Acknowledgement and Research, Bureau of Indian Affairs, Department of Interior, Washington DC.

Roe, M.D. (1994) 'Cowlitz (Indian Tribe)' in M.B. Davis (ed.), *Native America in the Twentieth Century* (pp. 147–9). New York: Garland Publishing.

Roe, M.D. (1998) '*The reproduction of ethnic identity and ethnic memories in a Native American people: The Cowlitz Indians of southwestern Washington state*' paper presented at the symposium entitled The Role of Memories in Ethnic Conflict conducted at the 24th International Congress of Applied Psychology, San Francisco, California.

Roe, M.D., W. Pegg, K. Hodges and R.A. Trimm (1999) 'Forgiving the other side: Social identity and ethnic memories in Northern Ireland' in J.P. Harrington and E. Mitchell (eds), *Politics and performance in contemporary Northern Ireland* (pp. 122–56). Amherst, MA: University of Massachusetts Press.

Roe, M.D. (2002) 'Contemporary Catholic and Protestant Irish America: Social Identities, Forgiveness, and Attitudes toward The Troubles of Northern Ireland' *Eire-Ireland,* 37 (1, 2), 153–74.

Rogers, P.J. (1984) 'Why teach history?' in A.K. Dickinson, P.J. Lee and P.J. Rogers (eds), *Learning History* (pp. 10–38). London: Heinemann Educational Books.

Rolston, B. (1992) *Drawing Support: Murals in the North of Ireland.* Belfast, Northern Ireland: Beyond the Pale.

Rolston, B. (1995) *Drawing Support 2: Murals of War and Peace.* Belfast, Northern Ireland: Beyond the Pale.

Rolston, B. (1996) *Turning the page without closing the book: The right to truth in the Irish context.* Dublin: Irish Reporter Publications.

Rosenberg, T. (1995) *The Haunted land: Facing Europe's ghost after communism.* New York: Vintage.

Ross, F. (1997) 'Blood feuds and childbirth: The TRC as Ritual' *Track Two,* 6 (3 and 4), 9–11.

Ross, M.H. (2000) '"Good-Enough" isn't so bad. Thinking about success and failure in ethnic conflict management' *Peace and Conflict: Journal of Peace Psychology,* 6 (l), 27–47.

Rubin, J.Z., D.G. Pruitee and S.H. Kim (1994) *Social conflict: Escalation, stalemate, and settlement,* 2nd edn. New York: McGraw-Hill.

Ruby, R.H. and J.A. Brown (1981) *Indians of the Pacific Northwest: A history.* Norman, Oklahoma: University of Oklahoma Press.

Russell, J. (1974) 'Sources of conflict' *Northern Teacher,* 11 (3), 3–11.

Rutkoff, P.M. (1981) *Revenge and revision.* Athens: Ohio University Press.

Salters, J. (1970) 'Attitudes towards society in Protestant and Roman Catholic school children in Belfast' Queen's University of Belfast, M.Ed. Thesis.

Santner, E. (1992) 'History beyond the pleasure principle' in S. Friedlander (ed.), *Probing the limits of representation: Nazism and the Final Solution* (pp. 141–55). Cambridge, MA: Harvard University Press.

Scheff, T.J. (1994) *Bloody revenge: Emotions, nationalism and war.* Boulder: Westview Press.

Schudson, M. (1995) 'Dynamics of Distortion in Collective Memory' in D.L. Schacter (ed.), *Memory Distortion: How Minds, Brains, and Societies Reconstruct the Past* (pp. 346–64). Cambridge, Mass: Harvard University Press.

Schuman, H. and C. Reiger (1992) 'Collective memory and collective memories' in M.A. Conway, D.C. Rubin, H. Spinnler and W.A. Wagenaar (eds), *Theoretical Perspectives On Autobiographical Memory* (pp. 323–36). Dordrecht: Kluwer Academic Publishers.

Schumann, H. and J. Scott (1989) 'Generations and Collective Memories' *American Sociological Review*, 54, 359–81.

Schumann, H., H. Akiyama and B. Knaüper (1998) 'Collective Memories of Germans and Japanese about the Past Half-century' *Memory*, 6, 427–54.

Schumann, H., R.F. Belli and K. Bischiping (1997) 'The generational basis of historical knowledge' in J.W. Pennebaker, D. Paez and B. Rimé (eds), *Collective memory of political events: Social psychological perspectives*, (pp. 47–77). Mahwah, NJ: Lawrence Erlbaum.

Schwartz, B. (1982) 'The Social Context of Commemoration: A Study in Collective Memory' *Social Forces*, 61, 374–402.

Schwartz, B. (1986) 'The recovery of Masada: A study in Collective Memory' *The Sociological Quarterly*, 27, 147–64.

Schwartz, B. (1991a) 'Social Change and Collective Memory: The Democratisation of George Washington' *American Sociological Review*, 56, 221–36.

Schwartz, B. (1991b) 'Iconography and Collective Memory: Lincoln's Image in the American Mind' *The Sociological Quarterly*, 32, 301–19.

Scribner, S. and K. Beach (1993) 'An Activity Theory Approach to Memory' *Applied Cognitive Psychology*, 7, 185–90.

Seixas, P. (1993) 'The community of inquiry as a basis for knowledge and learning: The case of history' *American Educational Research Journal*, 30, 305–24.

Sells, J.N. and T.D. Hargrave (1998) 'Forgiveness: A review of the theoretical and empirical literature' *Journal of Family Therapy*, 20, 21–36.

Shamir, I. (ed.) (1976) *The perpetuation of the memory of the fallen and its meaning*. Tel Aviv: Ministry of Defence Press (in Hebrew).

Sherif, M. (1966) *Group conflict and Co-operation: Their Social Psychology*. London: Routlege and Kegan Paul.

Shils, E. (1981) *Tradition*. Chicago: University of Chicago Press.

Shriver, D.W. Jr (1998) 'Is there forgiveness in politics? Germany, Vietnam and America' in R.D. Enright and J. North (eds), *Exploring Forgiveness* (pp. 131–49). Wisconsin: University of Wisconsin Press.

Simpson, G. and van Zyl, P. (1995) 'South Africa's Truth and Reconciliation Commission' occasional paper. Johannesburg: Centre for the Study of Violence and Reconciliation.

Sivan, E. (1991) *The 1948 generation: Myth, profile and memory*. Tel Aviv: Maarchot.

Slagle, A. (1989) 'Unfinished justice: Completing the restoration and acknowledgment of California Indian Tribes' *The American Indian Quarterly*, 13 (4), 325–45.

Smedes, L.B. (1998) 'Stations on the Journey from Forgiveness to Hope' in E.L. Worthington (ed.), *Dimensions of Forgiveness: Psychological Research and Theological Perspectives* (p. 341). Radno, P.A: Templeton Foundation Press.

Smith, A. (1999) 'Education and the peace process in Northern Ireland' paper presented at the annual meeting of the American Educational Research Association, Montreal, April. [http://cain.ulst.ac.uk/issues/education/docs/smith99.htm]

Smith, A. and S. Dunn (1990) *Extending inter school links: An evaluation of contact between Protestant and Catholic pupils in Northern Ireland*. Coleraine, Northern Ireland: Centre for the Study of Conflict, University of Ulster.

Smith, A.D. (1984) 'National Identity and Myths of Ethnic Descent' *Research in Social Movements, Conflict and Change*, 7, 95–130.

Smith, A. D. (1996) 'LSE Annual Lecture: The Resurgence of Nationalism? Myth and memory in the renewal of nations' *British Journal of Sociology*, 47, 575–98.

Smith, D.A. (1993) 'The Ethnic Sources of Nationalism' in M.E. Brown (ed.), *Ethnic Conflict and International Security* (pp. 27–41). Princeton University Press: Princeton.

Speller, G. (1992) *Metamorphosis of place and the loss of shared memories*. Socio-Environmental Metamorphoses: Builtscape, Landscape, Ethnocscape, Euroscape. Proceedings of the IAPS 12 International Conference, Marmaras, Chalkidiki, Greece, 11–14 July.

Staub, E. (1999) 'The origins and prevention of genocide, mass killing, and other collective violence' *Peace and Conflict: Journal of Peace Psychology*, 5 (4), 303–36.

Stevens, D. (1986) *Forgiveness and reconciliation in political perspective. Doctrine on Life*. Irish Council of Churches, February.

Stewart, A.T.Q. (1977) *The narrow ground: Aspects of Ulster, 1909–1969*. Belfast, Blackstaff Press.

Stokols, D. and M. Jacobi (1984) 'Traditional, present oriented, and futuristic modes of group environment relations' in K.J. Gergen and M.M. Gergen (eds), *Historical Social Psychology* (pp. 303–24). New Jersey: Lawrence Erlbaum and Associates.

Straub, J. (1993) 'Collective Memory and Collective Pasts as Constituents of Culture: An Action–Theoretical and Culture Psychological Perspective' *Schweizerische Zeitschrift fur Psychologie*, 52, 114–21.

Stuckless, N. and R. Goranson (1994) 'A selected bibiliography of literature on revenge' *Psychological Reports*, 75, 803–11.

Suarez-Orozco, M. (1991) 'The heritage of enduring a dirty war: Psychological aspects of terror in Argentina' *The Journal of Psychohistory*, 18 (4), 469–505.

Subkoviak, M.J., R.D. Enright, C. Wu, E.A. Gassin, S. Freedman, L.M. Olson and I. Sarinooulos (1995) 'Measuring interpersonal forgiveness in late adolescence and middle adulthood' *Journal of Adolescence*, 18, 641–55.

Tajfel, H. and J.C. Turner (1986) 'The Social Identity Theory of intergroup behaviour' in S. Worchel and W.G. Austin (eds), *Psychology of Intergroup Relations* (pp. 7–24). Chicago: Illinois: Nelson-Hall.

Tajfel, H. (ed.). (1982) *Social identity and intergroup relations*. Cambridge: Cambridge University Press.

Thelen, D. (1989) 'Memory and American History' *Journal of American History*, 75, 1117–29.

Thompson, P. (1988) *The Voice of the Past*. Oxford: Oxford University Press.

Tollefson, K.D. (1992) 'The political survival of landless Puget Sound Indians' *American Indian Quarterly*, 16 (2), 135–49.

Tollefson, K.D., M.L. Abbott and E. Wiggins (1996) 'Tribal estates: A comparative and case study' *Ethnology*, 35 (4), 321–38.

Tolölyan, K. (1989) 'Narrative Culture and the Motivation of the Terrorist' in J. Shotter and K. Gergen (eds), *Texts of Identity* (pp. 99–118). London: Sage.

Trew, K. (1992) 'Social Psychological Research on the Conflict' *The Psychologist*, 5, 342–4.

Trimble, J.E. (1989) 'Multilinearity of acculturation: Person-situation interactions' in D.M. Keats, D. Munro and L. Mann (eds), *Heterogeneity in cross-cultural psychology* (pp. 173–86). Rockland, MA: Swets and Zeitlinger.

Tugwell, M. (1981) 'Politics and Propaganda of the Provisional IRA' *Terrorism*, 5, 13–40.

Turner, J.C., P.J. Oakes, S.A. Haslam and C. McGary (1994) 'Self and collective: Cognition and social context' *Personality and Social Psychology Bulletin*, 20, 454–63.

Turney-High, H.H. (1949) *Primitive war*. Columbia: University of South Carolina Press.

Tylor, Sir E.B. (1958) *The Origin of Culture*. New York: Harper.

Uzzell, D. and M.-L. Stig-Sorensen (1993) 'Constructing and Deconstructing National Identities: The Role of the Past in the Present' paper presented at Changing European Identities: Social Psychological analyses of Social Change, Conference at Farnham Castle, Surrey, UK 7–9 May.

Valsiner, J. (1998) *The guided mind: A sociogenetic approach to personality*. Cambridge, MA: Harvard University Press.

Verbeek, P. and F.B.M. de Waal (2001) 'Peacemaking among preschool children' *Peace and Conflict: Journal of Peace Psychology*, 7 (1), 5–28.

von der Dunk, H.W. (1990) *Voorbij de verboden drempel: De shoah in ons geschiedbeeld* (Beyond the forbidden threshold: The shoah in our image of history). Amsterdam: Prometheus.

Walker, B.M. (1996) *Dancing to history's tune: History, myth, and politics in Ireland*. Belfast, Northern Ireland: Institute of Irish Studies, Queen's University of Belfast.

Ward, C. and A. Rana-Deuba (1999) 'Acculturation and Adaptation Revisited' *Journal of Cross-Cultural Psychology*, 30, 422–42.

Warwick, D.P. and C.A. Lininger (1975) *The sample survey: Theory and practice*. New York: McGraw-Hill.

Weaver, J. (ed.) (1998) *Native American religious identity: Unforgotten gods*. Maryknoll, NY: Orbis.

Wegner, D.M. (1987) 'Transactive Memory: A Contemporary Analysis of the Group Mind' in B. Mullen and G.R. Goethals (eds), *Theories of Group Behavior* (pp. 185–208). New York: Springer-Verlag.

Weinreich, P. (1988) 'The operationalization of ethnic identity' in J.W. Berry and R.C. Annis (eds), *Ethnic psychology: Research and practice with immigrants, refugees, native peoples, ethnic groups and sojourners* (pp. 149–68). Berwyn, PA: Swets North.

Wertsh, J. (1997) 'Collective memory: Issues from a sociohistorical perspective' in M. Cole, Y. Engeström and O. Vasquez (eds), *Mind, culture, and activity: Seminal papers from the Laboratory of Comparative Human Cognition* (pp. 226–32). Cambridge, UK: Cambridge University Press.

Wessells, M., M. Schwebel and A. Anderson (2001) 'Psychologists making a difference in the public arena: Building cultures of peace' in D.J. Christie, R.V. Wagner and D.D. Winter (eds), *Peace, conflict, and violence: Peace psychology for the 21st century* (pp. 350–62). Upper Saddle River, NJ: Prentice Hall.

White, J.P. and D.J. Mulvaney (1987) 'How many people?' in D.J. Mulvaney and J.P. White (eds), *Australians to 1788* (pp. 113–17). Sydney: Fairfax, Syme and Weldon.

White, R. (1970) *Nobody wanted war: Misperception in Vietnam and other wars*. Garden City, NY: Anchor Books.

Wichert, S. (1994) *Northern Ireland in 1945*. London: Longman.

Wilson, R. (2000) *The Politics of truth and reconciliation in South Africa: Legitimizing the post-apartheid state*. Law and Society Series. Cambridge: Cambridge University

Winegar, L.T. and J. Valsiner (1992) 'Re-contextualizing context: Analysis of metadata and some further elaborations' in L.T. Winegar and J. Valsiner (eds), *Children's development within social context. Vol. 2: Research and methodology* (pp. 249–66). Hillsdale, NJ: Erlbaum.

Winter, J. (1995) *Sites of memory, sites of mourning. The Great War in European cultural history*. Cambridge: Cambridge University Press.

Witztum, E. and Malkinson, R. (1993) 'Bereavement and perpetuation: The double face of the national myth' in R. Malkinson, S.S. Rubin and E. Witztum (eds), *Loss and bereavement in Jewish society in Israel* (pp. 231–58). Jerusalem: Kana (in Hebrew).

Worchel, S. (1999) *Written in blood: Ethnic identity and the struggle for human harmony*. New York: Worth Publishers.

Worthington, E.L. (1998) *Dimensions of Forgiveness: Psychological Research and Theological Perspectives*. Radno, PA: Templeton Foundation Press.

Wright, D. and G. Gaskell (1992) 'The construction and function of vivid memories' in M.A. Conway, D.C. Rubin, H. Spinnler and W.A. Wagenaar (eds), *Theoretical Perspectives On Autobiographical Memory* (pp. 275–93). Dordrecht: Kluwer Academic Publishers.

Yarwood, A.T. and M.J. Knowling (1982) *Race relations in Australia: A history*. Sydney: Methuen Australia.

Yunupingu, G. (1997) 'One-point plan will poison black Australia' *The Melbourne Age*, 26 May, p. 15.

Zerubavel, E. (1991) *The Fine Line*. London: University of Chicago Press.

Index